KEBRA NAGAST

BOOK OF THE GLORY OF KINGS

ANONYMOUS

Translated by

SIR E. A. WALLIS BUDGE

British Library Cataloguing in Publication Data

A catalogue record for this book is available from the British Library

ISBN-13: 9798884838482

Cover Illustration:
Ethiopian Icon

KEBRA NEGAST

From Brit. Mus. MS. Orient. No. 481, fol. 110a

God Almighty the Ancient of Days (*Daniel vii*, 9) surrounded by the " living creatures " seen by Ezekiel (*i*, 10)

PREFACE TO THE PRESENT EDITION

When the English translation of the "Book of the Glory of Kings" appeared in 1922 it received a generous welcome from the gentlemen of the Press, and the approval of it by the public generally was shown by the fact that within two months from the day of publication a reprint was called for. The amusing and interesting character of the book which piles up fancy tales, fables, legends, folk-lore, dogma, mysticism and pious remarks on a substratum of historical fact was frankly admitted by all the reviewers, but a few of them raised the question of the historicity of the Book of the Glory of Kings. It must be said at once that we shall never know whether the queen who visited SOLOMON was a pure-blooded ABYSSINIAN or an Arab queen from YAMAN or HADRAMAUT or some other part of the great Arabian peninsula. But the tradition that some "Queen of the South" did visit SOLOMON is so old and so widespread, that a kernel of historical fact, however small, must be hidden somewhere in it. It would not surprise me if SIDNEY SMITH or C. J. GADD one day published in the great Corpus of cuneiform texts from the tablets in the BRITISH MUSEUM a Sumerian or Babylonian inscription telling how some great queen from latter-day INDIA paid a visit to a king of one of the city states like ETANA, or MESANNIPADDA or the great SARGON of AGADE, to be instructed in the wisdom and civilization of his day. The story of such a visit would be noised abroad among the nations around by the caravan men, and the scribes of the day would incorporate it in their historical romances. It is quite possible that the story of SOLOMON and the Queen of SHEBA is based upon one which is far older. Something like this has actually happened with the history of GILGAMISH,[2] a king of URUK, in the Ethiopic history of the exploits of ALEXANDER THE GREAT. In the latter work the scribe tells us how the Macedonian king sought for the waters of life, and how he made his way through inpenetrable forests and arrived at the sea of the waters of death,[1] and how he tried to fly up into heaven,[3] &c., all of which is described in the Epic of GILGAMISH, the prototype of ALEXANDER to the scribe. The meeting of GILGAMISH with SIDURI the "SÂBITU" i.e. "inn-keeper" or "ale-wife" finds its counterpart in the meeting of ALEXANDER with KUNDAKA (CANDACE), the queen of ETHIOPIA, which country, by the way, ALEXANDER never invaded. ALEXANDER found such favour with KUNDAKA that she invited him to her private apartments and shared her bed with him. The beauty of KUNDAKA overcame ALEXANDER just as the beauty of MÂKĚDÂ overcame SOLOMON, and it is possible that GILGAMISH fell a victim to the "ale-wife". The object of the Ethiopian scribe, ancient or modern, was to make a "good story", and he never allowed facts, or anachronisms, or names of persons or places, or even possibility or probability to hamper him.

The next question is, How far are the ABYSSINIANS justified in claiming definite kinship with the SEMITES? In dealing with this question the

4

following facts must be considered. There is little doubt the aboriginal inhabitants of ABYSSINIA were negroes or negroids who came from the valley of the NILE. At a very early period, which must be called prehistoric, tribes and peoples who lived on the western side of the peninsula of ARABIA made their way across the sea from ASIA into AFRICA in the south at some place like BÂB-AL-MANDAB and in the north at some place in the peninsula of SINAI. In this way the influence of Asiatic peoples entered ABYSSINIA. Later a section of the HAMITES, whose language was akin to that of the LIBYANS, BERBERS, and EGYPTIANS, brought into ABYSSINIA a language which for convenience we may call "Ethiopic" though its more correct name is "Kushite". The translators of the Bible into "Ethiopic" identified, quite incorrectly, ABYSSINIA with KÛSH, the Hebrew name for the country which we now call NUBIA. Owing to the intermingling of SEMITES and HAMITES a Semitic element entered the Hamitic language at a very early period. The northern part of ABYSSINIA, that is, the mountainous section of it, became the principal settlement of the SEMITES, who are known as the "AGAW", and from them were probably descended many of the FALÂSHAS or "Abyssinian Jews".

In the eleventh or tenth century before CHRIST a further invasion of ABYSSINIA by Asiatic SEMITES took place, and it was they who taught the Abyssinians the elements of civilization. The principal tribe of the invaders was called "HABASHA", and they came from YAMAN in western SOUTH ARABIA. They gave the name of "HABESH" to this part of AFRICA in which they settled, and it is from this that the modern name of "ABYSSINIA" is derived. The immigration of SEMITES from ASIA went on steadily during the following centuries, and the newcomers introduced the writing which was current at that time in ARABIA, and trades, arts and crafts. Two or three centuries before the Christian era they succeeded in forming a kingdom, the capital of which was 'AKSÛM. The SEMITES who settled in Upper, Middle, and Lower ABYSSINIA became merchants and traders, and of such trade and commerce as existed at that time they were the originators and organizers. The SEMITES who settled in and about 'AKSÛM were known as the "'AG 'ÂZIYÂN", i.e. the "free", and the language they spoke is called "GĔ'ĔZ", now frequently called "ETHIOPIC". From this is derived the modern language of TIGRAY called "TIGRIÑA". The language of the SEMITES in Middle and Lower ABYSSINIA is known as "'AMÂRIÑÂ" or "AMHARIC" .The Abyssinians at that period had no literature.

Details of the downfall of the Semitic kingdom which had 'AKSÛM for its capital are wanting, but we know that its successor was ruled by kings who were pagans; among these were APHILAS, ENDYBIS, and ALALMIDIS ('ELLA 'AMÎDÂ), the father of 'EZÂNÂ, the 'Αειζανάς of the GREEKS, who reigned in the first half of the fourth century of our era. 'EZÂNÂ, who has been called the "CONSTANTINE OF ABYSSINIA" was the greatest king of ABYSSINIA known to history , and he adopted Christianity as the national religion of his country. With the coming of Christianity Abyssinian literature came into existence.

From the facts summarized briefly in the preceding paragraphs it is clear that the ABYSSINIANS or ETHIOPIANS, as the people themselves prefer to be called, owe more to the SEMITES than to the HAMITES, or NEGROES, or EGYPTIANS, or GREEKS, or any other people with whom they came in contact in the prehistoric or historic periods. The SEMITES found them negro savages, and taught them civilization and culture, and gave them the Holy Scriptures on which their whole literature is based, and set before their eyes shining examples of righteous kings, prophets, priests, and holy men. And from first to last there must have been a very large admixture of Semitic blood in the ABYSSINIANS introduced by marriage and concubinage.

The original form of the Legend of the Queen of SHEBA probably came into being soon after the great invasion of ABYSSINIA by the SEMITES in the tenth century before CHRIST. In the opinion of the ABYSSINIANS divine authority was given to it by Our Lord by His words quoted in the Gospels (Matt. xii. 42; Luke xi. 31), and they never doubted that SOLOMON was the father of the son of the Queen of SHEBA. It followed as a matter of course that the male descendants of this son were the lawful kings of ABYSSINIA, and as SOLOMON was an ancestor of CHRIST they were kinsmen of Our Lord, and they claimed to reign by divine right. This belief was probably shared by the kings of the Semitic kingdom of 'AKSÛM, which city was at a very early period regarded as a duplicate of JERUSALEM and was called the "ZION OF ABYSSINIA". When the ABYSSINIANS adopted Christianity in the second half of the fourth or the first half of the fifth century they decided to sever as far as possible their connexion with their pagan ancestors from ARABIA. The SEMITES who claimed kinship with the HEBREWS of JERUSALEM abandoned MAHRAM and the other gods of the MINAEANS and SABAEANS in favour of JAHWEH, the god of the HEBREWS. When the SEMITES who were Christians had the Holy Scriptures translated into GĚ'ĚZ the translators used a script which, though based on the old writings of the MINAEANS and SABAEANS, was different from it in some very important particulars. The old inscriptions, like Hebrew, Syriac, Arabic, &c., read from right to left, but the ABYSSINIANS decided to read their texts from left to right, as did the BABYLONIANS and ASSYRIANS. This decision was due probably to Greek influence. The letters of the old Arabian alphabets were entirely consonantal and vowels were expressed by the semi-vowel letters. Some genius, name unknown, discovered a way of expressing the vowels in GĚ'ĚZ by attaching short lines and minute circles to the consonants of the Sabaean alphabet and by modifying the forms of some of the consonants themselves. Thus the ABYSSINIANS turned the old Sabaean alphabet into a syllabary

The translators of the Bible into GĚ'ĚZ rejected HABESH, the old name of ABYSSINIA, and in their version definitely gave the name of ETHIOPIA ('ÎTĚYÔPĚYÂ) to the region, the capital of which was 'AKSÛM. They read that the "eunuch of great authority under CANDACE queen of the ETHIOPIANS 'was called' a man of ETHIOPIA" (Acts viii. 27), and as the country over which that queen ruled was the KÛSH of the Old Testament, they rendered that name by "ETHIOPIA" (e.g. Psalms lxviii. 32.; lxxxvii. 4). Strictly speaking KÛSH was UPPER NUBIA. The name HABESH was disliked by the indigenous peoples of the country , and though in the modern Amharic dictionaries HABASHÂ is still to be found, the present-day native hates to be called "HABASHIYY", for by him it is regarded as an abusive epithet. Thus the Abyssinian Christian gained a new national name, a new script, and a new literature.

As Christianity spread southwards the idea of the Solomonic ancestry of the kings of ETHIOPIA in the period between the sixth and the thirteenth centuries gained ground everywhere. During this period many kings who were not of the Solomonic line reigned, and a group of them called the ZÂGUÊ were masters of ETHIOPIA for about 330 years. At length there appeared a member of the Solomonic line called YEKUENÔ 'AMLÂK (1270-85) in SHOA, and with the help of the great saint TAKLA HAYMÂNÔT he expelled the ZÂGUÊ and became "King of the Kings of ETHIOPIA". In return for this help of the saint, YEKUENÔ 'AMLÂK agreed to give to the Church one-third of the revenues of his kingdom, and his successors have, on the whole, followed his example.

As regards the present edition of the Queen of Sheba little need be said. In the first edition of my translation of the KEBRA NAGAST (all vowels short) there were 31 plates containing monochrome photographs, reproductions of coloured illustrations copied from Ethiopic manuscripts of the sixteenth, seventeenth, and eighteenth centuries. The scenes and subjects represented were all of a religious character, but had no special reference to the Book of the Glory of Kings, for strangely enough that work is without illustrations. Nothing in a systematic way of publishing specimens of Ethiopian Art had been done before LADY MEUX published the coloured facsimiles of all the illustrations, both vignettes and full pages, from her two splendid manuscripts of the Miracles of the Virgin Mary and from the Life of Hanna the mother of the Virgin, and the Life of Mabâ' Sĕyon. I therefore added the 31 plates of illustrations from the manuscripts of the great MAKDALÂ Collection now in the BRITISH MUSEUM, thinking that they would give the reader a good idea of the character of Ethiopian art generally. But it must never be forgotten that the art represented on the plates is not indigenous, for it is borrowed directly from or is based upon the paintings which were executed for the kings of ETHIOPIA by FRANCISCO DI BRANCA-LEONE, a Venetian monk, who is commonly called "the Frank". He flourished in the reign of ZAR'A YÂ'KÔB (A.D. 1436-68). This monk came to ABYSSINIA with the view of converting the people to Christianity, and he is famous as "the Frank" who by the command of the king, carried on several debates with ABBÂ GÎYÔRGÎS on the faith. When the king discovered that he was a painter as well as a monk, he set him to work at painting pictures of Our Lady and the saints to be hung up in the churches, and it was he who painted for BA'EDA MÂRYÂM (A.D. 1468-78) the picture of the Virgin and the Infant CHRIST which exasperated the ABYSSINIANS. He represented the Virgin holding the Child on her left arm as was customary in Europe, but the ABYSSINIANS regarded the left hand as the "hand of dishonour", and they wanted to destroy the picture. This the king refused to permit, and it was hung in the 'ATRONSA MÂRYÂM, a church in the town of the same name in the south of AMHARÂ, on the 'ABÂY RIVER, and there it remained until the third year of the reign of THEOPHILUS

(A.D. 1709). In that year the GALLAS came and wrecked the church, and killed the priests, and the picture and the coffin containing the remains of BA'EDA MÂRYÂM were hurled over a precipice on SUNDAY, AUGUST 23.

The Introduction and Translation given in the first edition of the Queen of Sheba are repeated herein practically unaltered. The readings of two or three passages have been, I hope, improved, and a few references added. To write the literary history of the KEBRA NAGAST I believe to be impossible at present, owing to the lack of material. We can never expect to find out what was the original form of the Legend of the Queen of SHEBA, and it is impossible to assign dates to the various recensions of it which have been made in Coptic, Arabic, and Ethiopic. The sources of many of the legends reproduced in the great work are untraceable at present, and the unauthorized additions made to it by generations of scribes cannot with certainty be identified. It would be very interesting to know when the KEBRA NAGAST (all vowels short) began to be politically important, and regarded as the source of the invincibility of the ABYSSINIANS. The success of the British Expedition under GENERAL NAPIER in 1868 disturbed their equanimity somewhat, but they comforted themselves by remembering that it was directed against THEODORE, who was after all only an impostor. The natives everywhere helped the British Army because they wished to see the usurper smashed. Had they been hostile the result of the expedition would have been different. The battle of ADWA showed how the ABYSSINIANS could deal with an army of European soldiers, and "unconquered ABYSSINIA" is now the fiery, passionate cry of every patriot of ETHIOPIA from 'AKSÛM to the Equator.

48 Bloomsbury Street

Bedford Square, W.C. 1

August 22, 1932

Footnotes

1. For his authentic history see Sidney Smith, Early History of Assyria, p. 34.
2. See the Epic of Gilgamish (British Museum), London, 1929.
3. See the "Legend of Etana" in Jastrow, Religion of Babylonia and Assyria, p. 519f.

PREFACE TO THE FIRST EDITION

This volume contains a complete English translation of the famous Ethiopian work, The "KEBRA NAGAST", i.e. the "Glory of the Kings [of ETHIOPIA]". This work has been held in peculiar honour in ABYSSINIA for several centuries, and throughout that country it has been, and still is, venerated by the people as containing the final proof of their descent from the Hebrew Patriarchs, and of the kinship of their kings of the Solomonic line with CHRIST, the Son of God. The importance of the book, both for the kings and the people of ABYSSINIA, is clearly shown by the letter that King JOHN of ETHIOPIA wrote to the late Lord GRANVILLE in August, 1872. The king says: "There is a book called 'Kivera Negust' which contains the Law of the whole of ETHIOPIA, and the names of the SHÛMS [i.e. Chiefs], and Churches, and Provinces are in this book. I pray you find out who has got this book, and send it to me, for in my country my people will not obey my orders without it." (See *infra*, p. xxxv). The first summary of the contents of the KEBRA NAGAST was published by BRUCE as far back as 1813, but little interest was roused by his somewhat bald précis. And, in spite of the labours of PRÆTORIUS, BEZOLD, and HUGUES LE ROUX, the contents of the work are still practically unknown to the general reader in England. It is hoped that the translation given in the following pages will be of use to those who have not the time or opportunity for perusing the Ethiopic original.

The KEBRA NAGAST is a great storehouse of legends and traditions, some historical and some of a purely folk-lore character, derived from the Old Testament and the later Rabbinic writings, and from Egyptian (both pagan and Christian), Arabian, and Ethiopian sources. Of the early history of the compilation and its maker, and of its subsequent editors we know nothing, but the principal groundwork of its earliest form was the traditions that were current in SYRIA, PALESTINE, ARABIA, and EGYPT during the first four centuries of the Christian era. Weighing carefully all that has been written by DILLMANN, TRUMP, ZOTENBERG, WRIGHT, and BEZOLD, and taking into account the probabilities of the matter, it seems to me that we shall not be far wrong if we assign the composition of the earliest form of the KEBRA NAGAST to the sixth century A.D. Its compiler was probably a Coptic priest, for the books he used were writings that were accepted by the Coptic Church. Whether he lived in EGYPT, or in AKSÛM, or in some other part of ETHIOPIA matters little, but the colophons of the extant Ethiopic MSS. of the KEBRA NAGAST suggest that he wrote in Coptic.

In the succeeding centuries, probably as a result of the widespread conquests of MUHAMMAD and his KHALÎFAHS, the Coptic text was in whole or part translated into Arabic, and during the process of translation many additions were made to it, chiefly from Arabic sources. Last of all this Arabic version was translated into Ethiopic, and proper names underwent curious transformations in the process. According to the colophons of the MSS. in the BRITISH MUSEUM, OXFORD, and PARIS, the Arabic translation was made from the Coptic in the 409th "year of mercy", when GABRA MASKAL, commonly known as LÂLÎBALÂ, was reigning

9

over ETHIOPIA, i.e. between A.D. 1314 and 1344. And the same authorities say that the Ethiopic translation was made subsequently by one ISAAC, of whom nothing is known save that he was an enthusiastic Christian visionary and patriot. His knowledge of history and chronology was defective, and his comparative philology is unusually peculiar, even for the period in which he lived.

In the colophons ISAAC says: "I have toiled much for the glory of the kingdom of ETHIOPIA, and for the going forth (manifestation ?) of the heavenly ZION, and for the glory of the King of ETHIOPIA." These words throw some light upon ISAAC'S motive in translating the book, and supply the reason for his devoted labour. He firmly believed: [1]. That the lawful kings of ETHIOPIA were descended from SOLOMON, King of ISRAEL. [2]. That the Tabernacle of the Law of God, i.e. the Ark of the Covenant, had been brought from JERUSALEM to 'AKSÛM by MENYELEK, SOLOMON'S firstborn son, according to the ETHIOPIANS. 3. That the God of ISRAEL had transferred His place of abode on earth from JERUSALEM to 'AKSÛM (AXUM), the ecclesiastical and political capital of ETHIOPIA. The means employed by MENYELEK for obtaining possession of the Ark of the Covenant did not disturb ISAAC'S conscience in the least, nay he gloried in them, for manifestly MENYELEK was performing the Will of God in removing the tabernacle of ZION from JERUSALEM. God, according to ISAAC, was satisfied that the JEWS were unworthy to be custodians of the Ark wherein His Presence was, and the Ark wished to depart. ETHIOPIA had stretched out her hands to God (Psalm lxviii. 31), and He went to her, with the Ark, to preside over MENYELEK'S kingdom, which was established in accordance with the commands that He had given to MOSES and the prophets and priests of ISRAEL.

It will be remembered that the line of kings founded by SOLOMON continued to reign even after the ETHIOPIANS became Christians under the teaching of FRUMENTIUS and ADESIUS, the slaves of the merchant MEROPIUS, and that the line continued unbroken until the tenth century of our era. ISAAC knew that God then permitted the line to be broken, and allowed the ZÂGUÊ kings to reign over ETHIOPIA until the reign of YĔKÛNÔ 'AMLÂK, who restored the Solomonic line in 1270, and he makes no attempt to justify God's action in this matter, or to explain it. We learn, however, from the first section of the colophon, that he wondered why God had neglected to have the Arabic version of the KEBRA NAGAST translated into the "speech of ABYSSINIA" at an earlier date, and why 'ABU'L-'IZZ and 'ABU'L-FARAJ, who made the Arabic translation from the Coptic, did not make a rendering into Ethiopic also. In the explanation which he attempts to give, he reminds us that the Arabic translation appeared whilst the ZÂGUÊ kings were still reigning. As the KEBRA NAGAST was written to glorify the Solomonic line of kings, and its editors and translators regarded the ZÂGUÊ kings not only as non-ISRAELITES, but as "transgressors of the Law", the appearance of a translation of it in the vernacular whilst the ZÂGUÊ were still on the throne would be followed by the torture and death of its producers, and the destruction of their work.

There is extant in Ethiopian literature a legend to the effect that when

God made ADAM He placed in his body a "Pearl", which He intended should pass from it into the bodies of a series of holy men, one after the other, until the appointed time when it should enter the body of HANNÂ,[1] and form the substance of her daughter the VIRGIN MARY. Now this "Pearl" passed through the body of SOLOMON, an ancestor of CHRIST, and CHRIST and MENYELEK, the son of SOLOMON by the Queen of SHEBA, were sons of SOLOMON, and according to Ethiopian ideas they were akin to each other. But CHRIST was the Son of God, and, therefore, being the kinsman of CHRIST, MENYELEK was divine. And ISAAC the Ethiopian, holding this view, maintains in the KEBRA NAGAST that the kings of ETHIOPIA who were descended from MENYELEK were of divine origin, and that their words and deeds were those of gods.

Now the idea of the divine origin of kings in ETHIOPIA, the SÛDÂN, and EGYPT, is very old, and it appears to have been indigenous. According to a legend given in the WESTCAR PAPYRUS in BERLIN, three of the great kings of the Vth dynasty in EGYPT were the sons of the god RĀ by RUTTET, the wife of RUTTETUSER, high priest of RĀ, and before the close of that dynasty every king called himself "son of RĀ". Many a king of EGYPT states in his inscriptions that he reigned "in the egg", i.e. before he was born, and we are to understand that the egg was deposited in his mother by the form of the Sun-god, who was his father. Some of the sovereigns of the XVIIIth dynasty, certainly those who were the nominees of the priests of AMEN, were declared to be the actual children of AMEN, and to be of his substance. On the walls of the famous temple which the architect SENMUT built for Queen HATSHEPSUT in Western THEBES, there is a series of bas-reliefs in which the god AMEN is seen companying with the mother of that Queen, and HATSHEPSUT regarded herself as AMEN'S daughter. In the temple of Luxor there are bas-reliefs of a similar character, and the god AMEN is seen occupying the couch of the queen who became by him the mother of AMENHETEP III. This king was so thoroughly convinced of his divine origin that he caused an effigy of himself to be sculptured on the walls of the temple of SÛLB in the Egyptian SÛDÂN, together with the figures of the great gods of EGYPT. In fact he shared the worship of the people with the gods and goddesses of EGYPT. RAMESES THE GREAT was held to be the son of the god PTAH-TANEN, and in the inscription on a stele at ABU SIMBEL this god, in addressing the king, says: "I am thy father. Thou was begotten by the gods. All thy members are from the gods. I made myself assume the form of the RAM, the Lord of Tet-t, my seed stood in thy august mother"[2]

A thousand years later a story arose in EGYPT to the effect that ALEXANDER THE GREAT was the son of the god AMEN of EGYPT, and ALEXANDER'S councillors promptly took advantage of it to forward the fortunes of their lord. If, they argued, ALEXANDER is the son of AMEN, he is the lawful king of EGYPT, and the EGYPTIANS must acknowledge him as their king. But it was necessary for their purpose that AMEN should acknowledge ALEXANDER as his son, and they therefore took him to the Oasis of SÎWAH in the Libyan Desert, and presented him to the god AMEN of LIBYA. The god admitted that ALEXANDER was his son, the priesthood of AMEN accepted the declaration of their god, the EGYPTIANS believed that the holy blood of AMEN flowed in ALEXANDER'S veins, and as a result he became the king of the South and the North, and Governor of the Domain of HORUS without striking a blow. The native novelists and story-tellers, e.g. the PSEUDO CALLISTHENES, declared that when NECTANEBUS II, the last native king of EGYPT, fled from EGYPT he went to MACEDON, where he established himself as a magician. Here he became acquainted with Queen OLYMPIAS, who wished to find out from him if her husband, PHILIP, intended to put her away. An intimacy sprang up between NECTANEBUS and OLYMPIAS, and he appeared to the queen one night in the form of the god AMEN of LIBYA, arrayed in all the attributes of the god, and begot ALEXANDER THE GREAT. Tradition transferred the horns of AMEN to ALEXANDER, and ancient Arab writers call ALEXANDER "DHU'L-KARNÊN", i.e. "provided with two horns", a title that translates exactly one of the titles of AMEN, "Sept ābui"

ISAAC, the editor and translator of the KEBRA NAGAST, and his fellow countrymen saw nothing strange in the fact that MÂKĔDÂ, the virgin queen of SÂBA, gave herself to SOLOMON, for she believed him to be of divine origin, and he was to her as a god. Moreover, he was the custodian of the "Heavenly ZION, the Tabernacle of the Law of God", whence he obtained daily the renewal of his divinity, and power, and authority. The Tabernacle of the Law had much in common with the arks or divine tabernacles of the BABYLONIANS and EGYPTIANS, which formed the places of abode of figures of gods or their most characteristic emblems. The ark of BEL, the great god of BABYLON, contained a figure of the god, and the king visited it ceremonially once a year, and sued with tears for forgiveness, and grasped the hand or hands of the sacred figure. The chamber in which the figure abode was believed to have been built by the gods. On high days and holy days the ark was carried by the priests in procession. In EGYPT the arks of the gods were kept in chambers specially constructed for the purpose, and the figures of the gods were seated on thrones inside them. These arks were placed upon sledges or in boats and were carried by the priests in procession on great days of festival or on solemn days. We know from the inscriptions that the ark of AMEN was provided with doors that were kept bolted and sealed. On certain occasions the king had the right to break these seals and unbolt the doors, and look upon the face of the god. Thus, after his conquest of EGYPT, the Nubian king PIĀNKHI went to visit RĀ in his sanctuary near HELIOPOLIS. He was received by the KHERHEB priest, who prayed that the fiends might have no power over him. Having arrayed himself in the sacred seteb garment, and been censed and asperged, PIĀNKHI ascended the steps leading to the ark of RĀ and stood there alone. He broke the seal, drew the bolts, threw open the doors and looked upon the face of RĀ. Having adored the Mātet and Sektet Boats he drew together the doors and sealed them with his seal. In this way PIĀNKHI was recognized by RĀ as the king of all EGYPT. It is not clear whether it was a figure of RĀ or the holy benben stone, the symbol of the god, which PIĀNKHI looked upon. Many of the sacred arks of EGYPT contained no figures of gods, but only objects symbolic of them; in the temples of Osiris the arks contained portions of the body of this god.

The Ark of the Law which MENYELEK covered and stole from the Temple of JERUSALEM was probably a copy of that made by MOSES, and to all intents and purposes it was a rectangular box, made of hard wood plated with gold, and measuring about four feet long, two feet six inches wide, and two feet six inches deep. It was provided with a cover upon which rested the Mercy seat and figures of the Cherubim. In the KEBRA NAGAST no mention is made of the Mercy seat and the Cherubim, but we read there that MOSES made a case in shape like the "belly of a ship", and in this the Two Tables of the Law were placed. To the ETHIOPIANS this case symbolized the VIRGIN MARY; the case made by MOSES carried the Word in stone, and Mary carried the Word Incarnate. It cannot be assumed that the Ark stolen by MENYELEK was carried in a sacred boat like an Egyptian shrine, even though the "belly of a ship" is mentioned in connection with it. In several chapters of the KEBRA NAGAST the "chariot of the Tabernacle of the Law" is mentioned, a fact which suggests that in later days at least the sacred box was provided with a carriage or sledge. History is silent as to the place where the Tabernacle of the Law was finally deposited, but Ethiopian tradition asserts that it survived all the troubles and disasters that fell upon the ABYSSINIANS in their wars with the Muslims, and that it was preserved at 'AKSÛM until comparatively recent times.

In the short introduction that follows I have given a sketch of the literary history of the KEBRA NAGAST, with references to the authorities on the subject, and I have made an abstract of its contents in narrative form which will, I hope, be useful. A full discussion of every portion of the work, with extracts giving the original texts of the authorities used and quoted by ISAAC the scribe, would fill another volume, and the cost of printing, paper, and binding is now so great that the idea of producing such a book has been abandoned. A translation of the Arabic text describing how the Kingdom of DAVID was transferred from JERUSALEM to ETHIOPIA has been added, for this interesting document is practically unknown in England. The pictures of events described in the Old and New Testaments, given in this book, are taken from Ethiopic MSS. in the BRITISH MUSEUM; they show as nothing else can the religious beliefs and traditions of the ETHIOPIANS, and at the same time they serve as examples of the drawings and designs with which they illustrated their manuscripts. Nearly all of them depict Scriptural events described or referred to in the KEBRA NAGAST.

Footnotes

1. See the History of Hannâ, edited and translated by myself, in Lady Meux MSS. 2-5, p. 164.

2. Trans. Soc. Bibl. Arch., vol. vii, plate facing p. 119, ll. 3 and 4 (ed. Naville).

CONTENTS

INTRODUCTION

1. The Manuscripts of the KEBRA NAGAST and their Arrival in Europe.
The Labours of BRUCE, DILLMANN, PRÆTORIUS, WRIGHT, ZOTENBERG, and
BEZOLD. King JOHN'S Letter to Lord GRANVILLE. Date of Compilation of the
KEBRA NAGAST. The Ethiopian Work Based on Coptic and Arabic Sources, &c.

The KEBRA NAGAST, or the Book of the Glory of the Kings [of ETHIOPIA], has been held in the highest esteem and honour throughout the length and breadth of ABYSSINIA for a thousand years at least, and even to-day it is believed by every educated man in that country to contain the true history of the origin of the Solomonic line of kings in ETHIOPIA, and is regarded as the final authority on the history of the conversion of the ETHIOPIANS from the worship of the sun, moon, and stars to that of the Lord God of ISRAEL.

The existence of the KEBRA NAGAST appears to have been unknown in Europe until the second quarter of the sixteenth century, when scholars began to take an interest in the country of "PRESTER JOHN" through the writings of FRANCISCO ALVAREZ, chaplain to the Embassy which EMMANUEL, King of PORTUGAL, sent to DAVID, King of ETHIOPIA, under the leadership of DON RODERIGO DE LIMA (1520-1527). In the collection of documents concerning this Embassy, ALVAREZ included an account of the King of ETHIOPIA, and of the manners and customs of his subjects, and a description in Portuguese of the habits of the ETHIOPIANS (alcuni costumi di esso Serenissimo DAVID, e del suo paese e genti, tradotta di lingua ethiopica in Portogalese);[1] and in his Ho Preste Joam das Indias (COIMBRA, 1540), and his Historia de las cosas d'Etiopia (ANVERS 1557, SARAGOSSE 1561 and TOLEDO 1588) this account was greatly amplified.[2]

In the first quarter of the sixteenth century, P. N. GODINHO published some traditions about King SOLOMON and his son MĚNYĚLĚK or MĚNYĚLÎK, derived from the KEBRA NAGAST,[3] and further information on the subject was included by the Jesuit priest MANOEL ALMEIDA (1580-1646) in his Historia germal de Ethiopia, which does not appear to have been published in its entirety. MANOEL ALMEIDA was sent out as a missionary to ETHIOPIA, and had abundant means of learning about the KEBRA NAGAST at first hand, and his manuscript Historia is a valuable work. His brother, APOLLINARE, also went out to the country as a missionary, and was, with his two companions, stoned to death in TIGRÉ.

Still fuller information about the contents of the KEBRA NAGAST was supplied by F. BALTHAZAR TELLEZ (1595-1675), the author of the Historia general de Ethiopia Alta ov Preste Joã e do que nella obraram os Padres da Companhia de JESUS composta na mesma Ethiopia pelo Padre Manoel d'Almeyda. Abreviada com nova releçam e methodo pelo Padre Balthezar Tellez, COIMBRA, 1660, folio. The sources of his work were the histories of MANOEL

ALMEIDA, ALFONZO MENDEZ, JERONINO LOBO, and Father PAYS. The Historia of TELLEZ was well known to JOB LUDOLF, and he refers to it several times in his Historia Æthiopica, which was published at FRANKFORT in 1681, but it is pretty certain that he had no first-hand knowledge of the KEBRA NAGAST as a whole. Though he regarded much of its contents as fabulous, he was prepared to accept the statement of TELLEZ as to the great reputation and popularity which the book enjoyed in ABYSSINIA.

Little, apparently, was heard in Europe about the KEBRA NAGAST until the close of the eighteenth century when JAMES BRUCE of KINNAIRD (1730-1794), the famous African traveller, published an account of his travels in search of the sources of the NILE. When he was leaving GONDAR, RÂS MICHAEL, the all-powerful Wazîr of King TAKLA HAYMÂNÔT, gave him several most valuable Ethiopic manuscripts, and among them was a copy of the KEBRA NAGAST to which he attached great importance. During the years that BRUCE lived in ABYSSINIA he learned how highly this work was esteemed among all classes of ABYSSINIANS, and in the third edition of his Travels[4] (vol. iii, pp. 411-416) there appeared a description of its contents, the first to be published in any European language. Not content with this manuscript BRUCE brought away with him a copy of the KEBRA NAGAST which he had made for himself, and in due course he gave both manuscripts to the Bodleian Library, where they are known as "Bruce 93" and "Bruce 87" respectively. The former, which is the "Liber Axumea" of BRUCE'S Travels, was described at great length by DILLMANN,[5] who to his brief description of the latter added a transcript of its important colophon.[6] Thanks to DILLMANN, who printed the headings of all the chapters of the Fĕtha Nagasti in the original Ethiopic, there was no longer any doubt about the exact nature and contents of the work, though there was nothing in it to show exactly when and by whom the work was compiled.

In 1870 (?) FRANCIS PRÆTORIUS published,[7] with a Latin translation, the Ethiopic text of Chapters xix to xxxii of the KEBRA NAGAST edited from the manuscript at Berlin (Orient. 395), which LEPSIUS acquired from DOMINGO LORDA, and sent to the KÖNIGLICHE BIBLIOTHEK in 1843. To the Berlin text he added the variant readings supplied from the MSS. Orient. 818 and 819 in the BRITISH MUSEUM by Professor W. WRIGHT of CAMBRIDGE. In 1877 WRIGHT published a full description of the MS. of the KEBRA NAGAST in the MAKDALÂ Collection in the BRITISH MUSEUM. The work of Praetorius made known for the first time the exact form of the Ethiopian legend that makes the King of ETHIOPIA to be a descendant of SOLOMON, King of ISRAEL, by MÂKĔDÂ, the Queen of 'AZÊB, who is better known as the "Queen of SHEBA".

In August, 1868, the great collection of Ethiopic manuscripts, which the British Army brought away from MAKDALÂ after the defeat and suicide of King THEODORE, was brought to the BRITISH MUSEUM, and among them were two fine copies of the KEBRA NAGAST. Later these were numbered Oriental 818 and Oriental 819 respectively, and were described very fully and carefully by

Wright in his Catalogue of the Ethiopic MSS. in the British Museum, London, 1877,[8] No. cccxci, p. 297, and in the Zeitschrift der Deutschen Morgenländischen Gesellschaft, Bd. xxiv, pp. 614-615. It was the fate of Oriental 819, a fine manuscript which was written in the reign of 'ÎYÂSÛ I, A.D. 1682-1706, to return to ABYSSINIA, and this came about in the following manner. On 10 Aug., 1872, Prince KASA, who was subsequently crowned as King JOHN IV, wrote to Earl GRANVILLE thus: "And now again I have another thing to explain to you: that there was a Picture called QURATA REZOO, which is a Picture of our Lord and Saviour JESUS CHRIST, and was found with many books at MAGDALA by the English. This Picture King THEODORE took from GONDAR to MAGDALA, and it is now in England; all round the Picture is gold, and the midst of it coloured.

"Again there is a book called KIVERA NEGUST (i.e. KEBRA NAGAST), which contains the Law of the whole of ETHIOPIA, and the names of the SHUMS (i.e. Chiefs), Churches, and Provinces are in this book. I pray you will find out who has got this book, and send it to me, for in my Country my people will not obey my orders without it".

When a copy of this letter was sent to the BRITISH MUSEUM the Trustees decided to grant King JOHN'S request, and the manuscript was restored to him on 14 December, 1872. King JOHN'S letter proves that very great importance was attached to the KEBRA NAGAST by the Ethiopian peoples, even in the second half of the nineteenth century. M. HUGUES LE ROUX, a French envoy from the President of the French Republic to MENYELEK II, King of ETHIOPIA, went to ADDIS ALEM where the king was staying, in order to see this manuscript and to obtain his permission to translate it into French. Having made his request to MENYELEK II personally the king made a reply, which M. LE ROUX translates thus: "Je suis d'avis qu'un peuple ne se défend pas seulement avec ses armes, mais avec ses livres. Celui dont vous parlez est la fierté de ce Royaume. Depuis moi, l'Empereur, jusqu'au plus pauvre soldat qui marche dans les chemins, tous les Éthiopiens seront heureux que ce livre soit traduit dans la langue française et porté à la connaissance des amis que nous avons dans le monde. Ainsi l'on verra clairement quels liens nous unissent avec le peuple de Dieu, quels trésors ont été confiés à notre garde. On comprendra mieux pourquoi le secours de Dieu ne nous a jamais manqué contre les ennemis qui nous attaquaient". The king then gave orders that the manuscript was to be fetched from ADDIS ABEBA, where the monks tried to keep it on the pretext of copying the text, and in less than a week it was placed in the hands of M. LE ROUX, who could hardly believe his eyes. Having described the manuscript and noted on the last folio the words, "This volume was returned to the King of ETHIOPIA by order of the Trustees of the BRITISH MUSEUM, Dec. 14th, 1872. J. WINTER JONES, Principal Librarian". M. LE ROUX says: "Il n'y avait plus de doute possible: le livre que je tenais dans mes mains était bien cette version de l'histoire de la Reine de Saba et de Salomon, que Négus et Prêtres d'Éthiopie considèrent comme le plus authentique de toutes celles qui circulent dans les bibliothèques européennes et dans les monastètes abyssins. C'était le livre que Théodoros avait caché sous son oreiller, la nuit où il se suicida, celui que les soldats anglais avaient emporté à Londres, qu'un ambassadeur rendit à l'Empereur Jean, que ce même Jean feuilleta dans sa tente, le matin du jour où il tomba sous les cimeterres des Mahdistes, celui que les moines avaient dérobé".[9] With the help of a friend M. LE ROUX translated several of the Chapters of the KEBRA NAGAST, and in due course published his translation.[10]

The catalogues of the Ethiopic MSS. in OXFORD, LONDON and PARIS, which had been published by DILLMANN, WRIGHT and ZOTENBERG, supplied a good deal of information about the contents of the KEBRA NAGAST in general, but scholars felt that it was impossible to judge of the literary and historical value of the work by transcription and translations of the headings of the chapters only. In 1882 under the auspices of the Bavarian Government, DR. C. BEZOLD undertook to prepare an edition of the Ethiopic text edited from the best MSS., with a German translation, which the ROYAL BAVARIAN ACADEMY made arrangements to publish. After much unavoidable delay this work appeared in 1909, and is entitled Kebra Nagast. Die Herrlichkeit der Könige (Abhandlungen der Königlich Bayerischen Akademie, Band XXIII, Abth. 1, Munich, 1909 [Band LXXVII of the Denkschriften]). The text is prefaced by a learned introduction, which was greatly appreciated by Orientalists to whom the edition was specially addressed. The chief authority for the Ethiopic text in BEZOLD'S edition is the now famous manuscript which was sent as a gift to LOUIS PHILIPPE by SÂHLA (or SÂHLÛ) DĔNGĔL, King of ETHIOPIA, who died early in 1855. According to ZOTENBERG (Catalogue des manuscrits Éthiopiens, p. 6) this manuscript must belong to the thirteenth century; if this be so it is probably the oldest Ethiopic manuscript in existence. Though there seems to be no really good reason for assigning this very early date to the manuscript, there can be no doubt as to its being the oldest known Codex of the KEBRA NAGAST, and therefore BEZOLD was fully justified in making its text the base of his edition of that work. I have collated the greater part of the BRITISH MUSEUM Codex, Oriental 818, with his printed text, and though the variants are numerous they are not of great importance, in fact, as is the case in several other Codices of the KEBRA NAGAST, they are due chiefly to the haste or carelessness or fatigue of the scribe. As BEZOLD'S text represents the KEBRA NAGAST in the form that the Ethiopian priests and scribes have considered authoritative, I have made the English translation which is printed in the following pages from it.

Unfortunately, none of the Codices of the KEBRA NAGAST gives us any definite information about the compiler of the work - for it certainly is a compilation - or the time when he wrote, or the circumstances under which it was compiled. DILLMANN, the first European scholar who had read the whole book in the original Ethiopic, contented himself with saying in 1848, "de vero compositionis tempore nihil liquet" (Catalogus, p. 72), but later he thought it might be as old as the fourteenth century. ZOTENBERG (Catalogue, p. 222) was inclined to think that "it was composed soon after the restoration of the so-called Solomonic line of kings", that is to say, soon after the throne of ETHIOPIA was occupied by TASFÂ 'ÎYASÛS,or YĔKÛNÔ 'AMLÂK, who reigned from A.M. 6762-77, i.e. A.D. 1270-1285. A Colophon, (see pp. 228, 229)which is found in several of the Codices of the KEBRA NAGAST in OXFORD, LONDON and PARIS, states that the Ethiopic text was translated from the Arabic version, which, in turn, was translated from the Coptic. The Arabic translation was, it continues, made by 'ABU 'L-'IZZ and 'ABU 'L-FARAJ, in the "year of mercy" 409, during the reign of GABRA MASKAL ('AMDA SEYÔN I), i.e. between A.D. 1314 and 1344, when GEORGE was Patriarch of ALEXANDRIA. These statements are clear enough and definite enough, yet DILLMANN did not believe them, but thought that the whole Colophon was the result of the imagination of some idle scribe (ab otioso quodam librario inventa). The statements about the Ethiopic version being made from the Coptic through the Arabic, he treated as obvious fictions (plane fictitia esse), and he condemned the phrasing of the Colophon because he considered its literary style inferior to that used in the narrative of the KEBRA NAGAST itself (dictio hujus subscriptionis pessima est, et ab oratione eleganti libri ipsius quam maxime differt). ZOTENBERG (Catalogue, p. 223, col. 1) a very competent scholar, saw no reason for doubting the truth of the statements in the Colophon generally, but thought it possible that an Arab author might have supplied the fundamental facts of the narrative, and that the author or authors of the Ethiopic version stated that the original source of their work was a Coptic archetype in order to give it an authority and importance which it would not otherwise possess. On the other hand, WRIGHT merely regarded the KEBRA NAGAST as an "apocryphal work", and judging from the list of kings at the end of the work in Oriental 818, fol. 46B,which ends with YĔKWĔNÔ 'AMLÂK, who died in 1344, concluded that it was a product of the fourteenth century (Catalogue, p. 301, col. 2).

A careful study of the KEBRA NAGAST, made whilst translating the work into English, has convinced me that the opening statements in the Colophon are substantially correct, and that it is quite possible that in its original form the Arabic version of the book was translated from Coptic MSS. belonging to the Patriarchal Library at ALEXANDRIA, and copies of this Arabic translation, probably enlarged and greatly supplemented by the scribes in the various monasteries of EGYPT, would soon find their way into ETHIOPIA or ABYSSINIA, viâ the BLUE NILE. The principal theme of the KEBRA NAGAST, i.e. the descent of the Kings of ETHIOPIA from SOLOMON, King of ISRAEL, and the "Queen of the South, or the "Queen of SHEBA", was certainly well known in ETHIOPIA for centuries before the KEBRA NAGAST was compiled, but the general treatment of it in this work was undoubtedly greatly influenced by supplementary legends and additions, which in their simplest forms seem to me to have been derived from Coptic and even Syrian writers.

It is well known that the Solomonic line of kings continued to rule over ETHIOPIA until that somewhat mythical woman ESTHER, or JUDITH as some call her, succeeded in dethroning DELNA'AD and placing on the throne MARÂ TAKLA HÂYMÂNÔT, the first of the eleven ZÂGUÊ kings, who dispossessed the Solomonic kings for three hundred and fifty-four years (A.D. 914-1268) and reigned at AKSÛM. Written accounts of the descent of the kings of ETHIOPIA from SOLOMON must have existed in ETHIOPIA before the close of the ninth century A.D. and these were, no doubt, drawn up in Ethiopic and in Arabic. During the persecution of the Christians in EGYPT and ETHIOPIA by the MUHAMMADANS in the tenth, eleventh, and twelfth centuries, many churches and their libraries of manuscripts perished. We may, however, be sure that the Solomonic kings, who settled in the province of SHOA during the period of the ZÂGUÊ domination, managed to preserve chronological lists and other historical documents that contained the Annals of their predecessors.

The second part of the Colophon mentions 'ABU 'L-'IZZ and 'ABU 'L-FARAJ as being concerned with translating the book into Arabic, and makes one ISAAC (?), who was apparently the Ethiopian translator, ask why they did not translate it into Ethiopic. In answer to this question he says that the KEBRA NAGAST appeared during the period of the ZÂGUÊ rule, when it is obvious that the publication of any work that supported the claims of the Solomonic kings would meet with a very unfavourable reception, and cause the death of its editors and translators. Therefore it is fairly certain that the KEBRA NAGAST existed in Arabic in some form during the three and a half centuries of the ZÂGUÊ rule, and that no attempt was made to multiply copies of it in Ethiopic until the restoration of the line of Solomonic kings in the days of YĔKÛNÔ 'AMLÂK (A.D. 1270-1285). The Ethiopic work as we know it now is probably in much the same state as it was in the days of GABRA MASKAL. ('AMDA SĔYÔN) in the first half of the fourteenth century of our era. Of ISAAC we unfortunately know nothing, but there seem to be no good grounds for attributing the complete authorship of the KEBRA NAGAST to him. Yet he was evidently not merely a scribe or copyist, and when he speaks of the greatness of the toil which he undertook for the sake of the glory of the heavenly ZION, and ETHIOPIA and her king, he seems to suggest that he was the general redactor or editor who directed the work of his devoted companions YAMHARANA-'AB, HEZBA- KRESTÔS, ANDREW, PHILIP, and MAHÂRÎ-'AB.

Now, however important the KEBRA NAGAST may have been considered by the Ethiopians in bygone centuries, and notwithstanding the almost superstitious awe with which the book is still regarded in ABYSSINIA, we are hardly justified in accepting it as a connected historical document. But it is undoubtedly a very fine work, and many sections of it merit careful consideration and study. For many of the statements in it there are historical foundations, and the greater part of the narrative is based upon legends and sayings and traditions, many of which are exceedingly ancient. The legends and traditions are derived from many sources, and can be traced to the Old Testament and Chaldean TARGÛMS, to Syriac works like the "Book of the Bee", to Coptic lives of saints, to ancient Kur'ânic stories and commentaries, to apocryphal books like the "Book of ADAM and EVE", the "Book of ENOCH", "KÛFÂLÊ", the "Instructions of ST. PETER to his disciple CLEMENT" (i.e. the KALÊMĔNTÔS), the Life of HANNÂ, the Mother of the Virgin Mary", the "Book of the Pearl", and the "Ascension of ISAIAH", &c. Side by side with the extracts from these works we have long sections in which works attributed to GREGORY THAUMATURGUS, to TIMOTHEUS (?), Patriarch of CONSTANTINOPLE, and to CYRIL are quoted at great length.

The object of the author, or compiler, and the later editors of the KEBRA NAGAST (no matter what its original form may have been), was to glorify ETHIOPIA by narrating the history of the coming of the "spiritual and heavenly ZION", the Tabernacle of the Law of the God of ISRAEL, of her own free will from JERUSALEM to ETHIOPIA, and to make it quite clear that the King of ETHIOPIA was descended from SOLOMON, the son of DAVID, King of ISRAEL, and through him from Abraham and the early Patriarchs. But CHRIST also was descended from SOLOMON and the early Patriarchs, and he was the Son of God, so the King of ETHIOPIA being a kinsman of CHRIST was also a son of God, and he was therefore both God and king to his people. The KEBRA NAGAST was intended to make the people of ETHIOPIA believe that their country was specially chosen by God to be the new home of the spiritual and heavenly ZION, of which His chosen people the JEWS had become unworthy. This ZION existed originally in an immaterial form in heaven, where it was the habitation of God. MOSES made, under Divine directions, a copy of it in wood and gold, and placed in it the Two Tables of the Law, the pot of manna, the rod of AARON; and the SHECHINAH dwelt on it and in it. This material copy was called "ZION, the Tabernacle of the Law of God". When SOLOMON finished building his Temple ZION was established therein in the Holy of Holies, and from it God made known His commands when He visited the Temple. It was at all times held to be the visible emblem of God Almighty and the material duplicate of the immaterial ZION in heaven.

The fame of the wisdom of SOLOMON reached the ends of the earth, chiefly because he traded with merchants from the sea coast and from the countries to the south of PALESTINE on each side of the RED SEA. These merchants brought the precious woods and stones, and the scents, and the spices, and the rich stuffs and other objects with which he decorated the Temple and his own palace, and when their caravans returned home their servants described to eager listeners the great works that the King of ISRAEL was carrying out in JERUSALEM. Among the masters, or leaders, of these caravans was one TÂMRÎN, who managed the business affairs of a "Queen of the South", whom Arab writers call "BALKÎS", and Ethiopian writers "MÂKĔDÂ"; but neither of these names is ancient, and it is very doubtful if either represents in any way the true name of the southern queen. It is doubtful also if she was an Ethiopian, and it is far more probable that her home was SHĔBHÂ, or SABA, or SHEBA, in the south-west of ARABIA. As she was a worshipper of the sun she was probably a princess among the

SABAEANS. On the other hand, her ancestors may have been merely settlers in ARABIA, and some of them of Ethiopian origin. The KEBRA NAGAST says that she was a very beautiful, bright, and intelligent woman, but tells us nothing about her family. A manuscript at OXFORD (see DILLMANN, Catalogus Bibl. Bodl., p. 26), says that five kings reigned in ETHIOPIA before MÂKĔDÂ, viz. ARÂWÎ 400 years, ANGÂBÔ 200 years, GIEDUR 100 years, SIEBADÔ 50 years, and KAWNÂSYÂ 1 year. If these kings were indeed her ancestors she was probably a native of some country on the western shore of the RED SEA. Be this as it may, she must have been a woman of great enterprise and intelligence, for having heard what TÂMRÎN, the captain of her caravans, had told her about SOLOMON'S wisdom, she determined to go to JERUSALEM and to put to him a series of difficult questions that were puzzling her.

When MÂKĔDÂ arrived in JERUSALEM, she lodged in the splendid quarters which SOLOMON prepared for her, and she had frequent opportunities of conversing with the King. The more she saw him the more she was impressed with the handsomeness of his person, and with piety and wisdom, and with the eloquence of his speech, which he uttered in a low, musical and sympathetic voice. She spent several months in JERUSALEM as the King's guest, and one night after a great and splendid banquet which SOLOMON gave to the notables of his kingdom, in her honour, he took her to wife. When MÂKĔDÂ knew that she was with child, she bade farewell to SOLOMON, and having received from him a ring as a token, she returned to her own country, where her son MĔNYĔLĔK, or MĔNYĔLÎK, was born. In Ethiopic literature this son is often called WALDA-TABBÎB, i.e. "son of the wise man" (SOLOMON), or 'ĔBNA HAKÎM, or BAYNA-LEHKĔM, i.e. IBN AL-HAKÎM, or "the son of the wise man". When the boy reached early manhood he pressed MÂKĔDÂ to allow him to go to see his father SOLOMON in JERUSALEM, and his importunity was so great that at length she gave him the ring which SOLOMON had given her, and sent him thither under the care of TÂMRÎN. On his arrival at GÂZÂ the people in the city and everywhere in the district recognized his striking likeness to SOLOMON, and almost royal honours were paid to him by them. The same thing happened in JERUSALEM, and when the officials of SOLOMON'S palace were leading him to the presence chamber all the household knew without telling that a son was being taken in to his father. Father and son fell into each other's arms when they met, and the son had no need to prove his identity by producing the ring which his father had given to his beloved MÂKĔDÂ, for SOLOMON proclaimed straightway the young man's parentage, and made him to occupy the royal throne with him, after he had arrayed him in royal apparel.

SOLOMON spared no pains in providing both instruction and amusement for BAYNA-LĔHKĔM (BIN 'L-HAKÎM) whilst he was in JERUSALEM, for he hoped to keep him with him; but after a few months the young man was eager to get back to his mother and to his own country, and TÂMRÎN, the leader of MÂKĔDÂ'S caravans, wanted to be gone. BAYNA-LĔHKĔM, or MENYELEK, as we may now call him, saw that REHOBOAM must succeed SOLOMON on the throne of ISRAEL, and had no wish to occupy the subordinate position of a second son in JERUSALEM, and he therefore pressed SOLOMON to give him leave to depart. When the King had arranged that the elder sons of his nobles should accompany MENYELEK on his return to his mother's capital, DABRA MÂKĔDÂ, and had arranged with MENYELEK for the establishment of a duplicate Jewish kingdom in ETHIOPIA, he permitted him to depart. When MÂKĔDÂ was in JERUSALEM she learned that the Tabernacle ZION in the Temple of JERUSALEM was the abode of the God of ISRAEL, and the place where God Almighty was pleased to dwell, and in her letter to SOLOMON she begged him to send her, as a holy talisman, a portion of the fringe of the covering of the Tabernacle. SOLOMON told MENYELEK that he would grant MÂKĔDÂ'S request, but this satisfied neither MENYELEK nor his nobles, and, to speak briefly, MENYELEK and TÂMRÎN and the eldest sons of the Jewish notables who were destined to help MENYELEK to found his kingdom in ETHIOPIA, entered into a conspiracy together to steal the Tabernacle ZION and to carry it off to ETHIOPIA. Their object was to keep the God of ISRAEL with them, and this they expected to be able to effect by stealing the Tabernacle made of gold and wood (according to the pattern of the original Spirit-Tabernacle in heaven) which contained the Two Tables of the Law, the pot of manna, AARON'S rod, &c. One of the conspirators who had access to the chamber in which the Tabernacle ZION rested, removed it from under its curtain, and substituted a construction in wood of exactly the same size and shape, which he had caused to be made for the purpose. The theft was not discovered until MENYELEK, and TÂMRÎN, and their company of young JEWS and ETHIOPIANS were well on their road to the RED SEA, and though SOLOMON sent out swift horsemen to overtake them and cut them off, and himself followed with all the speed possible, the thieves made good their escape, and the King of ISRAEL returned to JERUSALEM in great grief. In due course MENYELEK reached his mother's capital, and he and the Tabernacle ZION were received with frantic rejoicings, and MÂKĔDÂ having abdicated in favour of her son, MENYELEK established in ETHIOPIA a kingdom modelled on that of ISRAEL, and introduced into his country the Laws of God and the admonitions of MOSES and the social rules and regulations with which the name of the great Lawgiver was associated in those days.

The KEBRA NAGAST tells us nothing about MENYELEK after his coronation, except that he carried on one or two campaigns against the enemies of his country, and the book is silent in respect of Queen MÂKĔDÂ'S history after her voluntary abdication. The author seems to expect his readers to assume that ETHIOPIA was ruled over by descendants of SOLOMON and Queen MÂKĔDÂ from the tenth century before CHRIST to about the tenth century A.D., i.e. for about two thousand years, and that the religion, laws, social customs, &c., of the ETHIOPIANS were substantially those of the Hebrews in PALESTINE under the kings of ISRAEL. In connection with this assumption reference may be made here briefly to a series of chapters which now form part of the KEBRA NAGAST, in which the author endeavours to prove that the kings of the MOABITES, PHILISTINES, EGYPTIANS, PERSIANS, BABYLONIANS and the BYZANTINES, are of Semitic origin. The fantastic legends which he invented or reproduced contain much falsified history and bad philology, but it would be interesting to know their source and their author; these chapters seem to suggest that he was a Semite, probably a Jew.

In another group of chapters, which can hardly have formed a part of the oldest version of the KEBRA NAGAST, the author summarizes the prophecies in the Old Testament that concern the Coming of the Messiah, and applies them to JESUS CHRIST with very considerable skill. And he devotes much space to the VIRGIN MARY, and quotes numerous passages from the Old Testament, with the view of identifying her symbolically with the Tabernacle of the Covenant.

2. English Translation of the Arabic Text Describing How the Kingdom of DAVID was Transferred from JERUSALEM to ETHIOPIA.[11]

[Here is] The Explanation of the Reason for the Transfer of the Kingdom of DAVID from his Son SOLOMON, King of ISRAEL, to the Country of the Negus, that is to say, to ABYSSINIA.

When the Lord, praise be unto Him! wished SOLOMON to build the House of the Lord in JERUSALEM, after the death of his father DAVID, the son of JESSE, who had reigned over the children of ISRAEL, and SOLOMON, in accordance with his most excellent desire, began to build the House of the Lord, praise be unto Him! SOLOMON the King gave the command that the stones for the building should be hewn in immense sizes. But the workmen were unable to hew such large blocks of stone, and their tools broke when they attempted the work, and they cried out to SOLOMON the King and besought him to think out in his wisdom some plan for lightening their labour. And SOLOMON entreated God, the bestower of wisdom, to suggest some means to him. And behold, SOLOMON summoned the hunters and commanded them to bring a young Rukh bird, and in accordance with his orders they brought a young Rukh bird. And he commanded them likewise to bring a brass pot with a space inside it sufficiently large to contain the Rukh bird; and the pot had three legs, each one cubit in height, and it stood upon the ground. Then SOLOMON commanded them to set down the Rukh bird in the palace and to put the brass pot over it, but the wings of the Rukh bird protruded from under the aforementioned pot, and raised it above the ground. Now when the [mother] Rukh bird returned to her nest in the high mountains, and did not find her young one there, she was disturbed, and she flew round and round over the earth seeking for it. And she flew over JERUSALEM and saw her young one under the aforementioned pot, but had not the power to seize it. And she mounted up into the heights and went towards the Paradise of God, in the eastern part of Eden, and she found below Paradise a piece of wood which had been cast down there as if for her to carry away. And then she seized it, and by reason of her great sorrow for her young one she took no rest until she had brought it to JERUSALEM, and hurled it down upon the brass pot. And by the might of God a miracle took place forthwith, for the pot split into two halves, and the mother Rukh saw her young, and caught it up and bore it off to her nest. And when SOLOMON and all the children of ISRAEL saw this miracle, with a loud voice they praised the Almighty (or, the Governor of the Universe), Who had bestowed upon a bird that was not endowed with reasoning powers the instinct to do that which human beings could not do. And straightway King SOLOMON commanded the stone-masons to take that piece of holy and blessed wood, and, when they had marked out and measured the stone which they wished to split, to lay the afore-mentioned piece of wood on the place marked. And when they had done this, by the might of God the stone split wheresoever they wished it to split, and they found their work easy. Then SOLOMON became certain in his mind that the Governor of the Universe regarded the building of the Holy Temple with favour. And when the construction of the Temple was finished, the afore-mentioned piece of wood remained in the entrance chamber of the forecourt of the porch, and as the building of the Temple had stopped the operative power of the afore-mentioned piece of wood came to an end, but it was still held in respect.

Now God, praise be unto Him! having willed that the kingdom of DAVID and his son SOLOMON should be transferred to the blessed land of ABYSSINIA, stirred up the Queen of that country to make a journey to JERUSALEM to hear some of the wisdom of SOLOMON, even as the Holy Gospel saith, "The Queen of the South shall rise up in the judgement and shall judge this generation, because she came from the ends of the earth to hear SOLOMON".[12] And behold, from the earliest times, the kingdom of ABYSSINIA was ruled over by royal princesses. And when the mother of this Queen was with child of her she saw a fat and handsome-looking goat, and she looked upon him with greedy desire, and said, "How handsome the beast is! And how handsome its feet are!" And she longed for it after the manner of women who are with child. And when the afore-mentioned daughter was fashioned completely in the womb of her mother, she had one foot like the foot of a man and another like the foot of a goat. Great and exalted be the Creator of the Universe, Who is to be praised! And when the mother of the Queen had brought forth this extraordinary being, and had reared her, and the maiden was ready for marriage, she (i.e. the maiden) did not want to marry any man because of her malformed foot; and she continued in her virginity until she began to reign. And when the thought to visit SOLOMON to hear his wisdom rose in her mind - as has already been mentioned - this had already been ordained in the wisdom of God, praise be unto Him! so that the kingdom of DAVID might last to the end of the world according to the word of DAVID by the Holy Ghost, "The Lord hath sworn a true oath to DAVID from which He will never turn aside: Of the fruit of thy loins I will seat upon thy throne. If they will keep the allegiance of My Covenant and of My testimony which I shall teach them, their children shall sit upon thy throne for ever".[13] And besides this passage there are many other passages in the Psalms and in the other Books that refer to this [oath]. This passage nevertheless showeth also that the kingdom was to be rent from the children of ISRAEL; and since they changed [the Covenant], and did not observe the truth, and ceased to believe in Him Who was expected, God rent from them Prophecy, Priesthood, and Sovereignty.

And when the afore-mentioned Queen arrived in JERUSALEM, and SOLOMON the King had heard of it, and was quite certain from the information, which he had received from his spies, that one of her feet was the foot of a goat, he planned a cunning plan in his wisdom, whereby he might be able to see her foot without asking [her to show it to him]. He placed his throne by the side of the courtyard of the Temple, and he ordered his servants to open the sluices so that the courtyard of the Temple might be filled with water. This was done, and the aforementioned piece of wood that was in the courtyard, having been brought there by the eagle (sic) from below Paradise, was submerged by the water, but no one noticed this thing which had been decreed aforetime by the wisdom of God. And behold when the Queen arrived at the gate of the Temple - now she was riding - she found the water there, and she determined to ride into the presence of King SOLOMON on her beast, but they made her to know that this was the door of the House of God, and that no one whatsoever might enter it riding on a beast. And they caused her to dismount from her beast, and her servants who were in attendance upon her supported her; and she stretched out her hand and drew up the lower parts of her cloak and her garments beneath it so that she might step into the water. Thus SOLOMON saw her feet without asking her [to show them to him]. And behold, she stepped into the water in the courtyard, and her foot touched that afore-mentioned piece of wood, and as the foot that was fashioned like the foot of a goat touched the wood, the Might of God made itself manifest, and the goat's foot became exactly like its fellow foot which was that of a man. And immediately she understood that mighty Power that had seized her great fear and trembling came upon her, but she [straightway] rejoiced and stepped further into the water, and at length she came into the presence of King SOLOMON. And SOLOMON welcomed her with gladness, and brought her up on his throne, and paid her honour, and permitted her to sit by his side. And the Queen informed him that she had come from the ends of the earth solely to worship in JERUSALEM and to hear his wisdom. Then she asked him questions, saying, "When I came to thy honourable kingdom and dipped my foot in to the water, that foot being the foot of a goat, my foot touched something that was submerged in the water, whereupon it became straightway like its fellow foot. Thereupon great fear and trembling came upon me, and then joy, because of that which had happened unto me through the compassion of the Governor of the Universe". And then she showed him both her feet. Then SOLOMON praised and glorified God, Who alone worketh mighty and wonderful things, and he testified to her that he had only made the water in order to cause her to lift her cloak so that he might see her foot, that is to say, the goat's foot. Then straightway he commanded that the water be made to go back to its place, and the courtyard became visible, and the piece of wood which she had touched with her foot stood out clearly. And SOLOMON related to her the story of the piece of wood. And when the Queen understood the matter truly she commanded that honour should be paid to the wood, and she decorated it with a collar of silver, and when SOLOMON saw her do this he also decorated the piece of wood with another collar of silver and assigned unto it a place in the Temple, in the Temple of the Lord. And it came to pass that each and every one of SOLOMON'S successors, who came to the Temple of God to pray, as soon as they heard the story of the piece of wood decorated it with silver rings. And from the days of SOLOMON to the coming of CHRIST this piece of wood was decorated with thirty collars of silver.

And it came to pass that, when the Lord, praise be unto Him! wished to complete His Dispensation, and to effect the deliverance of ADAM and his posterity from out of the hand of the accursed Enemy - whom may God put to everlasting shame - JUDAS made a covenant with the high priests and with the cunning folk among the JEWS to deliver CHRIST unto them, so that they might be able to condemn Him to death. And the high priests undertook to give JUDAS the afore-mentioned collars of silver on the wood, and they sent and had the piece of wood brought by night to the place where the high priests were, and they stripped off from it the afore-mentioned collars of silver, and delivered them over to JUDAS. And JUDAS took them and delivered the LORD CHRIST over to them, even as the Gospel saith. And when the morning of the fifth day of the week had come, on which they condemned the LORD CHRIST to death on the cross, they took the piece of wood afore-mentioned, and they commanded a carpenter to make a cross out of it, and they crucified the Redeemer upon it. And this is a clear proof, even as the Tongue of gold (i.e. CHRYSOSTOM) said that our father ADAM was led astray when he ate of the fruit of the tree in Paradise, and it was because of this that he was stripped of his glory and driven out from Paradise, and Satan reigned over him and over his race. And ADAM'S deliverance also took place by the Dispensation of God through the coming of this piece of wood from the region of Paradise. And it became an honoured thing to kings, and at length the King of Kings came and was crucified upon it. And He redeemed ADAM and his descendants from the hand of the Accursed One by means of a piece of wood, even as the fruit of a piece of wood had led him into error. And concerning this, DAVID the Prophet said in the Psalm,[14] "Declare ye among the nations that God reigneth from the wood". And this piece of wood became most honourable because the Body of our Lord was raised up on it, and at length when they laid it upon a dead body that body rose up again. And the similitude [of the Cross] became a protection to kings and a strengthening of the remainder of the Christians for evermore. And as for the thirty collars of silver aforementioned JUDAS cast them, back to the accursed JEWS, and after this he hanged himself and departed this life by reason of his love of money. And the JEWS took them and bought with them the field of the potter, and it is a place of burial for strangers unto this day. This is what happened through the piece of wood.

And now we will return to the subject with which we began, namely, how the kingdom of DAVID was removed to the country of ABYSSINIA, and will relate the conclusion of the story. Behold, SOLOMON the King paid honour to the Queen, and he made her and her retinue and her soldiers to alight by the side of his palace, and every day she visited him in order to hear his wisdom. And SOLOMON loved women passionately, and it came to pass that, when her visits to him multiplied, he longed for her greatly and entreated her to yield herself to him. But she would not surrender herself to him, and she said unto him, "I came to thee a maiden, a virgin; shall I go back despoiled of my virginity, and suffer disgrace in my kingdom?" And SOLOMON said unto her, "I will only take thee to myself in lawful marriage - I am the King, and thou shalt be the Queen." And she answered him never a word. And he said unto her. "Strike a covenant with me that I am only to take thee to wife of thine own free will - this shall be the condition between us: when thou shalt come to me by night as I am lying on the cushions of my bed, thou shalt become my wife by the Law of Kings." And behold she struck this covenant with him determining within herself that she would preserve her virginity from him; and this [happened] through the dispensation of God, the Most High, to Whom be praise! And SOLOMON by his wisdom instructed her for a number of days, and he did not again demand from her the surrender of her person, and the matter was good in her sight, because she thought that he had driven her out of his mind.

And after these things SOLOMON summoned the cooks and commanded them to prepare and cook food for all those who were in the palace, for himself and for the Queen, dainty and highly seasoned dishes, and he gave them pungent and aromatic and strong-smelling herbs and spices for this purpose, and the cooks did even as he had commanded them. Now when the Queen had eaten of these meats that were filled with spice and pepper and pungent herbs, she craved for cold water which she drank in large quantities by day and by night, but this did not help her to [quench her thirst]. And when the third night had come SOLOMON secretly gave the order to all those who were about the palace, both those who were inside it and those who were outside it, that none of them was to leave with the afore-mentioned Queen the smallest quantity of water to drink, and [he swore] that any one of them who showed her where water was or gave her any of the water which was his own should be put to death forthwith and without trial. And he commanded that, if any of them were to be asked for water by her during the night, they were to say unto her, "Thou wilt find no water except by the couch of the king." And it came to pass that when the night had come, a great and fiery heat rose up in the heart of the Queen because of the highly spiced food [that she had eaten], and she sought for water to drink, but found none, and she was sorely agitated and was smitten with death. Then she cried out with a loud voice to her servants, but they were unable to find any water to give her to drink. Then by reason of the consuming thirst that had seized upon her, she wandered into the palace and went round about to every one who had water therein to find some water to drink, and every person whom she asked said unto her, "Verily, by thy kingdom, thou wilt only find water to quench the flame of thy thirst by the bedside of the King." Then the Queen went back to her couch, but she could not control herself and keep still, and her spirit was about to depart from her body, and she was swooning. Then she made haste and went to the place where SOLOMON was, so that she might drink some water there. Now SOLOMON was in truth wide-awake, nevertheless he pretended to be asleep, and the Queen drank a very large quantity of water and assuaged her thirst, and she recovered her spirit, and she felt that her strength was restored after having [nearly] died. And when the Queen wanted to return to her couch, King SOLOMON started up hurriedly, and seized her, and said unto her, "Verily thou hast now become my wife according to the Law of Kings." And she remembered the covenant that existed between him and her. And she gave herself into his embrace willingly and yielded to his desire, according to that which she had covenanted with him.

And it came to pass that after these things she became with child by him, and she said unto him, "I am going to return to my country and to my kingdom, and what shall I do with thy child if it be that God shall desire to give him life?" And SOLOMON said unto her, "If God doth will this thing and thou dost bear to me a man child, so soon as he hath reached man's estate send him to me, and I will make him king, and thy kingdom shall be his; but if thou dost bear a woman child let her stay with thee." And the Queen said unto him, "If I send thee thy son how wilt thou be certain that he is thy son?" And SOLOMON gave her his ring, and said unto her, "Guard carefully this ring, and covenant with me that thou wilt not in the smallest degree break the conditions of the true and righteous covenant that existeth between us, and God, the Governor of the Universe, the God of Abraham, and ISAAC, and Jacob, the God of my father DAVID, shall be the witness between me and between thee. And when thou dost send my son to me, give him my ring, and let him wear it on his own hand, and I shall know that in very truth he is my son, and I will make him king and send him back to thee." And she accepted from SOLOMON this just covenant, and he and the Queen took farewell of each other, and she set out with her retinue to go to her own country, surrounded by the peace of God.

And behold, on her arrival in her own country the Queen fulfilled the number of her days, and she brought forth a man child, and she rejoiced with an exceedingly great joy, and she called him DAVID, according to the name of his grandfather, and she had him reared in great state and splendour. And when he had arrived at manhood's estate, he was hale, and strong, and wise, and understanding like his father. And it fell out on a day that he spake unto his mother and said unto her, "O my mother, who is my father? Did he, peradventure, die during my childhood?" Then the Queen answered and said unto him, "My son, thy father is alive, and he is SOLOMON, the son of DAVID, the Prophet of God and King of ISRAEL, and his Kingdom is in JERUSALEM. And behold, the seal of the kingdom of thy father is in my possession, and it is laid up ready for thee so that thou mayest become thereby king over the country of ABYSSINIA. And this is God's Will, and it is not due to me; the kingdom is no longer mine but thine, and thou, the King's son, art King." And this pleased the young man greatly, and he gave thanks to the Queen. And the Queen said unto him, "O my darling son, gather together for thy use gifts and soldiers, and get thee to JERUSALEM that thou mayest pray there, and see thy father and his kingdom, [and hear] his great wisdom, and that he may make thee king according to the covenant that existeth between him and me, the Governor of the Universe being witness between us." And thus saying, straightway she put his father's ring on his right hand. And by the Will of God - praise be unto Him! - he gathered together soldiers, and with them and the royal gifts he set out on his journey, and in due course he arrived in JERUSALEM. And when SOLOMON knew that a king was coming to him he commanded soldiers to meet him. And when the young man arrived at the gate of the palace of his father SOLOMON, the king was not certain that he was his son. And behold, when the young man came closer and saw the riding beast of his father standing there with his saddle on his back and his bridle in his mouth, straightway he leaped up and mounted him and pranced about, and unsheathed his sword with his hand. And when SOLOMON saw this the matter was grievous to him, but he hid his displeasure. And when they met [later] SOLOMON spoke openly what he had in his mind about the matter of the riding beast, and how the young man had mounted him and snatched the sword with his hand. And the young man said unto him, "The owner of this ring made me king of his kingdom when I was in my mother's womb, and this hath happened by the Will of God." And when SOLOMON had looked at the ring, and was certain about the matters connected with it, he was overcome with joy, and he stood up by his throne and threw his arms round the young man's neck, and he cried out, saying, "Welcome, my darling boy, [thou] son of DAVID." And straightway he put the crown of his father DAVID on his head, and made him to sit upon the throne of DAVID his father, and the trumpeters sounded their horns, and the proclaimers of tidings cried out, saying, "This is DAVID, the son of SOLOMON, the son of DAVID, the King of ISRAEL." And the matter was noised abroad, and the rumour spread about among all the tribes of the children of ISRAEL that the son of SOLOMON, the son of the Queen of the South, had come to his father SOLOMON, and that SOLOMON had made him ruler over the kingdom of his father DAVID, and had crowned him king, and had seated him upon his throne.

Now in the House of the Lord which SOLOMON had built and consecrated was the Tabernacle of the Covenant of God, and inside it were the two Tablets of stone that had been written by the Finger of God, and the rod of AARON, and the pot (or, chest) of manna. And this Tabernacle was covered with plates of gold and was draped with draperies of cloth woven with gold. And [in connection with the Tabernacle] a miracle which was seen by all the people of ISRAEL was wrought. Whensoever the priests prayed, and the supplications of themselves [and of the people] were presented before the Governor of the Universe, and they had made an end of their prostrations, the Tabernacle of the Covenant of God used to raise itself up from off the ground, and they [and the people] knew that in very truth their supplications had been accepted. And when they had made an end of their prostrations and the Tabernacle did not raise itself from off the ground, the priests knew of a certainty that some sin had been committed by themselves or by the people. Then they continued to make their supplications unto the Lord, and at the same time they searched out him that had done wrong, and they punished the guilty one, and when the Tabernacle raised itself up from off the ground they knew that God had removed His displeasure from them.

And it came to pass that the afore-mentioned king, the son of SOLOMON, went into the House of the Lord to pray, and he saw the Tabernacle of the Covenant of God raising itself up - a matter which it is impossible for the human mind to understand - and this was pleasing in his sight, and he determined to carry off the Tabernacle of the Covenant of God to his own country. And he broke the matter to his begetter SOLOMON, the King of ISRAEL, and he said unto him, "I am going to carry off the Tabernacle of the Covenant of God to my country." And SOLOMON said unto him, "O my darling son, thou canst not do this. Behold, there is no one except a priest who can carry the Tabernacle, and whosoever toucheth the Tabernacle except the priests, his soul departeth from him immediately. Moreover the children of ISRAEL have no protection whatsoever against their enemies except the Tabernacle of the Covenant of God." But these words did not satisfy him, and he said unto SOLOMON, "I ask of thee neither gold nor silver, for in my country men gather in heaps gold from its earth. I ask from thee nothing but the Tabernacle of the Covenant of God, so that it may protect me on my journey, and may be a support for my kingdom and for my soldiers in my country." And SOLOMON said unto his son, "O my son, if it be the Will of God, the Governor of the Universe, that thou shalt take away the Tabernacle with thee, it will be an easy thing for thee to do so. But when thou carriest away the Tabernacle do not let me know about it, and when thou goest away with it do not bid me farewell. For, behold, without doubt, the priests and the elders of the fortress of ISRAEL will make me to swear an oath by the Name of God concerning this matter, and when I have to swear an oath by the Name of God I must swear what is true."

Then the young man summoned to himself secretly a workman, who made a wooden case of the same length and breadth and depth and shape as the Tabernacle, and then the young man killed him by night. Then he brought in other artificers, and they overlaid the wooden case with plates of gold similar to those that covered the Tabernacle, and he treated those men even as he had treated the carpenter, and then the young man covered the case with draperies into which gold had been woven. Now whilst he was making his preparations for his departure SOLOMON the King knew nothing whatsoever about them. Then the young man summoned to him four of the priests who could be trusted, and he made them believe that he had done so in order to ask them to pray for him before his departure, and he gave them much gold to pray for him, and he bribed them to assist him whensoever he needed them. And when the night of his departure had arrived, these priests came to him in order to bid him farewell, and he took them into his own apartment, so that they might pray for him. And when they had entered and were in the apartment with him, he bound them in iron fetters for the night, and commanded his soldiers to mount and depart without sounding the trumpets. Then he took with him a company of his servants who were carrying spears in their hands, and he took those priests whom he had bound with iron fetters for the night so that they might not escape, and he went into the House of God. And he commanded the priests who were with him to carry away the Tabernacle of the Covenant of God, and then he deposited the case which he had had made to resemble it in the place thereof. And he went forth by night having with him the Tabernacle, which was carried by the priests, and he neither bade his father farewell nor allowed him to know of his departure. And this happened by the Dispensation of God the Most High, praise be unto Him! for the protection of the holy Tabernacle of His Covenant, so that it might abide for ever even as the Davidic kingdom, for even so did God make the promise to DAVID that the offspring of his loins should sit upon his throne for ever. And in this manner, enveloped in the protection of God, did the young man set out on his journey.

And it came to pass that, when the morning had come, the children of ISRAEL and the priests went into the House of God according to their wont to pray. And it came to pass that, when the priests had made an end of their prostrations and had presented their supplications unto the Governor of the Universe, the Tabernacle did not rise up into the air, and it did not stir from its place. And they said, "Behold, some folk have sinned"; and they ordered fasting and prayer for three days, and they searched among the people to find out who had committed sin and folly, but they found no [guilty] person. And after this the priests went up to the Tabernacle, and O what calamity, and terror, and grief were there for them when they did not find the Tabernacle of the Covenant of God and its holy things, but only an empty case resting upon the place where the Tabernacle had stood! Then they knew that of a certainty the son of King SOLOMON had taken it away. And they searched and made an examination into the number of the priests who were among the tribes of ISRAEL, but they were not able to find those priests whom the young man had taken with him, and thus it became clear to them that the sin lay with them (i.e. the four priests).

And behold, the priests and the elders of ISRAEL went to SOLOMON the King, and they were weeping and sorrowing because of the absence of the Tabernacle of the Covenant of God from its Holy Shrine, and they said unto SOLOMON, "It is thou who hast commanded thy son to take the Tabernacle." And SOLOMON wept and cried out in pain, and displayed exceedingly great sorrow, and he swore an oath to them, saying that he had not given his son permission to do this thing, and that he had not bidden him farewell, and that he knew nothing whatsoever about his departure or when it took place. And the priests and elders answered, saying, "May the King live! If this thing hath taken place without thy wish and without thy permission, despatch thou with us armed soldiers that we may pursue him and take from him the holy Tabernacle of the Covenant of God, so that we may bring it back to His sacred House." And SOLOMON gave them soldiers, and money, and provisions, and they set out in quest of the young man, and they rode on their way continuously for forty days. And they found merchants riding towards them on their return journey, and they enquired of them concerning the Tabernacle, and whether they had seen it. And the merchants answered them, saying, "We have seen a great king and his numerous soldiers, and the Box of the Covenant of God was with them. And they were travelling along like the clouds when they are driven before the attack of mighty winds for a very long distance at a time, and the natives of the villages through which we have passed informed us that they travelled each day the distance of a forty days' journey." And they returned defeated and disheartened, and weeping and regretting; but regret in no way helped them. And behold, the young man arrived in his country safe and sound, and his mother met him, and she abdicated in his favour, and he rose up as king on the throne of DAVID his father, and the kingdom of ABYSSINIA belonged to the throne of DAVID for ever and ever, and the Tabernacle of the Covenant of God remained therein.

This is what happened in respect of the Tabernacle of the Lord, and this is the reason why it was transferred to the country of the NĔGÛS; and this state of affairs continued until the birth of our Lord JESUS CHRIST of the pure MARY. And He completed His Dispensation upon earth and set free ADAM and his posterity. And after His Ascension into heaven the Disciples preached the Gospel in His Name in all the earth. And concerning the story of the eunuch, the Deputy of KANDÂKES, it is related that the cause of his visit to JERUSALEM was to pray [there]. And on his return journey the Holy Spirit sent to him the Apostle PHILIP, and the eunuch believed and was baptized; and when he went back to his native land he preached CHRIST therein, and all the people believed through him. And after this PÂRMENÂS, one of the Seven, went to them, and he baptized them, and consecrated for them priests and deacons, and he ordained that their Father should be of the throne of MARK the Evangelist. And the orthodox Faith was established in the country of ABYSSINIA, and the sovereignty of [the house of] DAVID remained fixed therein for ever and ever. Glory, and praise, and majesty, and honour, and supplication be unto the Holy Trinity for ever and ever! Amen. This is what is found [written] in the Histories of the ancient Fathers of the Coptic Church. Praise be unto the Giver of understanding and wisdom to His creatures; may His mercy be upon us for ever!

3.   *Legends of SOLOMON and the Queen of SHEBA in the KUR'ÂN and in Muhammadan literature*

The author, or editor, of the KUR'ÂN devoted a considerable section of Surah XXVII to the correspondence that passed between the Queen of SHEBA and King SOLOMON, and to their interviews. Among the many gifts that God bestowed upon SOLOMON were the understanding of the speech of birds, and knowledge of every kind. He was the lord of men, genii and birds. When he travelled through the air on his magical carpet of green silk, which was borne aloft by the wind according to the King's direction, the men stood on the right of it, and the spirits on the left, and a vast army of birds of every kind kept flying over the carpet to protect its occupants from the heat of the sun. One day when he was reviewing the birds he perceived that the lapwing was absent, and he asked why she was absent, and threatened to punish her for not making her appearance with the other birds. Very soon after he had spoken the lapwing appeared, and she excused herself for her absence by saying that she had been looking upon a country that the king had never seen, and that she had seen SÂBA, which was ruled over by a queen called "BALKÎS", who was very rich, and who sat upon a throne made of gold and silver and set with precious stones, eighty cubits long, forty cubits broad, and thirty cubits high. The queen and her people were idolaters and worshipped the sun, and they were under the influence of SATAN, who had turned them from the right way. Thereupon SOLOMON wrote the following letter to the Queen of SHEBA: "From the servant of God, SOLOMON, the son of DAVID, unto BALKÎS Queen of SHEBA. In the Name of the most merciful God. Peace be unto him who followeth the true direction. Rise not up against me, but come and render yourselves unto me." Having perfumed this letter with musk and sealed it with his wonderful seal, SOLOMON gave it to the lapwing and told the bird to go and drop it in SÂBA, and to turn aside afterwards and wait for the Queen's answer. The lapwing departed and delivered the letter, some saying that she flew into the Queen's private apartment through the window, and others that she dropped the letter into the Queen's bosom[15] as she was standing surrounded by her army. Having read the letter the Queen called upon her nobles to advise her what to do, but they reminded her that they were soldiers, who were ready to march against SOLOMON if she ordered them to do so, and that the letter was addressed to her and she must make the decision. Wishing to avoid invasion and the evils that would follow in its train, the Queen decided to send gifts to SOLOMON, and she despatched forthwith five hundred male and five hundred female slaves, five hundred ingots of gold, a crown studded with precious stones, and a large quantity of musk, amber, spices, precious woods, etc. The lapwing returned quickly to SOLOMON and told him what had happened, and that an embassy from the Queen bearing gifts was on its way. When the men of SÂBA arrived they were received by SOLOMON in a large square surrounded by a wall, the bricks of which were made of gold and silver. SOLOMON spoke slightingly of the Queen's gifts and sent the embassy back, bidding them tell their mistress that he would send invincible troops against her city, and that they would capture it and expel its inhabitants in disgrace. When BALKÎS received this message, she determined to go to SOLOMON and to tender her submission to him, and having locked up her throne in a certain strong fortress, and set a guard over it to protect it, she set out for JERUSALEM, accompanied by a large army. Whilst she was on her way SOLOMON said one day to his nobles, "Which of you will bring the Queen's throne here to me before she and her company arrive?" And an 'IFRÎT, one of the genii, whose aspect was most terrible, and who was called DHAKWÂN or SAKHR, said, "I will bring it to thee before thou hast finished thy session. Now SOLOMON used to sit in judgment until noon daily.[16] Some one who had knowledge of books and who was present seemed to think that the 'IFRÎT was demanding too much time in which to fulfil the King's urgent wish, and he said, I will bring thee the throne before thou canst cast thine eyes on an object and remove them again." The commentators are in doubt about the identity of the person who made this offer to SOLOMON, for some say he was ÂSAF, the son of BARKHÎYÂ, the wazîr of SOLOMON, and others that he was KHIDHR (ELIJAH), or GABRIEL, or some other angel, or even SOLOMON himself.[17] It is generally thought that the person was ÂSAF, for he knew the ineffable Name of God. Be this as it may, SOLOMON accepted the offer, and raising his eyes to heaven brought them down quickly to earth again, and when his eyes rested on the earth he saw the throne of BALKÎS standing before him. Then SOLOMON had the throne altered, with the view of preventing her knowing her own throne when she arrived. When BALKÎS came into his presence, he pointed to the throne, saying, "Is thy throne like unto this?" And she replied, "It is all one with this." Then BALKÎS was invited to go into the palace which SOLOMON had built specially for her reception. The walls were made of blocks of white glass, and the floor was made also of glass, over which water flowed, and in the running water fishes swam. When BALKÎS turned to enter the palace and saw the water, thinking that it was deep, she drew up the skirts of her garments before attempting to walk through it. By this act she uncovered her legs, and SOLOMON had proof that the rumour that the feet and legs of BALKÎS were covered with hair like the coat of an ass, was true. The sight of the glass building with its floor of glass amazed BALKÎS, who said, "O Lord, verily I have dealt unjustly with my own soul, and I resign myself, together with SOLOMON, unto God, the Lord of all creatures." Some commentators think that the Queen uttered these words partly in repentance for having worshipped the sun, and partly through fear of being drowned in the water which she saw before her. JALÂL AD-DÎN says that SOLOMON thought of marrying BALKÎS, but could not bring himself to do so because of the hair on her feet and legs. The devils who were always in attendance on SOLOMON removed the hair by the use of some infernal depilatory,[18] but it is doubtful if even then SOLOMON married her. AL-BEIDHAWÎ says that it is very doubtful who married BALKÎS, but is inclined to think that it was one of the chiefs of the Hamdân tribe.[19]

4. Modern Legends of SOLOMON and the Queen of SHEBA

A curious and interesting legend of the way in which King SOLOMON became the father of MENYELEK is found in a number of slightly varying versions among many of the tribes of Northern ABYSSINIA.[20] According to this the mother of MENYELEK was a Tigrê girl called ĔTĔYÊ AZÊB (i.e. Queen of the South), and her people worshipped a dragon or serpent, to which each man in turn had to present as an offering his eldest daughter, and large quantities of sweet beer and milk. When the turn of her parents came they tied her to a tree where the dragon used to come for his food, and soon after this seven saints came and seated themselves under the tree for the sake of the shade it gave. As they sat a tear dropped from the maiden above them, and when they looked up and saw her bound to the tree they asked her if she was a human being or a spirit, and she told them that she was a human being and, in answer to a further question, she told them that she was bound to the tree so that she might become food for the dragon. When the seven saints saw the dragon, one of them, Abbâ TCHÊHAMÂ, plucked at his own beard, another, Abbâ GARÎMÂ exclaimed "He hath frightened me", and a third, Abbâ MENTELÎT, cried out, "Let us seize him"; and he forthwith attacked the monster, and aided by his companions they killed him by smiting him with a cross. As they were killing him some blood spurted out from him and fell on the heel of ĔTĔYÊ AZÊB, and from that moment her heel became like the heel of an ass. The saints untied her fetters and sent her to her village, but the people drove her away, thinking that she had escaped from the dragon, and she climbed up into a tree and passed the night there. On the following day she fetched some people from the village and showed them the dead dragon, and they straightway made her their chieftainess, and she chose for her chief officer a maiden like herself. Soon after this ĔTĔYÊ AZÊB heard a report of the medical skill of King SOLOMON, and she determined to go to him so that he might restore her deformed heel to its original shape. She and her chief officer dressed their hair after the manner of men, and girded on swords, and departed to the Court of SOLOMON at JERUSALEM. Her arrival was announced to SOLOMON, who ordered his servants to bring the King of ABYSSINIA into his presence, and as soon as her deformed foot touched the threshold it recovered its natural form. SOLOMON had bread, meat, and beer brought in and set before the two women who were disguised as men, but they ate and drank so little that SOLOMON suspected that his guests were women. When night fell he caused two beds to be made for his guests in his own bedroom, and he hung up in the room a skin with honey[comb] in it, and he pierced the skin and the honey dropped down into a bowl set there to catch it, and SOLOMON and his guests betook themselves to their beds. At night the king was accustomed to keep vigil with his eyes closed, and to sleep with them half-open, and thus when the two women, who were longing to get off their beds and to go and drink honey from the bowl, saw him with his eyes half-open they thought that the king was awake, and they curbed their desire for the honey and lay still. After a time the king woke up and closed his eyes, but the women, thinking he was asleep, rose from their beds and went to the bowl of honey and began to eat. By this SOLOMON knew that his two guests were women, and he got up and went with them to their beds and lay with both of them. When he left them he gave to each woman a silver staff and a ring, and he said, "If the child be a girl let her take this staff and come to me, and if it be a boy let him take the ring and come to me"; and each woman being with child returned to her own country. In due course each woman gave birth to a son, and each told her child that SOLOMON was his father. When the boys grew up their mothers sent them to JERUSALEM, and the Queen of SHEBA gave her son, who resembled SOLOMON in every way, a mirror which she had brought when she visited SOLOMON, and told him to go with it to the king, who would hide from him, and not to speak to any other man who might be sitting on his throne. When the two youths arrived in JERUSALEM and SOLOMON knew that they claimed to be his sons, he gave orders for them to wait for an interview, and kept them waiting for three years. At the close of the third year he arrayed a friend in his royal robes, and seated him upon his throne, whilst he dressed himself in rags and went and sat in a stable, and then ordered the two young men to be admitted to the presence. When the young men entered the throne room the son of the Queen of SHEBA'S minister grasped the hand of the man on the throne, who personified SOLOMON, thinking that he was the king, but the son of the Queen of SHEBA, who was called "MENYELEK", stood upright and made no obeisance, and when he looked in the mirror which his mother had given him, and saw that the features of the occupant of the throne were entirely different from his own, he knew that he was not standing in the presence of SOLOMON. Then he turned about in all directions and looked at all the faces that were round about him, and found none resembling his own; after a time he looked up and saw SOLOMON gazing at him from the stable, and he knew him at once, and went to the stable and did homage to him as king. And SOLOMON said, "My true son! The other is also my son, but he is a fool." MENYELEK then took up his abode in JERUSALEM and assisted SOLOMON in ruling the kingdom, but after a time the people found that father and son did not always agree in their judicial decisions, and they became dissatisfied. On one occasion in the case of a trespass of cattle the king decided that the owner of the field might confiscate the cattle which had trespassed, but MENYELEK ordered him to accept six measures of grain instead of confiscating the cattle. Thereupon the people told the king that they would not be ruled by two chiefs, and that he must send his son back to his native country. When SOLOMON told his son of the people's complaint MENYELEK advised his father to say to them, "Is not MENYELEK my first-born son? I will send him away if you will send your first-born sons with him"; and the people agreed to send their first-born sons to ABYSSINIA with MENYELEK. When SOLOMON was arranging for MENYELEK'S departure he told him to take the Ark of MICHAEL with him, but MENYELEK, believing the Ark of MARY to be of greater importance, changed the covers of the two Arks, and took with him the Ark of MARY. A few days after the departure of MENYELEK a storm visited JERUSALEM, and SOLOMON told his servants to find out if the Ark of MARY was in its place, presumably with the idea of securing its protection against the storm. His servants went and looked and, seeing an Ark with the cover of MARY'S Ark upon it, assumed that it was the Ark of MARY, and reported to SOLOMON that the Ark of MARY was in its place. He then told them to take off the cover, and when they had done so they found that the Ark was MICHAEL'S, and though SOLOMON sent a messenger after MENYELEK to bring back the Ark of MARY, his son refused to give it up. Meanwhile MENYELEK and his party went on their way, and when they arrived at KAYĔH KÔR, a deacon who was carrying the Ark of MARY died, and was buried there. After the burial they wished to resume their journey, but the Ark of MARY refused to move. They then dug up the deacon's body, and laid it in a coffin, and buried it again, but still the Ark refused to move, and when MENYELEK again ordered them to dig up the body, they found a finger of the deacon outside the coffin. When they had placed the deacon's finger in the coffin with the rest of his body, the Ark of MARY allowed itself to be moved, and MENYELEK and his companions went on their way. In due course they came to TEGRÂY and arrived in AKSÛM, where they found SATAN building a house to fight against God. When they told him that the Ark of MARY had come he stopped building, threw down what he had built, and went away; and the stones which he had collected were used by MENYELEK in building a church to hold the Ark of MARY. One very large stone, which SATAN was carrying to his building when the news came of the arrival of the Ark of MARY, was dropped by him at once, and at the present day that stone stands on the same spot on which he dropped it.

5. The Contents of the KEBRA NAGAST Described

The book opens with an interpretation and explanation of the Three Hundred and Eighteen Orthodox Fathers concerning the children of ADAM, and the statement that the Trinity lived in ZION, the Tabernacle of the Law of God, which God made in the fortress of His holiness before He made anything else. The Trinity agreed to make man in God's image, and the Son agreed to put on the flesh of ADAM; man was made to take the place of SATAN and to praise God. In due course CHRIST, the second ADAM, was born of the flesh of MARY the Virgin, the Second ZION (Chap. 1).

In Chap. 2 ISAAC, the translator of the Ethiopic text, next quotes GREGORY the Illuminator, the son of ANAG, a native of BALKH, who was born about 257 A.D. and died about 330. Whilst GREGORY was suffering the tortures inflicted upon him by TIRIDATES III he pondered on the question, Of what doth the glory of kings consist? In the end he came to the conclusion that ADAM'S kingship bestowed upon him by God was greater than that of any of the Kings of ARMENIA.

Chaps. 3-6 deal with the birth of CAIN and ABEL; the face of CAIN was sullen and that of ABEL good tempered, and ADAM made ABEL his heir because of his pleasing countenance. CAIN and ABEL had twin sisters. CAIN'S sister LĔBHÛDHÂ had a good-tempered face, and ADAM gave her in marriage to ABEL; ABEL'S sister KALÎMATH had a sullen face like CAIN, and ADAM gave her in marriage to CAIN.[21] Moved by SATAN to envy, and filled with wrath against ADAM for taking his twin sister from him, CAIN rose up and slew ABEL.

41

ADAM was consoled for ABEL'S death by the birth of Seth. The descendants of CAIN were wicked men, and neglected God, and passed their time in singing lewd songs to stringed instruments and pipes and they lived lawless and abominable lives. ISAAC credits them with having produced the mule, and condemns the crossing of mares with asses. In the tenth generation from ADAM NOAH lived, and he refused to deal in any way with the children of CAIN, whose arrogance, pride, fraud, deceit, and uncleanness cried aloud to heaven. At length God sent the Flood, which destroyed everything on the earth except Eight Souls, and seven of every clean beast, and two of every unclean beast (Chap. 8). God made a covenant with NOAH not to destroy the earth again by a flood, and when NOAH died SHEM succeeded him (Chaps. 9 and 10). In Chap. 11 we have another declaration by the 318 Orthodox Fathers that: 1. The Tabernacle of the Law (i.e. the Ark of the Covenant) was created before the heavens, the earth and its pillars, the sea, and men and angels; 2. It was made by God for His own abode; 3. It is on the earth. The ZION wherein God dwelt in heaven before the creation was the type and similitude of the VIRGIN MARY.

The seven sons of CANAAN, who were the sons of HAM, seized seven cities that belonged to SHEM'S children, but eventually had to relinquish them. The nations seized by CANAAN'S sons were the CANAANITES, the PERIZZITES, the HIVITES, the HITTITES, the AMORITES, the JEBUSITES, the GIRGASITES. In the days of TERAH men made magical images, and placed on the tombs of their fathers statues, out of which devils spake and commanded them to offer up their sons and daughters as sacrifices to "filthy devils" (Chap. 12). TERAH'S son ABRAHAM, having proved for himself the powerlessness of idols, smashed the idols which his father sent him to sell, and then called upon the Creator of the Universe to be his God. A chariot of fire appeared (Chap. 13) and with it God, Who made a covenant with him, and told him to depart to another country. ABRAHAM took his wife, and departed to SALEM, where he reigned in righteousness according to God's command. He had a bodyguard of eighteen[22] stalwart men who wore crowns and belts of gold, and gold-embroidered tunics.

ISAAC and JACOB pleased God in their lives (Chap. 15), but REUBEN transgressed and the succession passed from him (Chap. 16); under the curse of JACOB, with whose concubine BILHAH REUBEN had lain, the children of REUBEN became leprous and scabby.

Chap. 17 describes the glory of ZION, i.e. the Tabernacle of the Law of God which God brought down from heaven to earth, and showed MOSES, and ordered him to make a copy of it. MOSES therefore made a box of acacia wood two and a half cubits long, one and a half cubits broad and one and a half cubits deep, i.e. a portable shrine measuring 3 ft. 9 in. by 2 ft. 3 in. by 2 ft. 3 in. or 4 ft. 2 in. by 2 ft. 6 in. by 2 ft. 6 in. In this shrine he placed the Two Tables of the Covenant, a gold pot containing one omer of manna, and the wonderful rod of AARON, which put forth buds when it was withered. This rod had been broken in two places and was in three pieces, and each piece became a separate and complete rod (see p. 13 and

Exod. xvi. 33, 34; Hebrews ix. 2; Numbers xvii. 10). We may note that in 2 Chron. v. 10, it is said that there was nothing in the Ark except the Two Tables which MOSES put therein in HOREB. MOSES covered the Ark with gold, inside and outside, and made all the vessels, hangings, &c., according to the patterns given to him by God. But there was something else in the Ark made by MOSES. By God's orders he made a case, presumably of gold, in the shape of the "belly of a ship" (p. 15), and in this the Two Tables were to rest. As the VIRGIN MARY is called the "new ship who carried the wealth of the world", this "belly of a ship" was a type of her. The case for the Two Tables symbolized her womb, the case carried the Word cut on stone, and MARY carried the Living Word incarnate. And the Ark made by MOSES was the abode of God, Who dwelt with the Two Tables.

With Chap 19 ISAAC, the translator of the KEBRA NAGAST, begins a long extract from an apocryphal work which "DOMITIUS, Archbishop of CONSTANTINOPLE", says he found among the manuscripts in the library of Saint SOPHIA. I have failed to identify either DOMITIUS or the work he quotes. According to this work the Emperor of ETHIOPIA and the Emperor of RÔMÊ (i.e. BYZANTIUM) are the sons of SHEM, and they divide the world between them (Chap. 20). From the same work we have a description of MÂKĔDÂ the "Queen of the South" (Matt. xii. 42), who was shrewd, intelligent in mind, beautiful in face and form, and exceedingly rich. She carried on a large business on land by means of caravans, and on sea by means of ships, and she traded with the merchants of INDIA and NUBIA and ASWÂN (SYENE). As the Queen came from the south her home was probably in Southern ARABIA, and she is far more likely to have been of ARAB than ETHIOPIAN origin. The head of her trading caravans was TÂMRÎN, a clever man of affairs who directed the operations of 520 camels and 73 ships (Chap. 22). At this time SOLOMON wanted gold, ebony and sapphires for the building of the Temple of God in JERUSALEM, and he opened negotiations with TÂMRÎN for the supply of the same. TÂMRÎN loaded his camels and took his goods to SOLOMON, who proved to be a generous customer, and his wisdom and handsome appearance and riches greatly impressed the merchant from the South. TÂMRÎN saw with amazement that SOLOMON was employing 700 carpenters and 800 masons on the building of the Temple (Chaps. 22, 23). When TÂMRÎN returned to his mistress he told the Queen all that he had seen at JERUSALEM, and day by day he described to her SOLOMON'S power and wisdom and the magnificence of the state in which he lived. Little by little, desire to see this wonderful man and to imbibe his wisdom grew in the Queen's mind, and at length she (Chap. 24) decided to go to JERUSALEM. Thereupon 797 camels and mules and asses innumerable were loaded, and she left her kingdom, and made her way direct to JERUSALEM.

When the Queen met SOLOMON she gave him rich presents, (Chap. 25), and he established her in a lodging, and supplied her with food and servants and rich apparel. The Queen was fascinated as much by his wisdom as by his physical perfections, and she marvelled at the extent and variety of his knowledge. When she saw him instructing the mason, the carpenter, the blacksmith, and directing all the workmen, and at the same time acting as judge and ruler of his people and household, her astonishment was unbounded.

During her stay in JERUSALEM MÂKĔDÂ conversed daily (Chaps. 26, 27) with SOLOMON, and she learned from him about the God of the Hebrews, the Creator of the heavens and the earth. She herself worshipped the sun, moon and stars, and trees, and idols of gold and silver, but under the influence of SOLOMON'S beautiful voice and eloquent words she renounced SÂBÂISM, and worshipped not the sun but the sun's Creator, the God of ISRAEL (Chap. 28). And she vowed that her seed after her should adore the Tabernacle of the God of ISRAEL, the abode of God upon earth. MÂKĔDÂ and SOLOMON exchanged visits frequently and the more she saw of him the more she appreciated his wisdom. The birds and the beasts also came to hear his wisdom, and SOLOMON talked to them, each in his own language, and they went back to their native lands and told their fellow creatures what they had seen and heard.

At length MÂKĔDÂ sent a message to SOLOMON, saying that the time had arrived for her to return to her own country. When SOLOMON heard this he pondered deeply and determined to company with her, for he loved her physical beauty and her shrewd native intelligence, and he wished to beget a son by her. SOLOMON had 400 wives and 600 concubines,[23] and among them were women from SYRIA, PALESTINE, the DELTA, UPPER EGYPT and NUBIA. Our translator, ISAAC, excuses SOLOMON for his excessive love of women, and says that he was not addicted to fornication, but only took these thousand women to wife that he might get sons by each of them. These children were to inherit the countries of his enemies and destroy idolaters. Moreover, SOLOMON lived under the Law of the Flesh, for the Holy Spirit was not given to men in his time. In answer to MÂKĔDÂ'S message SOLOMON sent her an invitation to a splendid banquet, which the Queen accepted, and she went to a place which he had prepared specially for her in the great tent (Chap. 29). The courses were ten in number, and the dishes were dainty, highly seasoned, and abundant, and the Queen was satisfied with their smell only. The tent was furnished with truly Oriental magnificence, scented oils had been sprinkled about with a lavish hand, the air was heavy with the perfumes of burning myrrh and cassia, and the Queen ate and drank heartily. When all the other guests had departed and SOLOMON and MÂKĔDÂ were alone, the King showed her a couch and invited her to sleep there. MÂKĔDÂ agreed on the condition that he did not attempt to take her by force, and in reply SOLOMON said that he would not touch her provided that she did not attempt to take anything that was in his house. Thereupon each vowed to respect the property of the other, and the Queen lay down to sleep. After a short time the highly-spiced meats began to have their effect, and the Queen was seized with violent thirst (Chap. 30). She got up and searched for water but found none. At length she saw a vessel of water by the King's bed, and thinking that he was asleep, she went and took up the vessel and was about to drink when SOLOMON jumped up, and stopped her, and accused her of breaking her oath not to steal anything of his. The agony of thirst was so great that the Queen retracted her oath, and SOLOMON allowed her to drink her fill, and then she retired with him to his couch and slept there. MÂKĚDÂ was a virgin Queen and had reigned over her country six years, when SOLOMON took her to wife. That same night SOLOMON saw a dream in which the sun came down from heaven, and shone brilliantly over ISRAEL, and then departed to ETHIOPIA to shine there for ever. Then a Sun far more brilliant came down and shone over ISRAEL, and the ISRAELITES rejected that Sun and destroyed it, and buried it; but that Sun rose again and ascended into heaven, and paid no further heed to ISRAEL. When SOLOMON understood the meaning of that vision he was greatly disturbed and troubled in his mind, for he knew that the departure of the sun from ISRAEL typified the departure of God.

At length MÂKĚDÂ departed from JERUSALEM, but before she left, SOLOMON gave her six thousand wagonloads of beautiful things, two specially constructed vehicles, one in which to travel over the sea, and one in which to travel through the air. Thus SOLOMON anticipated the motor boat and the airship. Besides all these things SOLOMON gave her the ring that was on his little finger (Chap. 31), as a token whereby she might remember him.

Nine months and five days after MÂKĚDÂ bade SOLOMON farewell she brought forth a man child, and in due course she arrived in her own country, where she was received with great joy and delight. She called her son BAYNA-LEHKEM, i.e. IBN AL-HAKÎM, "the son of the wise man", and he grew into a strong and handsome young man. At the age of twelve he questioned his mother as to his parentage, and in spite of rebuffs by her he continued to do so until she told him; ten years later no power could keep him in his own country, and MÂKĚDÂ sent him to JERUSALEM, accompanied by her old chief of caravans, TÂMRÎN (Chaps. 32, 33). With him she sent a letter to SOLOMON, telling him that in future a king should reign over her country, and not a virgin queen, and that her people should adopt the religion of ISRAEL. Finally she sent salutations to the Tabernacle of the Law of God, and begged SOLOMON to send her a portion of the fringe from the Covering of ZION, so that it might be treasured by her as a holy possession for ever. In saying farewell to her son, MÂKĚDÂ gave him the ring which SOLOMON had given her, so that if necessary he might use it as a proof that he was the son of MÂKĚDÂ by SOLOMON.

When the young man arrived at GÂZÂ, a district which SOLOMON had given to the Queen of SHEBA (Chap. 34), all the people were astonished at his close resemblance to SOLOMON, and some of them went so far so to declare that he was SOLOMON in person. The minds of the people were much exercised about the matter, and messengers were sent to SOLOMON from GÂZÂ announcing the arrival of a merchant who resembled him in face and features, and in form and stature, and in manners and carriage and behaviour. At that time SOLOMON was depressed, by reason of the miscarriage of his plans in respect of obtaining a large posterity, like "the stars of heaven and the sands on the seashore." He had married one thousand women, meaning to beget by them one thousand sons, but God only gave him three children! Therefore, when he heard of the arrival of the young merchant who resembled himself, he knew at once that it was his son by the Queen of SHEBA who had come to see him, and he sent out BENAIAH, the son of JEHOIADA, to meet him and to bring him to JERUSALEM (Chap. 35). In due course BENAIAH met BAYNA-LEHKEM, and he and his fifty guards escorted him into the presence of SOLOMON, who acknowledged him straightway, and embraced him, and kissed him on his forehead and eyes and mouth (Chap. 36). He then took him into his chamber and arrayed him in gorgeous apparel, and gave him a belt of gold and a gold crown, and set a ring upon his finger, and when he presented him to the nobles of ISRAEL, they accepted him as SOLOMON'S son and brought gifts to him. Then BAYNA-LEHKEM produced the ring which he had brought from his mother and gave it to SOLOMON, who said that it was unnecessary, for his face and stature proclaimed that he was his son.

Soon after this TÂMRÎN had an audience of SOLOMON, and he asked him to anoint BAYNA-LEHKEM king, to consecrate and to bless him and then to send him back to his mother as soon as possible, for such was her desire. This old and faithful servant was afraid that the luxurious living of SOLOMON'S house would have an ill effect upon his future king, and he was anxious to get him away from JERUSALEM as soon as possible. To this SOLOMON replied that after a woman had brought forth her son and suckled him she had nothing more to do with him, for a boy belongs to his father and a girl to her mother. And SOLOMON refused to give up his first-born son. But BAYNA-LEHKEM himself was anxious to leave JERUSALEM (Chap. 36), and he begged SOLOMON to give him a portion of the fringe of the Tabernacle of the Law of God, and to let him depart. He had no wish to live as SOLOMON'S second son in JERUSALEM, for he knew that SOLOMON had another son, REHOBOAM, who was six years old at that time and had been begotten in lawful marriage, whilst he himself was the son of an unmarried mother. SOLOMON promised to give him the kingdom of ISRAEL, and wives and concubines, and argued and pleaded with him long and earnestly, but to no purpose (Chap. 37); BAYNA-LEHKEM said that he had sworn by his mother's breasts to return to her quickly, and not to marry a wife in ISRAEL. To swear by a woman's breasts was a serious matter, and we have an echo of a somewhat similar ceremony in the Annals of the Nubian NASTASEN, King of NUBIA after 500 B.C. (?). This king paid a visit to the goddess BAST of TERT, his good mother, and he says that she gave him life, great old age, happiness, [and] her two breasts [on] the left (?) side, and placed him in her living, beautiful bosom."[24] We may be certain that NASTASEN swore to do something in return for the gracious kindness of the goddess BAST.

When SOLOMON saw that it was impossible to keep BAYNA-LEHKEM in JERUSALEM, he summoned the elders of ISRAEL (Chap. 38) and declared to them his intention of making the young man King of ETHIOPIA, and asked them to send their eldest sons with him to that far country to found a Jewish colony and kingdom there. The elders of course agreed to the king's request, and then ZADOK the priest and BENAIAH, the son of JEHOIADA, anointed BAYNA-LEHKEM king in the Holy of Holies (Chap. 39); the name which he received at his anointing was DAVID [II], the name of his grandfather. Then SOLOMON commanded ZADOK to describe to the young King of ETHIOPIA the curses that would fall upon him if he failed to obey God's commands (Chap. 40), and the blessings that would accrue to him if he performed the Will of God (Chap. 41). ZADOK did so, and then recited the Ten Commandments (Chap. 42) as given by MOSES, and a number of Hebrew laws concerning marriage, adultery, fornication, incest, sodomy, &c. The anointing of SOLOMON'S son to be king over ETHIOPIA was pleasing to the people, but all those whose first-born sons were to leave JERUSALEM with him sorrowed and cursed SOLOMON secretly in their hearts. In Chap. 43 we have a list of the names of those who were to hold positions of honour under DAVID II in ETHIOPIA, and Chap. 44 contains a series of warnings against abusing and reviling kings.

Now the children of ISRAEL who were to go to ETHIOPIA sorrowed greatly at the thought of leaving their country, but the matter that troubled them most was leaving the Tabernacle of the Law of God behind them (Chap. 45). At length AZARYAS suggested that they should take ZION with them, and having sworn his fellow sufferers to secrecy he declared to them the plan which he had devised. This was simple enough, for he determined to have a box made of the same size and shape as the Tabernacle, and when he had taken the Tabernacle out of the Holy of Holies, to set it in its place. He collected 140 double drachmas and employed a carpenter to construct the box he required. In the Arabic version of the story it is SOLOMON'S son who has the box made, and he puts the carpenter to death as soon as he had made it, knowing that dead men tell no tales. One night whilst these things were being carried out AZARYAS had a dream in which God told him to make BAYNA-LEHKEM offer up a sacrifice before he departed to ETHIOPIA, and during the performance of the ceremony to bring the Tabernacle out from the Holy of Holies into the fore part of the Temple (Chap. 46). SOLOMON agreed to the offering being made, and provided animals for sacrifice (Chap. 47). When the offering had been made, the Angel of the Lord appeared to AZARYAS (Chap. 48), and having opened the doors of the Holy of Holies with the keys which he had in his hand, he told him to go and bring in the box that had been made to replace the Tabernacle. When he had done this AZARYAS, and ELMEYAS, and ABESA, and MAKARI brought out the Tabernacle and carried it into the house of AZARYAS, and then they returned to the Temple and put together the box that was to replace the Tabernacle, and locked the doors, and came out. BAYNA-LEHKEM, who was well acquainted with all that had been done, then went and bade SOLOMON farewell, and received his father's blessing (Chap. 49). Then AZARYAS set the Tabernacle ZION upon a wagon and covered it over with baggage of all kinds (Chap. 50), and accompanied by the cries of men, the wailings of women, the howlings of dogs, and the screams of asses, it was driven out of JERUSALEM.

Both SOLOMON and his people knew instinctively that the glory of ISRAEL had departed with it. Then SOLOMON told ZADOK the priest to go into the Holy of Holies and bring out the covering of the Tabernacle, and to spread over the Tabernacle in its stead the new covering which he had had specially made for the purpose (Chap. 51); and thus saying he placed the new covering in the hands of the high priest. The Queen of SHEBA had asked him for a piece of the fringe of the covering of the Tabernacle, and she had repeated her request by the mouth of her son, and SOLOMON determined to send the complete covering to her. The text mentions the "five mice and ten emerods" which were given to ZION, but it is not clear whether SOLOMON meant them to be given to the Queen with the covering of the Tabernacle. Acting on SOLOMON'S instructions, ZADOK went and fetched the covering of the Tabernacle (Chap. 52), and gave it to BAYNA-LEHKEM, or DAVID, together with a chain of gold.

Then the wagons were loaded, and BAYNA-LEHKEM and his companions set out on their journey. The Archangel MICHAEL led the way, and he cut a path for them, and sheltered them from the heat. Neither man nor beast touched the ground with their feet, but were carried along above the ground with the speed of the bat and the eagle, and even the wagons were borne along without touching the earth (Chap. 52).

MICHAEL halted the company at GÂZÂ, which city SOLOMON had given to the Queen of SHEBA, and another day's march brought them to the frontier of EGYPT, and they encamped by "the River" (TAKKAZI), i.e. the NILE. Thus they had performed in one day a journey that generally took the caravans thirteen days to complete (Chap. 53). Whilst they were here his companions took the opportunity of revealing to DAVID the fact that they had carried off the Tabernacle ZION, and that it was there with them. AZARYAS told ELMEYAS to "beautify and dress our Lady", and when DAVID II saw her he rose up and skipped like a young sheep, and danced before the Tabernacle even as did his grandfather DAVID I (2 Sam. vi. 14). Then he stood up before ZION and made the address to her which is given in Chap. 54. When the natives heard that the Tabernacle of the Law of God was in their midst, they beat drums and played upon flutes and pipes, and the people shouted, and the pylons of the temples, and the idols that were in the forms of men, and dogs, and cats, fell down and were broken in pieces (Chaps. 54, 55). And AZARYAS dressed ZION, and spread their gifts before her, and he set her on a wagon with draperies of purple about her. On the following morning DAVID and his company resumed their journey, and men and beasts and wagons were all raised above the ground to the height of one cubit as before. They passed through the air like shadows, and the people ran alongside ZION and worshipped her. When they came to the RED SEA ZION passed over its waters, and the whole company were raised above them to a height of three cubits. The waves leaped up to welcome ZION, and the billows thundered forth praise of her, and the breakers roared their acclamations, and all the creatures in the sea worshipped her as she passed over them. In due course the company arrived at a place opposite

Mount SINAI and encamped in KÂDÊS, and then passing through MEDYÂM and BÊLÔNTÔS they came to ETHIOPIA, where they were received with great rejoicings. The description of the route followed by DAVID II is very vague, and it is clear that ISAAC'S geographical knowledge was incomplete.

Meanwhile ZADOK had returned from the Temple in JERUSALEM to SOLOMON'S palace and found the king very sorrowful, for he had been thinking over the dream which he had twenty-two years before, and feared that the glory of ISRAEL had either departed or was about to depart. ZADOK was greatly troubled when he heard what the king's dream was, and prophesied woe to ISRAEL if the Tabernacle had been carried off by DAVID. SOLOMON asked him if he had made sure that the Tabernacle was in the Holy of Holies the day before when he removed the outside covering to give it to DAVID, and ZADOK said he had not done so (Chap. 56). Then SOLOMON told him to go at once and see, and when he had gone into the Holy of Holies he found there nothing but the box which AZARYAS had had made to take the place of the Tabernacle. When ZADOK saw that ZION had departed he fainted, and BENAIAH found him lying there like a dead man. When ZADOK revived he cast ashes on his head, and went to the doors of the Temple and in a loud voice bewailed the loss of the glory and protection of ISRAEL. When SOLOMON heard the news he commanded men to make ready to pursue those who had stolen ZION, and to slay them when they found them (Chap. 57). When the soldiers were ready SOLOMON set himself at their head, and his mounted scouts rode in all haste to EGYPT, where they learned that the fugitives had left the place nine days before (Chap. 58). When SOLOMON himself arrived at GÂZÂ he found that the report which his scouts had made to him was true, and his heart sank. Near EGYPT he met envoys of PHARAOH who had been sent to him with presents, and he asked one of them for news of the thieves. This man told him that he had seen the company of DAVID II in CAIRO travelling through the air, and that all the statues of kings and gods in EGYPT had fallen down in the presence of the Tabernacle of ZION, and were dashed in pieces (Chap. 59). When SOLOMON heard this he returned to his tent and wept bitterly, and gave vent to the lamentations that form (Chap. 60).

When SOLOMON returned to JERUSALEM he went with the elders into the House of God, and he and ZADOK embraced each other and wept bitterly. Then they dried their tears and the elders made a long speech to SOLOMON in which they sketched the past history of the Ark of the Covenant, i.e. the Tabernacle ZION. They reminded him how the PHILISTINES captured it and carried it into the house of DAGON, and how they sent it away with sixty gold figures of mice, and sixty phalli, and how, when it came to JUDAH, the men of DAN slew the camels that drew the wagon on which it travelled, and cut up and burnt the wagon, and how it withdrew to its place and was ministered to by SAMUEL, and how it refused to be carried to the Valley of GILBOA, and how DAVID, the father of SOLOMON, brought it from SAMARIA to JERUSALEM. They proved to the king that the Tabernacle ZION could not have been carried off against God's will, and that if it was God's will it would return to JERUSALEM, and if it was not then it would not. Of one thing they were quite certain: the Tabernacle was able to take care of itself (Chap. 61).

When SOLOMON had heard all they had to say he agreed with them that the Will of God was irresistible, and called upon them to kneel down with him in the Holy of Holies (Chap. 62). When they had poured out prayer and supplication and dried their tears, SOLOMON advised them to keep the matter of the theft a secret among themselves, so that the uncircumcised might not boast over their misfortune. At his suggestion the elders set up the box which AZARYAS had made, and covered the boards over with gold, and decorated the box with coverings, and placed a copy of the Book of the Law inside it in lieu of the Two Tables. They remembered that JERUSALEM the free was as the heavens, and that their own earthly JERUSALEM was the Gate of Heaven, and they determined to do God's Will so that He Himself might be ever with them to watch over ISRAEL and to protect His people. The suggestion is that God would be a better protector than even the Tabernacle ZION.

But the loss of the Tabernacle ZION had a sad effect upon SOLOMON, for his love for God waned, and his wisdom forsook him, and he devoted himself to women during the last eleven years of his life. He married MÂKSHÂRÂ, an Egyptian princess, who first seduced his household into worshipping her idols, and then worked upon him with her beauty in such a way that he tolerated all she said and did (Chap. 63). When she knew that DAVID II had stolen the Tabernacle ZION, she reminded SOLOMON that his Lady ZION had been carried off, and that it would be better for him now to worship the gods of her fathers; but for a time he refused to forsake the God of ISRAEL. One day, however, overcome by her beauty he promised to do whatsoever she wished. Thereupon she tied a scarlet thread across the door of her gods, and she placed three locusts in the house of her gods. Then she called upon SOLOMON to enter without breaking the thread, and to kill the locusts and "pull out their necks." In some way, which I cannot explain, in doing this SOLOMON performed an act of worship of the Egyptian gods, and MÂKSHÂRÂ was content; besides this, to enter into an Egyptian temple was an offence against the God of ISRAEL (Chaps. 64, 65). In spite of his weakness and sin, SOLOMON is regarded in some respects as a type of CHRIST, and as he committed no sin like that of his father DAVID in the matter of the murder of URIAH, he is enumerated with the Patriarchs (Chap. 66).

When SOLOMON was sixty years of age he fell sick, and the Angel of Death drew nigh to him, and he wept and prayed for mercy (Chap. 67). And the Angel of God came to him and rebuked him for his excessive love of women and for marrying alien women. In a long speech the Angel refers to SOLOMON'S three sons, i.e. DAVID and REHOBOAM and 'ADRÂMÎ, his son by a Greek slave, and then he shows him how JOSEPH, and MOSES, and JOSHUA, were types of CHRIST, and how CHRIST should spring from SOLOMON'S seed and redeem mankind. In Chap. 68 the Angel prophesies concerning the VIRGIN MARY, and narrates to SOLOMON the history of the Pearl which passed from the body of ADAM to ABRAHAM, ISAAC, JACOB, PEREZ, JESSE, DAVID, SOLOMON, REHOBOAM, and JOACHIM, who passed it into the body of HANNA, the mother of the VIRGIN MARY. Finally, the Angel told SOLOMON that MICHAEL would remain with the Tabernacle in ETHIOPIA, and he (GABRIEL) with REHOBOAM, and URIEL with 'ADRÂMÎ. And SOLOMON gave thanks to God, and asked the Angel when the Saviour would come (Chap. 69), and the Angel replied, "After three and thirty generations." When the Angel told him that the ISRAELITES would crucify the Saviour, and be scattered over the face of the earth, SOLOMON wept, and the words of his lamentations fill the rest of Chap. 69.

SOLOMON died, and ZADOK anointed REHOBOAM king, and when he had laid a wooden tablet,[25] with SOLOMON'S

name inserted upon it, upon the Tabernacle, the people set him on the royal mule and cried, Hail! Long live the royal father (Chap. 70). Owing to REHOBOAM'S arrogant behaviour the people revolted, and they armed themselves and went to BÊTH EFRÂTÂ, and made JEROBOAM, the son of NEBAT, king over them. From REHOBOAM to JOACHIM, the grandfather of CHRIST, were forty-one generations. The VIRGIN MARY and JOSEPH the carpenter were akin, each being descended from DAVID, King of ISRAEL (Chap. 71).

According to traditions which ISAAC has grouped in Chap. 72, RÔM, RÔMÊ, or RÛM, i.e. BYZANTIUM, was originally the inheritance of JAPHET, the son of NOAH. He attributes the building of ANTIOCH, TYRE, PARTHIA (?) and CONSTANTINOPLE (?) to DARIUS, and says that from DARIUS to SOLOMON there were eighteen generations. One of his descendants, an astrologer and clockmaker called ZANBARÊS, prophesied that BYZANTIUM would pass into the possession of the sons of SHEM. His daughter married SOLOMON, who begot by her a son called 'ADRÂMÎ, and this son married 'ADLÔNYÂ, the daughter of BALTASÔR, the King of BYZANTIUM. When 'ADRÂMÎ was living in BYZANTIUM with his wife, his father-in-law, wishing to test his ability as a judge, set him to try a difficult case of trespass on the part of a flock of sheep on the one side and unlawful detention of property on the other (Chap. 72). He decided the case in such a way as to gain the approval of BALTASÔR, and in due course he reigned in his stead (Chap. 73). ISAAC further proves that the King of MEDYÂM (Chap. 74) and the King of BABYLON were SEMITES (Chap. 75). The narrative of KARMÎN and the false swearing of ZARYÔS and KÂRMÊLÔS, the flight of KARMÎN to BABYLON, the infidelity of the merchant's wife, and the exchange of children by the nurses, together make up a story more suitable for the "One Thousand Nights and a Night" than the KEBRA NAGAST. According to it NEBUCHADNEZZAR II was the son of KARMÎN, and therefore a SEMITE; the etymology given of the name is, of course, wholly wrong (Chap. 76). In Chap. 77 ISAAC tries to show that the King of PERSIA was a SEMITE, and that he was descended from PEREZ, a son of TAMAR. The incestuous origin of the MOABITES and AMALEKITES, as described in GENESIS, is repeated in Chaps. 78 and 79.

In Chap. 80 is the history of SAMSON with details of an apocryphal character. According to this, SAMSON married a woman of the PHILISTINES, and so transgressed the Will of God. The PHILISTINES made him act the buffoon, and in revenge he pulled the roof down upon them and slew 700,000 of them, and 700,000 more with iron and stone, and wood and the jaw-bone of an ass. When SAMSON died he left DELILAH, the sister of MAKSÂBÂ, wife of KWÔLÂSÔN, King of the PHILISTINES, with child. After SAMSON had slain KWÔLÂSÔN the two sisters lived together, and in due course each brought forth a man child. The boys grew up together, and their mothers dressed them in rich apparel, and hung chains round their necks, and gave them daggers to wear. One day AKAMHÊL, SAMSON'S son, asked his mother why he was not reigning over the city, and told her that he intended to reign over PHILISTIA. A little time later the two boys were eating with their mothers, and AKAMHÊL took from the dish a piece of meat as large as his two hands, and began to eat it. TEBRÊLÊS, the son of MAKSÂBÂ, snatched a piece of the meat from him, whereupon AKAMHÊL drew his dagger and cut off the head of TEBRÊLÊS, which fell into the dish. DELILAH seized the sword from the body of TEBRÊLÊS and tried to kill AKAMHÊL, but he hid behind a pillar and in turn tried to kill her. When MAKSÂBÂ strove to pacify him he turned on the two women like a wild bear and drove them from the apartment. Before she left MAKSÂBÂ gave him purple cloths from her couch, and promised him the throne of PHILISTIA, and that evening AKAMHÊL took possession of it and was acclaimed king. In Chaps. 82 and 83 the well-known story of ABRAHAM'S visit to EGYPT with SARAH is told, and a description of ISHMAEL'S kingdom is added.

ISAAC'S narrative now returns to MENYELEK. He and his company and ZION travelled from JERUSALEM to WAKÊRÔ in one day, and he sent messengers to MÂKĔDÂ, his mother, to announce their arrival (Chap. 84). In due course he arrived at DABRA MÂKĔDÂ (AXUM ?), the seat of his mother's Government, where the Queen was waiting to receive him. He pitched his tent in the plain at the foot of the mountain, and 32,000 stalled oxen and bulls were killed and a great feast was made. Seven hundred swordsmen were appointed to watch over ZION (Chap. 85), and the Queen and all her people rejoiced. On the third day MÂKĔDÂ abdicated in favour of her son MENYELEK, and she handed over to him 17,700 fine horses and 7,700 mares, 1,700 mules, robes of honour, and a large quantity of gold and silver (Chap. 86). Further, she made the nobles swear that henceforth no woman should rule over ETHIOPIA (Chap. 87), and that only the male offspring of her son DAVID should be kings of that country. At the coming of ZION to ETHIOPIA the people cast away their idols, and abandoned divination, and sorcery, and magic, and omens, and repented with tears, and adopted the religion of the HEBREWS. MENYELEK swore to render obedience to his mother, and AZARYAS was to be high priest and ALMEYAS Keeper of ZION, the Ark of the Covenant. MENYELEK then related to MÂKĔDÂ the story of his anointing by ZADOK in JERUSALEM, and when she heard it she admonished him to observe the Will of God, and to put his trust in ZION; and she called upon AZARYAS and ALMEYAS to help him to follow the path of righteousness (Chap. 88). She then addressed a long speech to her nobles (Chap. 89) and the new ISRAELITES, and prayed to God for wisdom and understanding. Her prayer was followed by an edict ordering every man to forsake the religion and manners and customs which he had formerly observed, and to adopt the new religion under penalty of the confiscation of his property and separation from his wife and children. In Chaps. 90 and 91, AZARYAS makes an address to MÂKĔDÂ and praises her for her wisdom. He compares favourably the country of ETHIOPIA with JUDAH, and says that, although the ETHIOPIANS are black of face, nothing can do them any harm provided that God lighteth their hearts. He then proclaims a number of laws, derived for the most part from the Pentateuch, and appends a list of clean and unclean animals. Curiously enough, a short paragraph is devoted to the explanation of the Queen's name MÂKĔDÂ (page 161). When AZARYAS had finished his exhortations he made preparations to "renew the Kingdom of DAVID", King of ISRAEL, in ETHIOPIA (Chap. 92), and with the blowing of the jubilee trumpets and music and singing and dancing and games of all kinds, MENYELEK, or DAVID II, was formally proclaimed King of ETHIOPIA. The boundaries of his kingdom are carefully described. After the three months that followed the proclamation of MENYELEK'S sovereignty, the Law of the Kingdom and the Creed of the ETHIOPIANS were written, presumably upon skins, and deposited in the Ark of the Covenant as a "memorial for the later days" (Chap. 93). ISAAC says that the belief of the Kings of RÔMÊ (RÛMÎ) and that of the Kings of ETHIOPIA was identical for 130 years, but that after that period the former corrupted the Faith of CHRIST by introducing into it the heresies of NESTORIUS, ARIUS and others.

Soon after MENYELEK had established his kingdom, he set out, accompanied by the Ark of the Covenant and MÂKĔDÂ (Chap. 94), to wage war against his enemies. He attacked the peoples to the west, south, and east of his country, and invaded the lands of the NUBIANS, EGYPTIANS, ARABIANS, and INDIANS; and many kings sent him tribute and did homage to him. The Ark of the Covenant went at the head of his army, and made the ETHIOPIANS victorious everywhere; many peoples were blotted out and whole districts laid waste. In Chap. 95 ISAAC couples the King of RÔMÊ with the King of ETHIOPIA, and condemns the JEWS for their ill-treatment of CHRIST, Who was born of the Pearl that was hidden in ADAM'S body when he was created. And ISAAC proclaims what the KEBRA NAGAST was written to prove, namely, that "the King of ETHIOPIA is more exalted and more honourable than any other king upon the earth, because of the glory and greatness of the heavenly ZION." Following several remarks, in which the JEWS are compared unfavourably with the ETHIOPIANS, comes a long extract from the writings of GREGORY, the "worker of wonders" (THAUMATURGUS), in which it is shown that the coming of CHRIST was known to the Prophets of ISRAEL, and passages from their books are quoted in support of this view. The beginning of all things was the Law which proclaimed CHRIST, and the Holy Spirit existed at the Creation. The brazen serpent was a symbol of CHRIST (Chap. 96). ABRAHAM was a type of God the Father, and ISAAC a symbol of CHRIST, the ram of sacrifice. EVE slew mankind, but the VIRGIN MARY gave them life. MARY was the "door", and that it was closed symbolized her virginity, which was God's seal upon her. She was the burning bush described by MOSES; she was the censer used by MOSES, the coals were CHRIST, and the perfume of the incense was His perfume (Chap. 97), on which prayer ascended to heaven. The chains of the censer were JACOB'S ladder. AARON'S rod was MARY, and the bud thereof was CHRIST (Chap. 98). The Ark made by MOSES was the abode of God on earth; it symbolized MARY, and the indestructible wood of which it was made symbolized the indestructible CHRIST. The pot that held the manna was MARY, and the manna was the body of CHRIST; the Words of the Law also were CHRIST. The Pearl in MARY'S body was CHRIST. The rock smitten by MOSES was CHRIST, and MOSES smote it lengthwise and breadthwise to symbolize the Cross of CHRIST. MOSES' ROD was the Cross, the water that flowed from the rock was the teaching of the Apostles. The darkness brought upon EGYPT for three days symbolized the darkness of the Crucifixion. The AMALEKITES symbolized the devils, and AARON and HÔR, who held up MOSES' hands, symbolized the two thieves who were crucified with CHRIST. In a parable given in Chap. 99 a king symbolizes CHRIST, and SATAN an arrogant servant and ADAM a humble servant.

The history of the angels who rebelled is given in Chap. 100. These angels were wroth with God for creating ADAM, and they reviled God and ADAM because of his transgression. God reminded them that ADAM was only a creature made of dust and water and wind and fire, whilst they were made of air and fire. They were made specially to praise God, whilst ADAM could be influenced by SATAN; had they been made of water and dust they would have sinned more than ADAM. In answer the angels said, "Make us even as ADAM, and put us to the test "; and God gave them flesh and blood and a heart like that of the children of men. Thereupon they came down to earth, mingled with the children of CAIN, and gave themselves up to singing, dancing, and fornication. The daughters of CAIN scented themselves to please the men who had been angels, and were debauched by any and every man who cared to take them. And they conceived, but were unable to bring forth their children in the natural way, and the children split open their mothers' bodies and came forth. These children grew up into giants, and their "height reached unto the clouds." God bore with them for 120 years, and then the waters of the Flood destroyed them. He told NOAH to build an Ark, and it was the wood of that Ark that saved him, as the wood of the Cross saved mankind when CHRIST died upon it.

In Chap. 101 God is made to declare by the mouth of MOSES that He is everywhere and in everything, and that everything supports itself on Him; He is the Master of everything, He fills everything, He is above the Seven Heavens and everything, He is beneath the deepest deep and the thickest darkness, and balances all creation. In Chap. 102 is a series of extracts from the Old and New Testaments which are to show that CHRIST was the Beginning, and that all things were made in and by Him. He was the Maker and Creator, the Light of Light, the God of God, the Refuge, the Feeder, and the Director. The Ark, or Tabernacle, symbolizes the horns of the altar and the tomb of CHRIST. The offering on the altar symbolizes and is the Body of CHRIST (Chap. 103). Returning to the Ark of NOAH (Chap. 104), the writer says that NOAH was saved by wood, ABRAHAM held converse with God in the wood of MANBAR, the thicket that caught the ram saved ISAAC, and the rods of wood that JACOB laid in running water saved him. The wood of the Ark made by MOSES was a means of salvation, even as was the wood of the Cross. The greater part of this Chapter appears to be a translation of a part of a homily by CYRIL, Archbishop of ALEXANDRIA, and it is possible that Chap. 105 is merely a continuation of Chap. 104. It deals with ABRAHAM'S visit to MELCHIZEDEK, who gave him the mystery of bread and wine, which is also celebrated in "our Passover." Prophecies concerning the Coming of CHRIST, collected from the Books of the Old Testament, are given in Chap. 106, but ISAAC or the copyists have made many mistakes as to their authorship, especially in the case of some of the Minor Prophets. Many appear to have been written down from memory. Another series of prophecies concerning CHRIST'S triumphal entry into JERUSALEM is given in Chap. 107, and CHRIST is identified with the unicorn. Prophecies dealing with the wickedness of the JEWS are given in Chap. 108, Chap. 109 consists of prophecies concerning the Crucifixion; in Chaps. 110 and 111 many prophecies foretelling the Resurrection and Ascension of CHRIST and His Second Coming are enumerated. The Patriarchs and Prophets were forerunners and symbols of CHRIST (Chap. 112), especially ISAAC, JACOB, MOSES, JOSEPH, and JONAH.

The chariot containing ZION, i.e. the vehicle on which the Tabernacle of the Law was borne, was in ETHIOPIA, and the Cross, which was discovered by Queen Helena, was in RÔMÊ (RÛMÎ), and the Archbishops asked GREGORY how long the chariot of ZION and the Cross were to remain where they were (Chap. 113). GREGORY replied that the Persians would attack the King of RÔMÊ, and defeat him, and make him a prisoner, together with the horse of the Cross, which would go mad, and rush into the sea and perish. But the nails of the Cross would shine in the sea until the Second Coming of CHRIST. On the other hand, the chariot of ZION would remain in ETHIOPIA, and the ETHIOPIANS would continue to be orthodox to the end of the world. At the Second Coming of CHRIST the Tabernacle of the Law shall return to Mount ZION in JERUSALEM (Chap. 114), and it shall be opened, and the JEWS shall be made to look upon the Words of the Law that they have despised, the pot of manna, and the rod of AARON. Chap. 115 described the judgement which shall fall upon the JEWS, who shall repent when it is too late and shall be cast into hell. Of the CHRISTIANS those who have sinned shall be punished according to the degree of their sins. One day with God is as a thousand years; some shall be punished for a whole day, some for twelve hours, some for three, and some for one hour. Others shall be tried and acquitted. In answer to a further question of the Archbishops GREGORY repeats (Chap. 116) that the chariot of ZION shall remain in ETHIOPIA until the Second Coming of CHRIST, and prophesies the war which the King of RÔMÊ will wage in ARMENIA, and the war which the ETHIOPIANS will make on the JEWS of NÂGRÂN.[26] The last Chapter (117) deals with the extermination of the JEWS and the ARMENIANS by the joint efforts of JUSTINUS, King of RÔMÊ, and KÂLÊB, King of ETHIOPIA, who are to meet in JERUSALEM, and exchange titles. The war of the ETHIOPIANS against the JEWS of NÂGRÂN is to be continued by GABRA MASKAL or LÂLÎBALÂ, after his father KÂLÊB has adopted the monastic life in the Monastery of Abbâ PANTALERN, and their defeat by him is declared to be a certainty. Parts of the text of this Chapter are difficult to understand.

Footnotes

1. Printed about 1533.

2. A French translation from the Spanish version of this work appeared in Paris in 1558, folio.

3. De Abassinorum rebus deque Æthiopiae Patriarchis, Libri I-III, Leyden, 1615, 8vo, p. 35.

4. Travels to Discover the Source of the Nile in the years 1768-1773, containing a Journey through Egypt, the three Arabias and Ethiopia. First edition in five vols., 1790; second edition in six vols., in 1805; 3rd edition in seven vols., 1813.

5. Cat. Codd. MSS. Bibliothecae Bodleianae, Oxford, 1848, No. xxvi, p. 68.

6. Ibid., p. 74 (No. xxvii).

7. Fabula de Regina Sabaea apud Æthiopes. Dissertatio inauguralis. Halle (No date).

8. A description of the very ancient copy of the KEBRA NAGAST in the Bibliothèque Nationale, which Zotenberg assigned to the thirteenth century, was published by him in his Catalogue des MSS. Éthiopiens, Paris, 1877, No. 5, p. 6.

9. Chez la Reine de Saba, Paris, 1914, pp. 110-121.

10. Ibid., pp. 125-227; see also a rendering of the French into English by Mrs. J. Van Vorst, entitled Magda, Queen of Sheba, New York and London, 1907, 8vo.

11. Translated from the Arabic text printed by Bezold, op. cit., p. xliv ff. A French paraphrase of the Arabic was printed by Amélineau in his Contes et Romans, Paris, 1888, tom. I, pp. 144 ff.

12. Luke xi. 31; see also 1 Kings x. 1; 2 Chron. ix. 1.

13. Psalm cxxxii. 11 f.

14. Psalm xcv (xcvi). 10. See the Douay Version, vol. ii, p. 176, and Swete, Old Test. in Greek, vol. ii, p. 342.

15. Ali Beidhawî's Commentary on the Kur'ân (ed. Fleischer, pt. 3, p. 67).

16. Al-Beidhawî, op. cit., p. 68.

17. Ibid., p. 69.

18. Commentary of Jalâl ad-Dîn MuHammad bin AHmad, Cairo edit. A.H. 1311, pt. 2, p. 60.

19. Ibid., p. 70.

20. See Littmann, Dr. E., The Legend of the Queen of Sheba in the Tradition of Axum, Leyden, 1904; Conti Rossini, Ricordi di un Soggiorno in Eritrea, Asmara, 1903.

21. See Malan, Book of Adam and Eve, London, 1882, p. 92 ff., and Bezold, Schatzöhle, Leipzig, 1883, p. 8.

22. In Genesis xiv. 14, ABRAHAM'S home-born armed servants numbered 318.

23. 1 Kings xi. 3, says 700 wives, princesses, and 300 concubines.

24. Budge, Annals of Nubian Kings, p. 153.

25. Several examples of such wooden tablets are exhibited among the Christian Antiquities in the White Wing of the British Museum.

26 See Pereira, Historia dos Martyres de Nagran, Lisbon, 1889.

THE GLORY OF KINGS

IN PRAISING GOD THE FATHER, THE SUSTAINER OF THE UNIVERSE, AND HIS SON JESUS CHRIST, THROUGH WHOM EVERYTHING CAME INTO BEING, AND WITHOUT WHOM NOTHING CAME INTO BEING, AND THE HOLY TRIUNE SPIRIT, THE PARACLETE, WHO GOETH FORTH FROM THE FATHER, AND DERIVETH FROM THE SON, WE BELIEVE IN AND ADORE THE TRINITY, ONE GOD, THE FATHER, AND THE SON, AND THE HOLY SPIRIT.

1. Concerning the Glory of Kings

The interpretation and explanation of the Three Hundred and Eighteen Orthodox [Fathers] concerning splendour, and greatness, and dignity, and how God gave them to the children of ADAM, and especially concerning the greatness and splendour of ZION, the Tabernacle (tâbôt) of the Law of God, of which He Himself is the Maker and Fashioner, in the fortress of His holiness before all created things, [both] angels and men. For the Father, and the Son, and the Holy Spirit with good fellowship and right good will and cordial agreement together made the Heavenly ZION to be the place of habitation of their Glory. And then the Father, and the Son, and the Holy Spirit said, "Let Us make man in Our similitude and likeness,"[1] and with ready agreement and good will They were all of this opinion. And the Son said, "I will put on the body of ADAM," and the Holy Spirit said, "I will dwell in the heart[s] of the Prophets and the Righteous," and this common agreement and covenant was [fulfilled] in ZION, the City of their Glory. And DAVID said, "Remember Thine agreement which Thou didst make of old for salvation, the rod of Thine inheritance, in Mount ZION wherein Thou dost dwell."[2]

And He made ADAM in His own image and likeness, so that He might remove SATAN because of his pride, together with his host, and might establish ADAM - His own plant - together with the righteous, His children, for His praises. For the plan of God was decided upon and decreed in that He said, "I will become man, and I will be in everything which I have created, I will abide in flesh." And in the days that came after, by His good pleasure there was born in the flesh of the Second ZION the second ADAM, Who was our Saviour CHRIST. This is our glory and our faith, our hope and our life, the Second ZION.[3]

Footnotes

1. Genesis i. 26.

2. Psalm lxxiv. 2.

3. i.e., the Virgin Mary, who is identified in Chapter II with the "Tabernacle of the Law of God, the heavenly and spiritual Zion."

2. Concerning the Greatness of Kings

Come then, let us go back, and let us consider, and let us begin [to state] which of the kings of the earth, from the first even unto the last, in respect of the Law and the Ordinances and honour and greatness, we should magnify or decry.

GREGORY, the worker of wonders and miracles,[4] who was cast into a cave because of [his] love for the martyrdom of CHRIST and suffered tribulation for fifteen years, said, "When I was in the pit I pondered over this matter, and over the folly of the Kings of ARMENIA, and I said, In so far as I can conceive it, [in] what doth the greatness of kings [consist]? Is it in the multitude of soldiers, or in the splendour of worldly possessions, or in extent of rule over cities and towns? This was my thought each time of my prayer, and my thought stirred me again and again to meditate upon the greatness of kings. And now I will begin."

Footnotes

4. The Gregory here referred to is not Thaumaturgus, but the "Illuminator", i.e., Gregor Lusavoritch, who flourished in the first quarter of the fourth century.

3. Concerning the Kingdom of ADAM

And I go up from ADAM and I say, God is King in truth, for Him praise is meet, and He appointed under Him ADAM to be king over all that He had created. And He drove him out of the Garden, because of his apostasy through the sin of the Serpent and the plotting of the Devil. And at that sorrowful moment CAIN was born, and when ADAM saw that the face of CAIN was ill-tempered (or, sullen) and his appearance evil he was sad. And then ABEL was born, and when ADAM saw that his appearance was good and his face good-tempered he said, "This is my son, the heir of my kingdom."

4. Concerning Envy

And when they had grown up together, SATAN had envy of him, and he cast this envy into the heart of CAIN, who was envious [of ABEL] first, because of the words of his father ADAM, who said, "He who hath the good-tempered face shall be the heir of my kingdom"; and secondly, because of his sister with the beautiful face, who was born with him and who had been given unto ABEL, even as God commanded them to multiply and fill the earth - now the face of the sister who had been born with ABEL resembled that of CAIN, and their father had transferred them (i.e., the two sisters) when giving them [in marriage]; - and thirdly, because when the two [brothers] offered up sacrifice, God accepted the offering of ABEL and rejected the offering of CAIN. And because of this envy CAIN killed ABEL. Thus fratricide was first created through SATAN'S envy of the children of ADAM. And having killed his brother, CAIN fell into a state of trembling and horrible fright, and he was repulsed by his father and his Lord. And [then] SETH was born, and ADAM looked upon him and said, "Now hath God shown compassion upon me, and He hath given unto me the light of my face. In sorrowful remembrance I will console myself (?) with him. The name of him that shall slay my heir shall be blotted out, even to his ninth generation."

5. *Concerning the Kingdom of SETH*

And ADAM died, and SETH reigned in righteousness. And SETH died, and HÊNÔS (ENOS) reigned. And HÊNÔS (ENOS) died, and KÂYNÂN (CAINAN) reigned. And KÂYNÂN (CAINAN) died, and MALÂL'ÊL (MAHALALEEL) reigned. And MALÂL'ÊL (MAHALALEEL) died, and YÂRÔD (JARED) reigned. And YÂRÔD died, and HÊNÔKH (ENOCH) reigned in righteousness, and he feared God, and [God] hid him so that he might not see death. And he became a king in his flesh in the Land of the Living. And after ENOCH disappeared MÂTÛSÂLÂ (METHUSELAH) reigned. And MÂTÛSÂLÂ died, and LÂMÊKH (LAMECH) reigned. And LÂMÊKH died, and NÔH (NOAH) reigned in righteousness, and he pleased God in all his works.

6. *Concerning the Sin of CAIN*

And that accursed man CAIN, the murderer of his brother, multiplied evil, and his seed did likewise, and they provoked God to wrath with their wickedness. They had not the fear of God before their eyes, and they never kept in mind that He had created them, and they never prayed to Him, and they never worshipped Him, and they never called upon Him, and they never rendered service to Him in fear; nay, they ate, and they drank, and they danced, and they played upon stringed instruments, and sang lewd songs thereto, and they worked uncleanness without law, without measure, and without rule. And the wickedness of the children of CAIN multiplied, until at length in the greatness of their filthiness they introduced the seed of the ass into the mare, and the mule came into being, which God had not commanded - even like those who give their children who are believers unto those who deny God, and their offspring become the seed of the filthy GOMORRAITES, one half of them being of good and one half of them of evil seed. And as for those who do [this] wickedness, their judgment is ready, and their error is lasting.

7. *Concerning NOAH*

Now NOAH was a righteous man. He feared God, and kept the righteousness and the Law which his fathers had declared unto him - now NOAH was the tenth generation from ADAM - and he kept in remembrance and did what was good, and he preserved his body from fornication, and he admonished his children, bidding them not to mingle with the children of CAIN, the arrogant tyrant, the divider of the kingdom, [who] walked in the counsel of the Devil, who maketh evil to flourish. And he taught them everything that God hated - pride, boastfulness of speech, self-adulation, calumniation, false accusation, and the swearing of false oaths. And besides these things, in the wickedness of their uncleanness, which was unlawful and against rule, man wrought pollution with man, and woman worked with woman the abominable thing.

8. Concerning the Flood

And this thing was evil before God, and He destroyed them with the water of the Flood, which was colder than ice. He opened the doors of heaven, and the cataracts of the Flood poured down; and He opened the fountains that were under the earth, and the fountains of the Flood appeared on the earth. And the sinners were blotted out, for they reaped the fruit of their punishment. And with them perished all beasts and creeping things, for they were all created for the gratification of ADAM, and for his glory, some to provide him with food, and some for his pleasure, and some for the names to the glorification of his Creator so that he might know them, even as DAVID saith, "And Thou hast set everything under his feet";[5] for his sake they were created, and for his sake they were destroyed, with the exception of Eight Souls, and seven of every kind of clean beasts and creeping things, and two of every kind of unclean beast and creeping thing.

Footnotes

5. Psalm viii. 6.

9. Concerning the Covenant of NOAH

And then NOAH the righteous man died, and SHEM reigned in wisdom and righteousness, for he was blessed by NOAH, saying, "Be God to thy brother." And to HAM he said, "Be servant to thy brother." And he said unto JAPHET, "Be thou servant to SHEM my heir, and be thou subject unto him."[6] And again, after the Flood, the Devil, our Enemy, did not cease from his hostility against the children of NOAH, but stirred up CANAAN, the son of HAM, and he became the violent tyrant (or usurper) who rent the kingdom from the children of SHEM. Now they had divided the earth among them, and NOAH had made them swear by the Name of his God that they would not encroach on each other's boundaries, and would not eat the beast that had died of itself or had been rent [by wild animals], and that they would not cultivate harlotry against the law, lest God should again become angry with them and punish them with a Flood. And as for NOAH, he humbled himself, and offered up sacrifice, and he cried out, and groaned, and wept. And God held converse with NOAH, who said [unto Him], "If Thou wilt destroy the earth a second time with a Flood, blot Thou me out with those who are to perish." And God said unto him, "I will make a covenant with thee that thou shalt tell thy children they shall not eat the beast that hath died of itself or that hath been torn by wild beasts, and they shall not cultivate harlotry against the law; and I, on My part, [covenant] that I will not destroy the earth a second time with a Flood, and that I will give unto thy children Winter and Summer, Seedtime and Harvest, Autumn and Spring.[7]

Footnotes

6. Compare Genesis ix. 25-27.
7. Genesis viii. 21; and compare Genesis ix. 4.

10. Concerning ZION

"And I swear by Myself and by ZION, the Tabernacle of My covenant, which I have created for a mercy seat and for the salvation of men, and in the latter days I will make it to come down to thy seed, that I will have pleasure in the offerings of thy children upon earth, and the Tabernacle of My covenant shall be with them for ever. And when a cloud hath appeared [in the sky], so that they may not fear and may not imagine that a Flood [is coming] I will make to come down from My habitation of ZION the Bow of My Covenant, that is to say, the rainbow, which shall the Tabernacle of My Law. And it shall come to pass that, when their sins multiply, and I am wishful to be wroth with them, I will remember the Tabernacle of My Covenant, and I will set the rainbow [in the sky], and I will put away Mine anger and will send My compassion. And I will not forget My word, and that which hath gone forth from My mouth I will not overlook. Though heaven and earth pass away My word shall not pass away."[8]

And the Archbishops who were there answered and said to the blessed GREGORY, "Behold now, we understand clearly that before every created thing, even the angels, and before the heavens and the earth, and before the pillars of heaven, and the abysses of the sea, He created the Tabernacle of the Covenant, and this which is in heaven goeth about upon the earth."

Footnotes
8. Matthew xxiv. 35.

11. The Unanimous Declaration of the Three Hundred and Eighteen Orthodox Fathers

And they answered and said unto him, "Yea, verily the Tabernacle of the Covenant was the first thing to be created by Him, and there is no lie in thy word; it is true, and correct, and righteous, and unalterable. He created ZION before everything else to be the habitation of His glory, and the plan of His Covenant was that which He said, 'I will put on the flesh of ADAM, which is of the dust, and I will appear unto all those whom I have created with My hand and with My voice.' And if it had been that the heavenly ZION had not come down, and if He had not put on the flesh of ADAM, then God the Word would not have appeared, and our salvation would not have taken place. The testimony (or proof) is in the similitude; the heavenly ZION is to be regarded as the similitude of the Mother of the Redeemer, MARY. For in the ZION which is builded there are deposited the Ten Words of the Law which were written by His hands, and He Himself, the Creator, dwelt in the womb of MARY, and through Him everything came into being."

12. Concerning CANAAN[9]

Now, it was CANAAN who rent the kingdom from the children of SHEM, and he transgressed the oath which his father NOAH had made them to swear.

And the sons of CANAAN were seven mighty men, and he took seven mighty cities from the land of SHEM, and set his sons over them; and likewise he also made his own portion double. And in later days God took vengeance upon the sons of CANAAN, and made the sons of SHEM to inherit their country. These are the nations whom they inherited: the CANAANITES, the PERIZZITES, the HIVITES, the HITTITES, the AMORITES, the JEBUSITES, and the GIRGASITES; these are they whom CANAAN seized by force from the seed of SHEM. For it was not right for him to invade [his] kingdom, and to falsify the oath, and because of this they ceased to be, and their memorial perished, through transgressing [God's] command, and worshipping idols, and bowing down to those who were not gods.

And after the death of SHEM ARPHAXAD reigned, and after the death of ARPHAXAD KÂYNÂN[10] (CAINAN) reigned, and after the death of KÂYNÂN SÂLÂ (SALAH) reigned, and after him EBER reigned, and after him PÂLÊK (PELEG) reigned, and after him RÂGÂW (REU) reigned, and after him SÊRÔH (SERUG) reigned, and after him NÂKHÔR (NAHOR) reigned, and after him TÂRÂ (TERAH) reigned. And these are they who made magical images, and they went to the tombs of their fathers and made an image (or, picture) of gold, and silver, and brass, and a devil used to hold converse with them out of each of the images of their fathers, and say unto them, "O my son So-and-so, offer up unto me as a sacrifice the son whom thou lovest." And they slaughtered their sons and their daughters to the devils, and they poured out innocent blood to filthy devils.

Footnotes
9. The son of Ham (Genesis x. 6).
10. There is some confusion here; Cainan was the son of Enos (Gen. v. 9).

13. Concerning ABRAHAM

And TÂRÂ (TERAH) begot a son and called him "ABRAHAM" (or, ABRÂM). And when ABRAHAM was twelve years old his father TERAH sent him to sell idols. And ABRAHAM said, "These are not gods that can make deliverance"; and he took away the idols to sell even as his father had commanded him. And he said unto those unto whom he would sell them, "Do ye wish to buy gods that cannot make deliverance, [things] made of wood, and stone, and iron, and brass, which the hand of an artificer hath made?" And they refused to buy the idols from ABRAHAM because he himself had defamed the images of his father. And as he was returning he stepped aside from the road, and he set the images down, and looked at them, and said unto them, "I wonder now if ye are able to do what I ask you at this moment, and whether ye are able to give me bread to eat or water to drink?" And none of them answered him, for they were pieces of stone and wood; and he abused them and heaped revilings upon them, and they spake never a word. And he buffeted the face of one, and kicked another with his feet, and a third he knocked over and broke to pieces with stones, and he said unto them, "If ye are unable to deliver yourselves from him that buffeteth you, and ye cannot requite with injury him that injureth you, how can ye be called 'gods'? Those who worship you do so in vain, and as for myself I utterly despise you, and ye shall not be my gods." Then he turned his face to the East, and he stretched out his hands and said, "Be Thou my God, O Lord, Creator of the heavens and the earth, Creator of the sun and the moon, Creator of the sea and the dry land, Maker of the majesty of the heavens and the earth, and of that which is visible and that which is invisible; O Maker of the universe, be Thou my God. I place my trust in Thee, and from this day forth I will place my trust in no other save Thyself." And then there appeared unto him a chariot of fire which blazed, and ABRAHAM was afraid and fell on his face on the ground; and [God] said unto him, "Fear thou not, stand upright." [11] And He removed fear from him.

Footnotes
11. Compare Genesis xv. 1.

14. Concerning the Covenant of ABRAHAM

And God held converse with ABRÂM, and He said unto him, "Fear thou not. From this day thou art My servant, and I will establish My Covenant with thee and with thy seed after thee, and I will multiply thy seed, and I will magnify thy name exceedingly. And I will bring down the Tabernacle of My Covenant upon the earth seven generations after thee, and it shall go round about with thy seed, and shall be salvation unto thy race and afterwards I will send My Word for the salvation of ADAM and his sons for ever. And at this moment these who are of thy kinsmen are evil men (or, rebels), and My divinity, which is true, they have rejected. And as for thee, that day by day they may not seduce thee, come, get thee forth out of this land, the land of thy fathers, into the land which I will show thee, and I will give it unto thy seed after thee."[12] And ABRÂM made obeisance to God, and was subject to his God. And [God] said unto him, "Thy name shall be ABRAHAM"; and He gave him the salutation of peace and went up into heaven. And ABRAHAM returned to his abode, and he took SÂRÂ (SARAH) his wife, and went forth and did not go back to his father, and his mother, and his house, and his kinsfolk; and he forsook them all for God's sake. And he arrived in the city of SÂLÊM, and dwelt there and reigned in righteousness, and did not transgress the commandment of God. And God blessed him exceedingly, and at length he possessed [3]18 stalwart servants, who were trained in war, and who stood before him and performed his will. And they wore tunics richly embroidered with gold, and they had chains of gold about their necks, and belts of gold round their loins, and they had crowns of gold on their heads; and by means of these men ABRAHAM vanquished [his] foe. And he died in glory in God, and was more gracious and excellent than those who were before him. He was gracious, and held in honour, and highly esteemed.

Footnotes
12. Compare Genesis xii. and xiii. 14-17.

15. Concerning ISAAC and JACOB

And ISAAC his son became king, and he did not transgress the commandment of God; and he was pure in his soul and in his body, and he died in honour. And his son JACOB reigned, and he also did not transgress the commandment of God, and his possessions became numerous, and his children were many; and God blessed him and he died in honour.

16. Concerning RÔBÊL (REUBEN)

And after him, JACOB'S firstborn son transgressed the commandment of God, and the kingdom departed from him and from his seed, because he had defiled his father's wife;[13] now it is not right to transgress the law which God hath commanded. And his father cursed him, and God was wroth with him, and he became the least among his brethren, and his children became leprous and scabby; and although he was the firstborn son [of JACOB] the kingdom was rent from him.[14] And his younger brother reigned, and he was called JUDAH because of this.[15] And his seed was blessed, and his kingdom flourished, and his sons were blessed. And after him FÂRÊS (PHAREZ) his son reigned. And he died and 'ISÂRÔM (HEZRON) his son reigned. And after him his son 'ORNI (OREN[16] ?) reigned, and after him ARÂM (ARAM[17]) his son reigned, and after him AMÎNÂDÂB his son reigned, and after him NÂSÔN (NAASSON) his son reigned, and after him SÂLÂ (SALMON ?) his son reigned, and after him BÂ'OS (BOAZ) his son reigned, and after him 'IYÛBÊD (OBED) his son reigned, and after him Ě'SÊY (JESSE) his son reigned. And this is what I say [concerning] the kingdom: The blessing of the father [was] on the son, so that it (i.e., the kingdom) was blessed with prosperity. And as for the kingship over ISRAEL, after the death of JESSE DAVID reigned in righteousness, and in integrity, and in graciousness.

Footnotes
13. Genesis xxxv. 22; xlix. 4.
14. 1 Chronicles v. 1.
15. Here the name Judah is considered to be derived from the Ethiopic root hêd, "to carry off by force".
16. See 1 Chronicles ii. 25.
17. Matthew i. 4.; Luke iii. 33.

17. Concerning the Glory of ZION

And as concerning ZION, the Tabernacle of the Law of God: at the very beginning, as soon as God had stablished the heavens, He ordained that it should become the habitation of His glory upon the earth. And willing this He brought it down to the earth, and permitted MOSES to make a likeness of it. And He said unto him, "Make an ark (or, tabernacle) of wood that cannot be eaten by worms, and overlay it with pure gold. And thou shalt place therein the Word of the Law, which is the Covenant that I have written with Mine own fingers, that they may keep My law, the Two Tables of the Covenant."[18] Now the heavenly and spiritual [original] within it is of divers colours, and the work thereof is marvellous, and it resembleth jasper, and the sparkling stone, and the topaz, and the hyacinthine stone (?), and the crystal, and the light, and it catcheth the eye by force, and it astonisheth the mind and stupefieth it with wonder; it was made by the mind of God and not by the hand of the artificer, man, but He Himself created it for the habitation of His glory. And it is a spiritual thing and is full of compassion; it is a heavenly thing and is full of light; it is a thing of freedom and a habitation of the Godhead, Whose habitation is in heaven, and Whose place of movement is on the earth, and it dwelleth with men and with the angels, a city of salvation for men, and for the Holy Spirit a habitation. And within it are a GOMOR of gold [containing] a measure of the manna which came down from heaven; and the rod of AARON which sprouted after it had become withered though no one watered it with water, and one had broken it in two places, and it became three rods being [originally only] one rod.

And MOSES covered [the Ark] with pure gold, and he made for it poles wherewith to carry it and rings [in which to place them], and they carried it before the people until they brought it into the land of [their] inheritance, which is JERUSALEM, the City of ZION. And when they were crossing the JORDAN and the priests were carrying it, the waters stood upright like a wall until all the people had passed over, and after all the people had passed over the priests passed over bearing the Ark, and they set it down in the city of JUDAH, the land of [their] inheritance. And prophets were appointed over the children of ISRAEL in the Tabernacle of Testimony, and the priests wore the ephod, so that they might minister to the Tabernacle of Testimony, and the high priests offered up offerings, so that they might obtain remission of their own sins and of the sins of the people likewise.

And God commanded MOSES and AARON to make holy vessels for the Tabernacle of Testimony for the furnishing of the Holy of Holies, namely, vessels of gold, bowls and pots, pitchers and sacred tables, netted cloths and tops for pillars, lamps and vessels for filling them, torch-holders and snuffers, tongs, candlesticks, and rings and rods for carrying them, large bowls and lavers, embroidered curtains and hangings, crowns and worked vestments, purple cloths and leather work, carpets and draperies, unguents for anointing priests and kings, hyacinthine and purple hangings, rugs of double thickness and hangings of silk (?), skins of kids and red hides of rams, and sardius stones, and rubies, and sapphires, and emeralds [and to place them] in the Tabernacle of Witness, where dwelleth ZION, the habitation of His glory. [And God told them] to make for it the "belly of a ship" with the Two Tables, which were written by the fingers of God - ZION shall rest upon them - And thou shalt make for it a tabernacle of wood that the worms cannot eat, whereon ZION shall rest, two cubits and half a cubit shall be the length thereof, and a cubit and half a cubit the breadth thereof, and thou shalt cover it with pure gold, both the outside thereof and the inside thereof. And thou shalt make the fittings and the cover thereof of fine gold, and there shall be rings round about it; and thou shalt make in the four sides four holes for the carrying-poles. And thou shalt make it of wood that the worms cannot eat, and thou shalt cover it with pure gold, and in this ye shall carry the Tabernacle of the Law.

In this wise did God command MOSES on Mount SINAI, and He showed him the work thereof, and the construction and the pattern of the Tent, according to which he was to make it. And it (i.e., ZION) was revered and had exceedingly great majesty in ISRAEL, and it was acknowledged by God to be the habitation of His glory. And He Himself came down on the mountain of His holiness, and He held converse with His chosen ones, and He opened to them [a way of] salvation, and He delivered them from the hand of their enemies. And he spake with them from the pillar of cloud, and commanded them to keep His Law and His commandments, and to walk in the precepts of God.

Footnotes
18. See Exodus xxv. 10 ff.

18. *How the Orthodox Fathers and Bishops Agreed*

And again the Council of the Three Hundred and Eighteen answered and said, "Amen. This is the salvation of the children of ADAM. For since the Tabernacle of the Law of God hath come down, they shall be called, 'Men of the house of God', even as DAVID saith, 'And His habitation is in ZION.'[19] And again he saith by the mouth of the Holy Ghost, 'And My habitation is here, for I have chosen it. And I will bless her priests, and I will make her poor to be glad. And unto DAVID will I give seed in her, and upon the earth one who shall become king, and moreover, in the heavens one from his seed shall reign in the flesh upon the throne of the Godhead. And as for his enemies they shall be gathered together under his footstool, and they shall be sealed with his seal.'"

Footnotes
19. Psalm ix. 11.

19. *How this Book came to be found*

And DĚMÂTĚYÔS (the Patriarch TIMOTHEUS (?) who sat from 511 to 517), the Archbishop of RÔM (i.e., CONSTANTINOPLE, BYZANTIUM), said, "I have found in the Church of [Saint] SOPHIA among the books and the royal treasures a manuscript [which stated] that the whole kingdom of the world [belonged] to the Emperor of RÔM and the Emperor of ETHIOPIA."

20. *Concerning the Division of the Earth*

From the middle of JERUSALEM, and from the north thereof to the south-east is the portion of the Emperor of RÔM; and from the middle of JERUSALEM from the north thereof to the south and to WESTERN INDIA is the portion of the Emperor of ETHIOPIA. For both of them are of the seed of SHEM, the son of NOAH, the seed of ABRAHAM, the seed of DAVID, the children of SOLOMON. For God gave the seed of SHEM glory because of the blessing of their father NOAH. The Emperor of RÔM is the son of SOLOMON, and the Emperor of ETHIOPIA is the firstborn and eldest son of SOLOMON.

21. *Concerning the Queen of the South*

And how this Queen was born I have discovered written in that manuscript, and in this manner also doth the Evangelist mention that woman. And our Lord JESUS CHRIST, in condemning the Jewish people, the crucifiers, who lived at that time, spake, saying: "The Queen of the South shall rise up on the Day of Judgment and shall dispute with, and condemn, and overcome this generation who would not hearken unto the preaching of My word, for she came from the ends of the earth to hear the wisdom of SOLOMON."[20] And the Queen of the South of whom He spake was the Queen of ETHIOPIA. And in the words "ends of the earth" [He maketh allusion] to the delicacy of the constitution of women, and the long distance of the journey, and the burning heat of the sun, and the hunger on the way, and the thirst for water. And this Queen of the South was very beautiful in face, and her stature was superb, and her understanding and intelligence, which God had given her, were of such high character that she went to JERUSALEM to hear the wisdom of SOLOMON; now this was done by the command of God and it was His good pleasure. And moreover, she was exceedingly rich, for God had given her glory, and riches, and gold, and silver, and splendid apparel, and camels, and slaves, and trading men (or, merchants). And they carried on her business and trafficked for her by sea and by land, and in INDIA, and in 'ASWÂN (SYENE).

Footnotes
20. Matthew xii. 42; Luke xi. 31.

22. Concerning TÂMRÎN, the Merchant

And there was a certain wise man, the leader of a merchant's caravan, whose name was TÂMRÎN, and he used to load five hundred and twenty camels, and he possessed about three and seventy ships.

Now at that time King SOLOMON wished to build the House of God, and he sent out messages among all the merchants in the east and in the west, and in the north and in the south, bidding the merchants come and take gold and silver from him, so that he might take from them whatsoever was necessary for the work. And certain men reported to him concerning this rich ETHIOPIAN merchant, and SOLOMON sent to him a message and told him to bring whatsoever he wished from the country of ARABIA, red gold, and black wood that could not be eaten by worms, and sapphires. And that merchant, whose name was TÂMRÎN, the merchant of the Queen of ETHIOPIA, went to SOLOMON the King; and SOLOMON took whatsoever he desired from him, and he gave to the merchant whatsoever he wished for in great abundance. Now that merchant was a man of great understanding, and he saw and comprehended the wisdom of SOLOMON, and he marvelled [thereat], and he watched carefully so that he might learn how the King made answer by his word, and understand his judgment, and the readiness of his mouth, and the discreetness of his speech, and the manner of his life, and his sitting down and his rising up, and his occupations, and his love, and his administration, and his table, and his law. To those to whom SOLOMON had to give orders he spake with humility and graciousness, and when they had committed a fault he admonished them [gently]. For he ordered his house in the wisdom and fear of God, and he smiled graciously on the fools and set them on the right road, and he dealt gently with the maidservants. He opened his mouth in parables, and his words were sweeter than the purest honey; his whole behaviour was admirable, and his whole aspect pleasant. For wisdom is beloved by men of understanding, and is rejected by fools.

And when that merchant had seen all these things he was astonished, and he marvelled exceedingly. For those who were wont to see SOLOMON held him in complete affection, and he [became] their teacher; and because of his wisdom and excellence those who had once come to him did not wish to leave him and go away from him. And the sweetness of his words was like water to the man who is athirst, and like bread to the hungry man, and like healing to the sick man, and like apparel to the naked man. And he was like a father to the orphans. And he judged with righteousness and accepted the person of no man (i.e., he was impartial). He had glory, and riches, which God had given unto him, in great abundance, namely, gold, and silver, and precious stones, and rich apparel, and cattle, and sheep, and goats innumerable. Now in the days of SOLOMON the King gold was as common as bronze, and silver as lead, and bronze and lead and iron were as abundant as the grass of the fields and the reeds of the desert; and cedarwood was also abundant. And God had given him glory, and riches, and wisdom, and grace in such abundance that there was none like unto him among his predecessors, and among those who came after him there was none like unto him.

23. How the Merchant returned to ETHIOPIA

And it came to pass that the merchant TÂMRÎN wished to return to his own country, and he went to SOLOMON and bowed low before him, and embraced him and said unto him, "Peace be to thy majesty! Send me away and let me depart to my country to my Lady, for I have tarried long in beholding thy glory, and thy wisdom, and the abundance of dainty meats wherewith thou hast regaled me. And now I would depart to my Lady. Would that I could abide with thee, even as one of the very least of thy servants, for blessed are they who hear thy voice and perform thy commands! Would that I could abide here and never leave thee! but thou must send me away to my Lady because of what hath been committed to my charge, so that I may give unto her her property. And as for myself, I am her servant." And SOLOMON went into his house and gave unto him whatever valuable thing he desired for the country of ETHIOPIA, and he sent him away in peace. And TÂMRÎN bade him farewell, and went forth, and journeyed along his road, and came to his Lady, and delivered over to her all the possessions which he had brought. And he related unto her how he had arrived in the country of JUDAH [and] JERUSALEM, and how he had gone into the presence of SOLOMON the King, and all that he had heard and seen. And he told her how SOLOMON administered just judgment, and how he spake with authority, and how he decided rightly in all the matters which he enquired into, and how he returned soft and gracious answers, and how there was nothing false about him, and how he appointed inspectors over the seven hundred woodmen who hauled the timber and the eight hundred masons who hewed the stone, and how he sought to learn from all the merchants and dealers concerning the cunning craft and the working thereof, and how he received information and imparted it twofold, and how all his handicraft and his works were performed with wisdom.

And each morning TÂMRÎN related to the Queen [about] all the wisdom of SOLOMON, how he administered judgment and did what was just, and how he ordered his table, and how he made feasts, and how he taught wisdom, and how he directed his servants and all his affairs on a wise system, and how they went on their errands at his command, and how no man defrauded another, and how no man purloined the property of his neighbour, and how there was neither a thief nor a robber in his days. For in his wisdom he knew those who had done wrong, and he chastised them, and made them afraid, and they did not repeat their evil deeds, but they lived in a state of peace which had mingled therein the fear of the King.

All these things did TÂMRÎN relate unto the Queen, and each morning he recalled the things that he had seen with the King and described them unto her. And the Queen was struck dumb with wonder at the things that she heard from the merchant her servant, and she thought in her heart that she would go to him; and she wept by reason of the greatness of her pleasure in those things that TÂMRÎN had told her. And she was exceedingly anxious to go to him, but when she pondered upon the long journey she thought that it was too far and too difficult to undertake. And time after time she asked TÂMRÎN questions about SOLOMON, and time after time TÂMRÎN told her about him, and she became very wishful and most desirous to go that she might hear his wisdom, and see his face, and embrace him, and petition his royalty. And her heart inclined to go to him, for God had made her heart incline to go and had made her to desire it.

24. How the Queen made ready to set out on her Journey

And the Queen said unto them, "Hearken, O ye who are my people, and give ye ear to my words. For I desire wisdom and my heart seeketh to find understanding. I am smitten with the love of wisdom, and I am constrained by the cords of understanding; for wisdom is far better than treasure of gold and silver, and wisdom is the best of everything that hath been created on the earth. Now unto what under the heavens shall wisdom be compared? It is sweeter than honey, and it maketh one to rejoice more than wine, and it illumineth more than the sun, and it is to be loved more than precious stones. And it fatteneth more than oil, and it satisfieth more than dainty meats, and it giveth [a man] more renown than thousands of gold and silver. It is a source of joy for the heart, and a bright and shining light for the eyes, and a giver of speed to the feet, and a shield for the breast, and a helmet for the head, and chain-work for the neck, and a belt for the loins. It maketh the ears to hear and hearts to understand, it is a teacher of those who are learned, and it is a consoler of those who are discreet and prudent, and it giveth fame to those who seek after it. And as for a kingdom, it cannot stand without wisdom, and riches cannot be preserved without wisdom; the foot cannot keep the place wherein it hath set itself without wisdom. And without wisdom that which the tongue speaketh is not acceptable. Wisdom is the best of all treasures. He who heapeth up gold and silver doeth so to no profit without wisdom, but he who heapeth up wisdom - no man can filch it from his heart. That which fools heap up the wise consume. And because of the wickedness of those who do evil the righteous are praised; and because of the wicked acts of fools the wise are beloved. Wisdom is an exalted thing and a rich thing: I will love her like a mother, and she shall embrace me like her child. I will follow the footprints of wisdom and she shall protect me for ever; I will seek after wisdom, and she shall be with me for ever; I will follow her footprints, and she shall not cast me away; I will lean upon her, and she shall be unto me a wall of adamant; I will seek asylum with her, and she shall be unto me power and strength; I will rejoice in her, and she shall be unto me abundant grace. For it is right for us to follow the footprints of wisdom, and for the soles of our feet to stand upon the threshold of the gates of wisdom. Let us seek her, and we shall find her; let us love her, and she will not withdraw herself from us; let us pursue her, and we shall overtake her; let us ask, and we shall receive; and let us turn our hearts to her so that we may never forget her. If [we] remember her, she will have us in remembrance; and in connection with fools thou shalt not remember wisdom, for they do not hold her in honour, and she doth not love them. The honouring of wisdom is the honouring of the wise man, and the loving of wisdom is the loving of the wise man. Love the wise man and withdraw not thyself from him, and by the sight of him thou shalt become wise; hearken to the utterance of his mouth, so that thou mayest become like unto him; watch the place whereon he hath set his foot, and leave him not, so that thou mayest receive the remainder of his wisdom. And I love him merely on hearing concerning him and without seeing him, and the whole story of him that hath been told me is to me as the desire of my heart, and like water to the thirsty man."

And her nobles, and her slaves, and her handmaidens, and her counsellors answered and said unto her, "O our Lady, as for wisdom, it is not lacking in thee, and it is because of thy wisdom that thou lovest wisdom. And to for us, if thou goest we will go with thee, and if thou sittest down we will sit down with thee; our death shall be with thy death, and our life with thy life." Then the Queen made ready to set out on her journey with great pomp and majesty, and with great equipment and many preparations. For, by the Will of God, her heart desired to go to JERUSALEM so that she might hear the Wisdom of SOLOMON; for she had hearkened eagerly. So she made ready to set out. And seven hundred and ninety-seven camels were loaded, and mules and asses innumerable were loaded, and she set out on her journey and followed her road without pause, and her heart had confidence in God.

25. How the Queen came to SOLOMON the King
And she arrived in JERUSALEM, and brought to the King very many precious gifts which he desired to possess greatly. And he paid her great honour and rejoiced, and he gave her a habitation in the royal palace near him. And he sent her food both for the morning and evening meal, each time fifteen measures by the Kôrî of finely ground white meal, cooked with oil and gravy and sauce in abundance,

and thirty measures by the Kôrî of crushed white meal wherefrom bread for three hundred and fifty people was made, with the necessary platters and trays, and ten stalled oxen, and five bulls, and fifty sheep, without (counting) the kids, and deer, and gazelles and fatted fowls, and a vessel of wine containing sixty gerrât measures, and thirty measures of old wine, and twenty-five singing men and twenty-five singing women, and the finest honey and rich sweets, and some of the food which he himself ate, and some of the wine whereof he drank. And every day he arrayed her in eleven garments which bewitched the eyes. And he visited her and was gratified, and she visited him and was gratified, and she saw his wisdom, and his just judgments and his splendour, and his grace, and heard the eloquence of his speech. And she marvelled in her heart, and was utterly astonished in her mind, and she recognized in her understanding, and perceived very clearly with her eyes how admirable he was; and she wondered exceedingly because of what she saw and heard with him - how perfect he was in composure, and wise in understanding, and pleasant in graciousness, and commanding in stature. And she observed the subtlety of his voice, and the discreet utterances of his lips, and that he gave his commands with dignity, and that his replies were made quietly and with the fear of God. All these things she saw, and she was astonished at the abundance of his wisdom, and there was nothing whatsoever wanting in his word and speech, but everything that he spake was perfect.

And SOLOMON was working at the building of the House of God, and he rose up and went to the right and to the left, and forward and backward. And he showed the workmen the measurement and weight and the space covered [by the materials], and he told the workers in metal how to use the hammer, and the drill, and the chisel (?), and he showed the stone-masons the angle [measure] and the circle and the surface [measure]. And everything was wrought by his order, and there was none who set himself in opposition to his word; for the light of his heart was like a lamp in the darkness, and his wisdom was as abundant as the sand. And of the speech of the beasts and the birds there was nothing hidden from him, and he forced the devils to obey him by his wisdom. And he did everything by means of the skill which God gave him when he made supplication to Him; for he did not ask for victory over his enemy, and he did not ask for riches and fame, but he asked God to give him wisdom and understanding whereby he might rule his people, and build His House, and beautify the work of God and all that He had given him [in] wisdom and understanding.

26. How the King held converse with the Queen
And the Queen MÂKĔDÂ spake unto King SOLOMON, saying, "Blessed art thou, my lord, in that such wisdom and understanding have been given unto thee. For myself I only wish that I could be as one of the least of thine handmaidens, so that I could wash thy feet, and hearken to thy wisdom, and apprehend thy understanding, and serve thy majesty, and enjoy thy wisdom. O how greatly

have pleased me thy answering, and the sweetness of thy voice, and the beauty of thy going, and the graciousness of thy words, and the readiness thereof. The sweetness of thy voice maketh the heart to rejoice, and maketh the bones fat, and giveth courage to hearts, and goodwill and grace to the lips, and strength to the gait. I look upon thee and I see that thy wisdom is immeasureable and thine understanding inexhaustible, and that it is like unto a lamp in the darkness, and like unto a pomegranate in the garden, and like unto a pearl in the sea, and like unto the Morning Star among the stars, and like unto the light of the moon in the mist, and like unto a glorious dawn and sunrise in the heavens. And I give thanks unto Him that brought me hither and showed thee to me, and made me to tread upon the threshold of thy gate, and made me to hear thy voice."

And King SOLOMON answered and said unto her, "Wisdom and understanding spring from thee thyself. As for me, [I only possess them] in the measure in which the God of ISRAEL hath given [them] to me because I asked and entreated them from Him. And thou, although thou dost not know the God of ISRAEL, hast this wisdom which thou hast made to grow in thine heart, and [it hath made thee come] to see me, the vassal and slave of my God, and the building of His sanctuary which I am establishing, and wherein I serve and move round about my Lady, the Tabernacle of the Law of the God of ISRAEL, the holy and heavenly ZION. Now, I am the slave of my God, and I am not a free man; I do not serve according to my own will but according to His Will. And this speech of mine springeth not from myself, but I give utterance only to what He maketh me to utter. Whatsoever He commandeth me that I do; wheresoever He wisheth me to go thither I go; whatsoever He teacheth me that I speak; that concerning which He giveth me wisdom I understand. For from being only dust He hath made me flesh, and from being only water He hath made me a solid man, and from being only an ejected drop, which shot forth upon the ground would have dried up on the surface of the earth, He hath fashioned me in His own likeness and hath made me in His own image."

27. Concerning the Labourer

And as SOLOMON was talking in this wise with the Queen, he saw a certain labourer carrying a stone upon his head and a skin of water upon his neck and shoulders, and his food and his sandals were [tied] about his loins, and there were pieces of wood in his hands; his garments were ragged and tattered, the sweat fell in drops from his face, and water from the skin of water dripped down upon his feet. And the labourer passed before SOLOMON, and as he was going by the King said unto him, "Stand still"; and the labourer stood still. And the King turned to the Queen and said unto her, "Look at this man. Wherein am I superior to this man? And in what am I better than this man? And wherein shall I glory over this man? For I am a man and dust and ashes, who to-morrow will become worms and corruption, and yet at this moment I appear like one who will never die. Who would make any complaint against God if He were to give unto this man as He hath given to me, and if He were to make me even as this man is? Are we not both of us beings, that is to say men? As is his death, [so] is my death; and as is his life [so] is my life. Yet this man is stronger to work than I am, for God giveth power to those who are feeble just as it pleaseth Him to do so." And SOLOMON said unto the labourer, "Get thee to thy work."

And he spake further unto the Queen, saying, "What is the use of us, the children of men, if we do not exercise kindness and love upon earth? Are we not all nothingness, mere grass of the field, which withereth in its season and is burnt in the fire? On the earth we provide ourselves with dainty meats, and [we wear] costly apparel, but even whilst we are alive we are stinking corruption; we provide ourselves with sweet scents and delicate unguents, but even whilst we are alive we are dead in sin and in transgressions; being wise, we become fools through disobedience and deeds of iniquity; being held in honour, we become contemptible through magic, and sorcery, and the worship of idols. Now the man who is a being of honour, who was created in the image of God, if he doeth that which is good becometh like God; but the man who is a thing of nothingness, if he committeth sin becometh like unto the Devil - the arrogant Devil who refused to obey the command of his Creator - and all the arrogant among men walk in his way, and they shall be judged with him. And God loveth the lowly-minded, and those who practise humility walk in His way, and they shall rejoice in His kingdom. Blessed is the man who knoweth wisdom, that is to say, compassion and the fear of God."

And when the Queen heard this she said, "How thy voice doth please me! And how greatly do thy words and the utterance of thy mouth delight me! Tell me now: whom is it right for me to worship? We worship the sun according as our fathers have taught us to do, because we say that the sun is the king of the gods. And there are others among our subjects [who worship other things]; some worship stones, and some worship wood (i.e., trees), and some worship carved figures, and some worship images of gold and silver. And we worship the sun, for he cooketh our food, and moreover, he illumineth the darkness, and removeth fear; we call him 'Our King', and we call him 'Our Creator', and we worship him as our god; for no man hath told us that besides him there is another god. But we have heard that there is with you, ISRAEL, another God Whom we do not know, and men have told us that He hath sent down to you from heaven a Tabernacle and hath given unto you a Tablet of the ordering of the angels, by the hand of MOSES the Prophet. This also we have heard - that He Himself cometh down to you and talketh to you, and informeth you concerning His ordinances and commandments."

28. How SOLOMON gave Commandments to the Queen

And the King answered and said unto her, "Verily, it is right that they (i.e., men) should worship God, Who created the universe, the heavens and the earth, the sea and the dry land, the sun and the moon, the stars and the brilliant bodies of the heavens, the trees and the stones, the beasts and the feathered fowl, the wild beasts and the crocodiles, the fish and the whales, the hippopotamuses and the water lizards, the lightnings and the crashes of thunder, the clouds and the thunders, and the good and the evil. It is meet that Him alone we should worship, in fear and trembling, with joy and with gladness. For He is the Lord of the Universe, the Creator of angels and men. And it is He Who killeth and maketh to live, it is He Who inflicteth punishment and showeth compassion, Who raiseth up from the ground him that is in misery, Who exalteth the poor from the dust, Who maketh to be sorrowful and Who to rejoice, Who raiseth up and Who bringeth down. No one can chide Him, for He is the Lord of the Universe, and there is no one who can say unto Him, 'What hast Thou done?' And unto Him it is meet that there should be praise and thanksgiving from angels and men. And as concerning what thou sayest, that 'He hath given unto you the Tabernacle of the Law,' verily there hath been given unto us the Tabernacle of the God of ISRAEL, which was created before all creation by His glorious counsel. And He hath made to come down to us His commandments, done into writing, so that we may know His decree and the judgment that He hath ordained in the mountain of His holiness."

And the Queen said, "From this moment I will not worship the sun, but will worship the Creator of the sun, the God of ISRAEL. And that Tabernacle of the God of ISRAEL shall be unto me my Lady, and unto my seed after me, and unto all my kingdoms that are under my dominion. And because of this I have found favour before thee, and before the God of ISRAEL my Creator, Who hath brought me unto thee, and hath made me to hear thy voice, and hath shown me thy face, and hath made me to understand thy commandment." Then she returned to [her] house.

And the Queen used to go [to SOLOMON] and return continually, and hearken unto his wisdom, and keep it in her heart. And SOLOMON used to go and visit her, and answer all the questions which she put to him, and the Queen used to visit him and ask him questions, and he informed her concerning every matter that she wished to enquire about. And after she had dwelt [there] six months the Queen wished to return to her own country, and she sent a message to SOLOMON, saying, "I desire greatly to dwell with thee, but now, for the sake of all my people, I wish to return to my own country. And as for that which I have heard, may God make it to bear fruit in my heart, and in the hearts of all those who have heard it with me. For the ear could never be filled with the hearing of thy wisdom, and the eye could never be filled with the sight of the same."

Now it was not only the Queen who came [to hear the wisdom of SOLOMON], but very many used to come from cities and countries, both from near and from far; for in those days there was no man found to be like unto him for wisdom (and it was not only human beings who came to him, but the wild animals and the birds used to come to him and hearken unto his voice, and hold converse with him), and then they returned to their own countries, and every one of them was astonished at his wisdom, and marvelled at what he had seen and heard.

And when the Queen sent her message to SOLOMON, saying that she was about to depart to her own country, he pondered in his heart and said, "A woman of such splendid beauty hath come to me from the ends of the earth! What do I know? Will God give me seed in her?" Now, as it is said in the Book of KINGS, SOLOMON the King was a lover of women.[21] And he married wives of the HEBREWS, and the EGYPTIANS, and the CANAANITES, and the EDOMITES, and the ÎYÔBÂWÎYÂN (MOABITES ?), and from RÎF[22] and KUĔRGUĔ,[23] and DAMASCUS, and SÛREST (SYRIA), and women who were reported to be beautiful. And he had four hundred queens and six hundred concubines. Now this which he did was not for [the sake of] fornication, but as a result of the wise intent that God had given unto him, and his remembering what God had said unto ABRAHAM, "I will make thy seed like the stars of heaven for number, and like the sand of the sea."[24] And SOLOMON said in his heart, "What do I know? Peradventure God will give me men children from each one of these women." Therefore when he did thus he acted wisely, saying, "My children shall inherit the cities of the enemy, and shall destroy those who worship idols."

Now those early peoples lived under the law of the flesh, for the grace of the Holy Spirit had not been given unto them. And to those [who lived] after CHRIST, it was given to live with one woman under the law of marriage. And the Apostles laid down for them an ordinance, saying, "All those who have received His flesh and His blood are brethren. Their mother is the Church and their father is God, and they cry out with CHRIST Whom they have received, saying, 'Our Father, Who art in heaven.'" And as concerning SOLOMON no law had been laid down for him in respect of women, and no blame can be imputed to him in respect of marrying [many] wives. But for those who believe, the law and the command have been given that they shall not marry many wives, even as Paul saith, "Those who marry many wives seek their own punishment. He who marrieth one wife hath no sin."[25] And the law restraineth us from the sister [-in-law],[26] in respect of the bearing of children. The Apostles speak [concerning it] in the [Book of] Councils.[27]

Footnotes

21. 1 Kings xi. 1.
22. Upper Egypt.
23. See YâKût, IV, p. 250.
24. Genesis xxii. 17.
25. Compare 1 Corinthians vii.
26. Compare Leviticus xviii. 18.
27. Guidi (apud Bezold) compares No. 19 of the Apocryphal Canones Apostolorum.

29. Concerning the Three Hundred and Eighteen [Patriarchs]

Now we ordain even as did they. We know well what the Apostles who were before us spake. We the Three Hundred and Eighteen have maintained and laid down the orthodox faith, our Lord JESUS CHRIST being with us. And He hath directed us what we should teach, and how we should fashion the faith.

[The Narrative of SOLOMON and the Queen of SHEBA continued]

And King SOLOMON sent a message unto the Queen, saying, "Now that thou hast come here why wilt thou go away without seeing the administration of the kingdom, and how the meal[s] for the chosen ones of the kingdom are eaten after the manner of the righteous, and how the people are driven away after the manner of sinners? From [the sight of] it thou wouldst acquire wisdom. Follow me now and seat thyself in my splendour in the tent, and I will complete thy instruction, and thou shalt learn the administration of my kingdom; for thou hast loved wisdom, and she shall dwell with thee until thine end and for ever." Now a prophecy maketh itself apparent in [this] speech.

And the Queen sent a second message, saying, "From being a fool, I have become wise by following thy wisdom, and from being a thing rejected by the God of ISRAEL, I have become a chosen woman because of this faith which is in my heart; and henceforth I will worship no other god except Him. And as concerning that which thou sayest, that thou wishest to increase in me wisdom and honour, I will come according to thy desire." And SOLOMON rejoiced because of this [message], and he arrayed his chosen ones [in splendid apparel], and he added a double supply to his table, and he had all the arrangements concerning the management of his house carefully ordered, and the house of King SOLOMON was made ready [for guests] daily. And he made it ready with very great pomp, in joy, and in peace, in wisdom, and in tenderness, with all humility and lowliness; and then he ordered the royal table according to the law of the kingdom.

And the Queen came and passed into a place set apart in splendour and glory, and she sat down immediately behind him where she could see and learn and know everything. And she marvelled exceedingly at what she saw, and at what she heard, and she praised the God of ISRAEL in her heart; and she was struck with wonder at the splendour of the royal palace which she saw. For she could see, though no one could see her, even as SOLOMON had arranged in wisdom for her. He had beautified the place where she was seated, and had spread over it purple hangings, and laid down carpets, and decorated it with miskât (moschus), and marbles, and precious stones, and he burned aromatic powders, and sprinkled oil of myrrh and cassia round about, and scattered frankincense and costly incense in all directions. And when they brought her into this abode, the odour thereof was very pleasing to her, and even before she ate the dainty meats therein she was satisfied with the smell of them. And with wise intent SOLOMON sent to her meats which would make her thirsty, and drinks that were mingled with vinegar, and fish and dishes made with pepper. And this he did and he gave them to the Queen to eat. And the royal meal had come to an end three times and seven times,[28] and the administrators, and the counsellors, and the young men and the servants had departed, and the King rose up and he went to the Queen, and he said

78

unto her - now they were alone together - "Take thou thine ease here for love's sake until daybreak." And she said unto him, "Swear to me by thy God, the God of ISRAEL, that thou wilt not take me by force. For if I, who according to the law of men am a maiden, be seduced, I should travel on my journey [back] in sorrow, and affliction, and tribulation."

Footnotes
28. i.e., three courses and seven courses had been consumed.

30. Concerning how King SOLOMON swore to the Queen

And SOLOMON answered and said unto her, "I swear unto thee that I will not take thee by force, but thou must swear unto me that thou wilt not take by force anything that is in my house." And the Queen laughed and said unto him, "Being a wise man why dost thou speak as a fool? Shall I steal anything, or shall I carry out of the house of the King that which the King hath not given to me? Do not imagine that I have come hither through love of riches. Moreover, my own kingdom is as wealthy as thine, and there is nothing which I wish for that I lack. Assuredly I have only come in quest of thy wisdom." And he said unto her, "If thou wouldst make me swear, swear thou to me, for a swearing is meet for both [of us], so that neither of us may be unjustly treated. And if thou wilt not make me swear I will not make thee swear." And she said unto him, "Swear to me that thou wilt not take me by force, and I on my part will swear not to take by force thy possessions"; and he swore to her and made her swear.

And the King went up on his bed on the one side [of the chamber], and the servants made ready for her a bed on the other side. And SOLOMON said unto a young manservant, "Wash out the bowl and set in it a vessel of water whilst the Queen is looking on, and shut the doors and go and sleep." And SOLOMON spake to the servant in another tongue which the Queen did not understand, and he did as the King commanded, and went and slept. And the King had not as yet fallen asleep, but he only pretended to be asleep, and he was watching the Queen intently. Now the house of SOLOMON the King was illumined as by day, for in his wisdom he had made shining pearls which were like unto the sun, and moon, and stars [and had set them] in the roof of his house.

And the Queen slept a little. And when she woke up her mouth was dry with thirst, for the food which SOLOMON had given her in his wisdom had made her thirsty, and she was very thirsty indeed, and her mouth was dry; and she moved her lips and sucked with her mouth and found no moisture. And she determined to drink the water which she had seen, and she looked at King SOLOMON and watched him carefully, and she thought that he was sleeping a sound sleep. But he was not asleep, and he was waiting until she should rise up to steal the water to [quench] her thirst. And she rose up and, making no sound with her feet, she went to the water in the bowl and lifted up the jar to drink the water. And SOLOMON seized her hand before she could drink the water, and said unto her, "Why hast thou broken the oath that thou hast sworn that thou wouldst not take by force anything that is in my house?" And she answered and said unto him in fear, "Is the oath broken by my drinking water?" And the King said unto her, "Is there anything that thou hast seen under the heavens that is better than water?" And the Queen said, "I have sinned against myself, and thou art free from [thy] oath. But let me drink water for my thirst." Then SOLOMON said unto her, "Am I perchance free from the oath which thou hast made me swear?" And the Queen said, "Be free from thy oath, only let me drink water." And he permitted her to drink water, and after she had drunk water he worked his will with her and they slept together.

And after he slept there appeared unto King SOLOMON [in a dream] a brilliant sun, and it came down from heaven and shed exceedingly great splendour over ISRAEL. And when it had tarried there for a time it suddenly withdrew itself, and it flew away to the country of ETHIOPIA, and it shone there with exceedingly great brightness for ever, for it willed to dwell there. And [the King said], "I waited [to see] if it would come back to ISRAEL, but it did not return. And again while I waited a light rose up in the heavens, and a Sun came down from them in the country of JUDAH, and it sent forth light which was very much stronger than before." And[29] ISRAEL, because of the flame of that Sun entreated that Sun evilly and would not walk in the light thereof. And that Sun paid no heed to ISRAEL, and the ISRAELITES hated Him, and it became impossible that peace should exist between them and the Sun. And they lifted up their hands against Him with staves and knives, and they wished to extinguish that Sun. And they cast darkness upon the whole world with earthquake and thick darkness, and they imagined that that Sun would never more rise upon them. And they destroyed His light and cast themselves upon Him and they set a guard over His tomb wherein they had cast Him. And He came forth where they did not look for Him, and illumined the whole world, more especially the First Sea and the Last Sea, ETHIOPIA and RÔM. And He paid no heed whatsoever to ISRAEL, and He ascended His former throne.

And when SOLOMON the King saw this vision in his sleep, his soul became disturbed, and his understanding was snatched away as by [a flash of] lightning, and he woke up with an agitated mind. And moreover, SOLOMON marvelled concerning the Queen, for she was vigorous in strength, and beautiful of form, and she was undefiled in her virginity; and she had reigned for six years in her own country, and, notwithstanding her gracious attraction and her splendid form, had preserved her body pure. And the Queen said unto SOLOMON, "Dismiss me, and let me depart to my own country." And he went into his house and gave unto her whatsoever she wished for of splendid things and riches, and beautiful apparel which bewitched the eyes, and everything on which great store was set in the country of ETHIOPIA, and camels and wagons, six thousand in number, which were laden with beautiful things of the most desirable kind, and wagons wherein loads were carried over the desert, and a vessel wherein one could travel over the sea, and a vessel wherein one could traverse the air (or winds), which SOLOMON had made by the wisdom that God had given unto him.

Footnotes

29. The remainder of this paragraph is a comment by the author of this work.

31. Concerning the sign which SOLOMON gave the Queen

And the Queen rejoiced, and she went forth in order to depart, and the King set her on her way with great pomp and ceremony. And SOLOMON took her aside so that they might be alone together, and he took off the ring that was upon his little finger, and he gave it to the Queen, and said unto her, "Take [this] so that thou mayest not forget me. And if it happen that I obtain seed from thee, this ring shall be unto it a sign; and if it be a man child he shall come to me; and the peace of God be with thee! Whilst I was sleeping with thee I saw many visions in a dream, [and it seemed] as if a sun had risen upon ISRAEL, but it snatched itself away and flew off and lighted up the country of ETHIOPIA; peradventure that country shall be blessed through thee; God knoweth. And as for thee, observe what I have told thee, so that thou mayest worship God with all thy heart and perform His Will. For He punisheth those who are arrogant, and He showeth compassion upon those who are humble, and He removeth the thrones of the mighty, and He maketh to be honoured those who are needy. For death and life are from Him, and riches and poverty are bestowed by His Will. For everything is His, and none can oppose His command and His judgment in the heavens, or in the earth, or in the sea, or in the abysses. And may God be with thee! Go in peace." And they separated from each other.

32. How the Queen brought forth and came to her own Country

And the Queen departed and came into the country of BÂLÂ ZADÎSÂRĔYÂ nine months and five days after she had separated from King SOLOMON. And the pains of childbirth laid hold upon her, and she brought forth a man child, and she gave it to the nurse with great pride and delight. And she tarried until the days of her purification were ended, and then she came to her own country with great pomp and ceremony. And her officers who had remained there brought gifts to their mistress, and made obeisance to her, and did homage to her, and all the borders of the country rejoiced at her coming. Those who were nobles among them she arrayed in splendid apparel, and to some she gave gold and silver, and hyacinthine and purple robes; and she gave them all manner of things that could be desired. And she ordered her kingdom aright, and none disobeyed her command; for she loved wisdom and God strengthened her kingdom.

And the child grew and she called his name BAYNA-LEHKEM. And the child reached the age of twelve years, and he asked his friends among the boys who were being educated with him, and said unto them, "Who is my father?"

And they said unto him, "SOLOMON the King." And he went to the Queen his mother, and said unto her, "O Queen, make me to know who is my father." And the Queen spake unto him angrily, wishing to frighten him so that he might not desire to go [to his father] saying, "Why dost thou ask me about thy father? I am thy father and thy mother; seek not to know any more." And the boy went forth from her presence, and sat down. And a second time, and a third time he asked her, and he importuned her to tell him. One day, however, she told him, saying, "His country is far away, and the road thither is very difficult; wouldst thou not rather be here?" And the youth BAYNA-LEHKEM was handsome, and his whole body and his members, and the bearing of his shoulders resembled those of King SOLOMON his father, and his eyes, and his legs, and his whole gait resembled those of SOLOMON the King. And when he was two and twenty years old he was skilled in the whole art of war and of horsemanship, and in the hunting and trapping of wild beasts, and in everything that young men are wont to learn. And he said unto the Queen, "I will go and look upon the face of my father, and I will come back here by the Will of God, the Lord of ISRAEL."

33. How the King of ETHIOPIA travelled

And the Queen called TÂMRÎN, the chief of her caravan men and merchants, and she said unto him, "Get ready for thy journey and take this young man with thee, for he importuneth me by night and by day. And thou shalt take him to the King and shalt bring him back hither in safety, if God, the Lord of ISRAEL, pleaseth." And she prepared a retinue suitable to their wealth and honourable condition, and made ready all the goods that were necessary for the journey, and for presenting as gifts to the King, and all that would be necessary for ease and comfort by the way. And she made ready everything for sending him away, and she gave to the officers who were to accompany him such moneys as they would need for him and for themselves on the journey. And she commanded them that they were not to leave him there, but only to take him to the King, and then to bring him back again to her, when he should assume the sovereignty over her land.

Now there was a law in the country of ETHIOPIA that [only] a woman should reign, and that she must be a virgin who had never known man, but the Queen said [unto SOLOMON], "Henceforward a man who is of thy seed shall reign, and a woman shall nevermore reign; only seed of thine shall reign and his seed after him from generation to generation. And this thou shalt inscribe in the letters of the rolls in the Book of their Prophets in brass, and thou shalt lay it in the House of God, which shall be built as a memorial and as a prophecy for the last days. And the people shall not worship the sun and the magnificence of the heavens, or the mountains and the forests, or the stones and the trees of the wilderness, or the abysses and that which is in the waters, or graven images and figures of gold, or the feathered fowl which fly; and they shall not make use of them in divining, and they shall not pay adoration unto them. And this law shall abide for ever. And if there be anyone who shall transgress this law, thy seed shall judge him for ever. Only give us the fringes of the covering of the holy heavenly ZION, the Tabernacle of the Law of God, which we would embrace (or, greet). Peace be to the strength of thy kingdom and to thy brilliant wisdom, which God, the Lord of ISRAEL our Creator, hath given unto thee."

And the Queen took the young man aside and when he was alone with her she gave him that symbol which SOLOMON had given her, that is to say, the ring on his finger, so that he might know his son, and might remember her word and her covenant which she had made [with him], that she would worship God all the days of her life, she and those who were under her dominion, with all [the power] which God had given her. And then the Queen sent him away in peace.

And the young man [and his retinue] made straight their way and they journeyed on and came into the country of the neighbourhood of GÂZÂ. Now this is the GÂZÂ which SOLOMON the King gave to the Queen of ETHIOPIA. And in the Acts of the Apostles LUKE the Evangelist wrote, saying, "He was the governor of the whole country of GÂZÂ, an eunuch of Queen HENDAKÊ, who had believed on the word of LUKE the Apostle."[30]

Footnotes
30. Acts viii. 27

34. How the young man arrived in his mother's country

And when the young man arrived in his mother's country he rejoiced there in the honour [which he received], and in the gifts [that were made] to him. And when the people saw him they thought him to be the perfect likeness of SOLOMON the King. And they made obeisance to him, and they said unto him, "Hail, the royal father liveth!" And they brought unto him gifts and offerings, fatted cattle and food, as to their king. And [the people of] the whole country of GÂZÂ, as far as the border of JUDAH, were stirred up and they said, "This is King SOLOMON." And there were some who said, "The King is in JERUSALEM building his house" - now he had finished building the House of God - and others said, "This is SOLOMON the King, the son of DAVID." And they were perplexed, and they disputed with one another, and they sent off spies mounted on horses, who were to seek out King SOLOMON and to find out if he were actually in JERUSALEM, or if he were with them [in GÂZÂ]. And the spies came to the watchmen of the city of JERUSALEM, and they found King SOLOMON there, and they made obeisance to him, and they said unto him, "Hail, may the royal father live! [Our] country is disturbed because there hath come into it a merchant who resembleth thee in form and appearance, without the smallest alteration or variation. He resembleth thee in noble carriage and in splendid form, and in stature and in goodly appearance; he lacketh nothing in respect of these and is in no way different from thyself. His eyes are gladsome, like unto those of a man who hath drunk wine, his legs are graceful and slender, and the tower of his neck is like unto the tower of DAVID thy father. He is like unto thee exactly in every respect, and every member of his whole body is like unto thine."

And King SOLOMON answered and said unto them, "Where is it then that he wisheth to go?" And they answered and said unto him, "We have not enquired of him, for he is awesome like thyself. But his own people, when we asked them, 'Whence have ye come and whither do ye go?' said, 'We have come from the dominions of HENDAKÊ (CANDACE) and ETHIOPIA, and we are going to the country of JUDAH to King SOLOMON.'" And when King SOLOMON heard this his heart was perturbed and he was glad in his soul, for in those days he had no children, except a boy who was seven years old and whose name was ÎYÔRBE'ÂM (REHOBOAM). It happened to SOLOMON even as Paul stateth, saying, "God hath made foolishness the wisdom of this world,"[31] for SOLOMON had made a plan in his wisdom and said, "By one thousand women I shall beget one thousand men children, and I shall inherit the countries of the enemy, and I will overthrow [their] idols." But [God] only gave him three children. His eldest son was the King of ETHIOPIA, the son of the Queen of ETHIOPIA, and was the firstborn of whom [God] spake prophetically, "God sware unto DAVID in righteousness, and repented not, 'Of the fruit of thy body will I make to sit upon thy throne.'"[32] And God gave unto DAVID His servant grace before Him, and granted unto him that there should sit upon the throne of Godhead One of his seed in the flesh, from the Virgin, and should judge the living and the dead, and reward every man according to his work, One to whom praise is meet, our Lord JESUS CHRIST, for ever and ever, Amen. And He gave him one on the earth who should become king over the Tabernacle of the Law of the holy, heavenly ZION, that is to say, the King of ETHIOPIA. And as for those who reigned, who were not [of] ISRAEL, that was due to the transgression of the law and the commandment, whereat God was not pleased.

Footnotes
31. 1 Corinthians i. 20.
32. 2 Samuel vii. 17; Psalm cxxxii. 11.

35. How King SOLOMON sent to his son the commander of his army
And SOLOMON the King sent the commander of his army, on whose hand he was wont to lean, with gifts and meat and drink to entertain that traveller. And the commander set out with a great number of wagons, and he came to BAYNA LEHKEM, and embraced him, and gave him everything that SOLOMON the King had sent unto him. And he said unto him, "Make haste and come with me, for the heart of the King is burnt up as with fire with the love of thee. Peradventure he will find out for himself whether thou art his own son or his brother; for in thine

appearance and in thy conversation (or, manner) thou art in no way different from him. And now, rise up quickly, for my lord the King said unto me, 'Haste and bring him hither to me in honour, and comfort, and with suitable service, and in joy and gladness.'" And the young man answered and said unto him, "I thank God, the Lord of ISRAEL, that I have found grace with my lord the King without having seen his face; his word hath rejoiced me. And now I will put my trust in the Lord of ISRAEL that He will show me the King, and will bring me back safely to my mother the Queen, and to my country ETHIOPIA."

And JOAS (?), the son of YÔDÂHÊ,[33] the commander of the army of King SOLOMON, answered and said unto BAYNA LEHKEM, "My lord, this is a very small matter, and thou wilt find far greater joy and pleasure with my lord the King. And as concerning what thou sayest, 'my mother' and 'my country', SOLOMON the King is better than thy mother, and this our country is better than thy country. And as for thy country, we have heard that it is a land of cold and cloud, and a country of glare and burning heat, and a region of snow and ice. And when the sons of NOAH, SHEM, and HAM, and JAPHET, divided the world among them, they looked on thy country with wisdom and saw that, although it was spacious and broad, it was a land of whirlwind and burning heat, and [therefore] gave it to CANAAN, the son of HAM, as a portion for himself and his seed for ever. But the land that is ours is the land of inheritance (i.e., the promised land), which God hath given unto us according to the oath that He swore to our fathers, a land flowing with milk and honey, where sustenance is [ours] without anxiety, a land that yieldeth fruit of every kind in its season without exhausting labour, a land which God keepeth watch over continually from one year to the beginning of the revolution of the next. All this is thine, and we are thine, and we will be thine heirs, and thou shalt dwell in our country, for thou art the seed of DAVID, the lord of my lord, and unto thee belongeth this throne of ISRAEL."

And the headmen of the merchant TÂMRÎN answered and said unto BENAIAH, "Our country is the better. The air (i.e., climate) of our country is good, for it is without burning heat and fire, and the water of our country is good, and sweet, and floweth in rivers, moreover the tops of our mountains run with water. And we do not do as ye do in your country, that is to say, dig very deep wells [in search of] water, and we do not die through the heat of the sun; but even at noonday we hunt wild animals, namely, the wild buffaloes, and gazelles, and birds, and small animals. And in the winter God taketh heed unto us from [one] year to the beginning of the course of the next. And in the springtime the people eat what they have trodden with the foot as [in] the land of EGYPT, and as for our trees they produce good crops of fruit, and the wheat, and the barley, and all our fruits, and cattle are good and wonderful. But there is one thing that ye have wherein ye are better than we are, namely wisdom, and because of it we are journeying to you."

And JOAS (read BENAIAH), the commander of the army of King SOLOMON, answered [saying], "What is better than wisdom? For wisdom hath founded the earth, and made strong the heavens, and fettered the waves of the sea so that it might not cover the earth. However, rise up and let us go to my lord, for his heart is greatly moved by love for thee, and he hath sent me to bring thee [to him] with all the speed possible."

And the son of the Queen rose up, and arrayed JOAS (BENAIAH), the son of YÔDÂHÊ, and the fifty men who were in his retinue, in gorgeous raiment, and they rose up to go to JERUSALEM to SOLOMON the King. And when they came nigh unto the place where the horses were exercised and trained, JOAS (BENAIAH), the son of YÔDÂHÊ, went on in front, and came to the place where SOLOMON was, and he told him that [the son of the Queen] was well-favoured in his appearance, and that his voice was pleasant, and that he resembled him in form, and that his whole bearing was exceedingly noble. And the King said unto him, "Where is he? Did I not send thee forth to bring him as quickly as possible?" And JOAS (BENAIAH) said unto him, "He is here, I will bring him quickly." And JOAS (BENAIAH) went and said unto the young man, "Rise up, O my master, and come"; and making BAYNA LEHKEM to go quickly he brought him to the King's Gate. And when all the soldiers saw him they made obeisance unto him, and they said, "Behold, King SOLOMON hath gone forth from his abode." And when the men who were inside came forth, they marvelled, and they went back to their places, and again they saw the King upon his throne; and wondering they went forth again and looked at the young man, and they were incapable of speaking and of saying anything. And when JOAS (BENAIAH), the son of YÔDÂHÊ, came in again to announce to the King the arrival of the young man, there was none standing before the King, but all ISRAEL had thronged outside to see him.

Footnotes

33. There is a mistake here. The author had in his mind Joab, the captain of David's host. Several of the MSS. have the reading "Benyâs", i.e., Benaiah, the son of Jehoiada (see 1 Kings ii. 35), who was put in Joab's room.

36. How King SOLOMON held intercourse with his son

And JOAS (BENAIAH), the son of YÔDÂHÊ, went out and brought BAYNA LEHKEM inside. And when King SOLOMON saw him he rose up, and moved forward to welcome him, and he loosed the band of his apparel from his shoulder, and he embraced him, with his hands [resting] on his breast, and he kissed his mouth, and forehead, and eyes, and he said unto him, "Behold, my father DAVID hath renewed his youth and hath risen from the dead." And SOLOMON the King turned round to those who had announced the arrival of the young man, and he said unto them, "Ye said unto me, 'He resembleth thee,' but this is not my stature, but the stature of DAVID my father in the days of his early manhood, and he is handsomer than I am." And SOLOMON the King rose up straightway, and he went into his chamber, and he arrayed the young man in apparel made of cloth embroidered with gold, and a belt of gold, and he set a crown upon his head, and a ring upon his finger. And having arrayed him in glorious apparel which bewitched the eyes, he seated him upon his throne, that he might be equal in rank to himself. And he said unto the nobles and officers of ISRAEL, "O ye who treat me with contumely among yourselves and say that I have no son, look ye, this is my son, the fruit that hath gone forth from my body, whom God, the Lord of ISRAEL, hath given me, when I expected it not."

And his nobles answered and said unto him, "Blessed be the mother who hath brought forth this young man, and blessed be the day wherein thou hadst union with the mother of this young man. For there hath risen upon us from the root of JESSE a shining man who shall be king of the posterity of our posterity of his seed. Concerning his father none shall ask questions, and none shall say, 'Whence is his coming?' Verily he is an ISRAELITE of the seed of DAVID, fashioned perfectly in the likeness of his father's form and appearance; we are his servants, and he shall be our king." And they brought unto him gifts, each according to his greatness. And the young man took that ring which his mother had given him when they were alone together, and he said unto his father, "Take this ring, and remember the word which thou didst speak unto the Queen, and give unto us a portion of the fringe of the covering of the Tabernacle of the Law of God, so that we may worship it all our days, and all those who are subject unto us, and those who are in the kingdom of the Queen." And the King answered and said unto him, "Why givest thou me the ring as a sign? Without thy giving me a sign I discovered the likeness of thy form to myself, for thou art indeed my son."

And the merchant TÂMRÎN spake again unto King SOLOMON, saying, "Hearken, O King, unto the message which thy handmaiden, the Queen my mistress, sent by me: 'Take this young man, anoint him, consecrate him, and bless him, and make him king over our country, and give him the command that a woman shall never again reign [in this country], and send him back in peace. And peace be with the might of thy kingdom, and with thy brilliant wisdom. As for me, I never wished that he should come where thou art, but he urged me exceedingly that he should be allowed to come to thee. And besides, I was afraid for him lest he should fall sick on the journey, either through thirst for water, or the heat of the sun, and I should bring my grey hairs down to the grave with sorrow. Then I put my trust in the holy, heavenly ZION, the Tabernacle of the Law of God, that thou wilt not withhold it in thy wisdom. For thy nobles cannot return to their houses and look upon their children, by reason of the abundance of wisdom and food which thou givest them, according to their desire, and they say, The table of SOLOMON is better for us than enjoying and gratifying ourselves in our own houses. And because of this I, through my fear, sought protection so that thou mightest not stablish him with thee, but mightest send him [back] to me in peace, without sickness and suffering, in love and in peace, that my heart might rejoice at having encountered thee.'"

And the King answered and said unto him, "Besides travailing with him and suckling him, what else hath a woman to do with a son? A daughter belongeth to the mother, and a boy to the father. God cursed EVE, saying, 'Bring forth children in anguish[34] and with sorrow of heart, and [after] thy bringing forth shall take place thy return to thy husband'; with an oath He said, 'Bring forth,' and having sworn, thy return to thy husband [shall follow]. As for this my son, I will not give him to the Queen, but I will make him king over ISRAEL. For this is my firstborn, the first of my race whom God hath given me."

And then SOLOMON sent unto the young man evening and morning dainty meats, and apparel of honour, and gold and silver. And he said unto him, "It is better for thee to dwell here in our country with us, where the House of God is, and where the Tabernacle of the Law of God is, and where God dwelleth." And the young man his son sent a message unto him, saying, "Gold, and silver, and [rich] apparel are not wanting in our country. But I came hither in order to hear thy wisdom, and to see thy face, and to salute thee, and to pay homage to thy kingdom, and to make obeisance to thee, and then [I intended thee] to send me away to my mother and to my own country. For no man hateth the place where he was born, and everyone loveth the things of his native country. And though thou givest me dainty meats I do not love them, and they are not suitable for my body, but the meats whereby I grow and become strong are those that are gratifying to me. And although [thy] country pleaseth me even as doth a garden, yet is not my heart gratified therewith; the mountains of the land of my mother where I was born are far better in my sight. And as for the Tabernacle of the God of ISRAEL, if I adore it where I am, it will give me glory, and I shall look upon the House of God which thou hast builded, and I will make offering and make supplication to it there. And as for ZION, the Tabernacle of the Law of God, give me [a portion of] the fringe of the covering thereof, and I will worship it with my mother and with all those who are subject to my sovereignty. For my Lady the Queen hath already rooted out all those who served idols, and those who worshipped strange objects, and stones and trees, and she hath rooted them out and hath brought them to ZION, the Tabernacle of the Law of God. For she had heard from thee and had learned, and she did according to thy word, and we worship God." And the King was not able to make his son consent to remain [in JERUSALEM] with all [his persuadings].

Footnotes
34. See Genesis iii. 16.

37. How SOLOMON asked His Son Questions

And again SOLOMON held converse with his son when he was alone, and he said unto him, "Why dost thou wish to depart from me? What dost thou lack here that thou wouldst go to the country of the heathen? And what is it that driveth thee to forsake the kingdom of ISRAEL?"

And his son answered and said unto him, "It is impossible for me to live here. Nay, I must go to my mother, thou favouring me with thy blessing. For thou hast a son who is better than I am, namely ÎYÔRBE'ÂM (REHOBOAM) who was born of thy wife lawfully, whilst my mother is not thy wife according to the law."

And the King answered and said unto him, "Since thou speakest in this wise, according to the law I myself am not the son of my father DAVID, for he took the wife of another man whom he caused to be slain in battle, and he begot me by her; but God is compassionate and He hath forgiven him. Who is wickeder and more foolish than men? and who is as compassionate and as wise as God? God hath made me of my father, and thee hath He made of me, according to His Will. And as for thee, O my son, thou fearer of our Lord God, do not violence to the face of thy father, so that in times to come thou mayest not meet with violence from him that shall go forth from thy loins, and that thy seed may prosper upon the earth. My son REHOBOAM is a boy six years old, and thou art my firstborn son, and thou hast come to reign, and to lift up the spear of him that begot thee. Behold, I have been reigning for nine and twenty years, and thy mother came to me in the seventh year of my kingdom; and please God, He shall make me to attain to the span of the days of my father. And when I shall be gathered to my fathers, thou shalt sit upon my throne, and thou shalt reign in my stead, and the elders of ISRAEL shall love thee exceedingly; and I will make a marriage for thee, and I will give thee as many queens and concubines as thou desirest. And thou shalt be blessed in this land of inheritance with the blessing that God gave unto our fathers, even as He covenanted with NOAH His servant, and with ABRAHAM His friend, and the righteous men their descendants after them down to DAVID my father. Thou seest me, a weak man, upon the throne of my fathers, and thou shalt be like myself after me, and thou shalt judge nations without number, and families that cannot be counted. And the Tabernacle of the God of ISRAEL shall belong to thee and to thy seed, whereto thou shalt make offerings and make prayers to ascend. And God shall dwell within it for ever and shall hear thy prayers therein, and thou shalt do the good pleasure of God therein, and thy remembrance shall be in it from generation to generation."

And his son answered and said unto him, "O my lord, it is impossible for me to leave my country and my mother, for my mother made me to swear by her breasts that I would not remain here but would return to her quickly, and also that I would not marry a wife here. And the Tabernacle of the God of ISRAEL shall bless me wheresoever I shall be, and thy prayer shall accompany me whithersoever I go. I desired to see thy face, and to hear thy voice, and to receive thy blessing, and now I desire to depart to my mother in safety."

38. How the King planned to send away his son with the children of the nobles

And then SOLOMON the King went back into his house, and he caused to be gathered together his councillors, and his officers, and the elders of his kingdom, and he said unto them, "I am not able to make this young man consent [to dwell here]. And now, hearken ye unto me and to what I shall say unto you. Come, let us make him king of the country of ETHIOPIA, together with your children; ye sit on my right hand and on my left hand, and in like manner the eldest of your children shall sit on his right hand and on his left hand. Come, O ye councillors and officers, let us give [him] your firstborn children, and we shall have two kingdoms; I will rule here with you, and our children shall reign there. And I put my trust in God that a third time He will give me seed, and that a third king will be to me. Now BALTÂSÔR, the King of RÔM, wisheth that I would give my son to his daughter, and to make him with his daughter king over the whole country of RÔM. For besides her he hath no other child, and he hath sworn that he will only make king a man who is of the seed of DAVID my father. And if we rule there we shall be three kings. And REHOBOAM shall reign here over ISRAEL. For thus saith the prophecy of DAVID my father: 'The seed of SOLOMON shall become three heads of kingdoms upon the earth.' And we will send unto them priests, and we will ordain laws for them, and they shall worship and serve the God of ISRAEL under the three royal heads. And God shall be praised by the race of His people ISRAEL, and be exalted in all the earth, even as my father wrote in his Book, saying, 'Tell the nations that God is king';[35] and again he said, 'Announce to the peoples His work, praise Him and sing ye unto Him'; and again he saith, 'Praise God with a new song. His praise is in the congregation of the righteous, ISRAEL shall rejoice in his Creator.'[36] Unto us belongeth the glory of sovereignty and we will praise our Creator. And the nations who serve idols shall look upon us, and they shall fear us, and make us kings over them, and they shall praise God and fear Him. And now, come ye, let us make this young man king, and let us send him away with your children, ye who possess wealth and position. According to the position and wealth that ye have here shall your children [rule] there. And they shall see the ordering of royalty, and we will establish them according to our law, and we will direct them and give them commands and send them away to reign there."

And the priests, and the officers, and the councillors answered and said unto him, "Do thou send thy firstborn, and we will send our children also according to thy wish. Who can resist the commandment of God and the king? They are the servants of thee and of thy seed as thou hast proclaimed. If thou wishest, thou canst sell them and their mothers to be slaves; it is not for us to transgress thy command and the command of the Lord thy God." And then they made ready to do for them (i.e., their children) what it was right to do, and to send them into the country of ETHIOPIA, so that they might reign there and dwell there for ever, they and their seed from generation to generation.

Footnotes
35. Compare Psalm xcv.
36. Compare Psalm xcvi.

39. How they made the Son of SOLOMON King

And they made ready the ointment of the oil of kingship, and the sounds of the large horn, and the small horn, and the flute and the pipes, and the harp and the drum filled the air; and the city resounded with cries of joy and gladness. And they brought the young man into the Holy of Holies, and he laid hold upon the horns of the altar, and sovereignty was given unto him by the mouth of ZADOK the priest, and by the mouth of JOAS (BENAIAH) the priest, the commander of the army of King SOLOMON, and he anointed him with the holy oil of the ointment of kingship. And he went out from the house of the Lord, and they called his name DAVID, for the name of a king came to him by the law. And they made him to ride upon the mule of King SOLOMON, and they led him round about the city, and said, "We have appointed thee from this moment"; and then they cried out to him, "Bâh [Long] live the royal father!" And there were some who said, "It is meet and right that thy dominion of ETHIOPIA shall be from the River of EGYPT to the west of the sun (i.e., to the setting sun); blessed be thy seed upon the earth! - and from SHOA to the east of INDIA, for thou wilt please [the people of these lands]. And the Lord God of ISRAEL shall be unto thee a guide, and the Tabernacle of the Law of God shall be with all that thou lookest upon. And all thine enemies and foes shall be overthrown before thee, and completion and finish shall be unto thee and unto thy seed after thee; thou shalt judge many nations and none shall judge thee." And again his father blessed him and said unto him, "The blessing of heaven and earth shall be thy blessing," and all the congregation of ISRAEL said, "Amen." And his father also said unto ZADOK the priest, "Make him to know and tell him concerning the judgment and decree of God which he shall observe there" [in ETHIOPIA].

40. How ZADOK the priest gave commands to DAVID the King

And ZADOK the priest answered and said unto the young man, "Hearken unto what I shall say unto thee. And if thou wilt perform it thou shalt live to God, and if thou dost not God will punish thee, and thou shalt become the least of all the nations, and thou shalt be vanquished by thy foes. And God shall turn away His face from thee, and thou shalt be dismayed, and sad, and sorrowful in thy heart, and thy sleep shall be without refreshing and health. And hearken unto the word of God, and perform it, and withdraw not thyself either to the right hand or the left, in respect of that which we command thee this day; and thou shalt serve no other god. And if thou wilt not hear the word of God, then hearken to all the curses here mentioned which shall come upon thee. Cursed shalt thou be in the field, cursed shalt thou be in the city. Cursed shall be the fruit of thy land, cursed shall be the fruit of thy belly, and the herds of thy cattle, and the flocks of thy sheep. And God shall send upon thee famine and pestilence, and He shall destroy that whereto thou hast put thine hand, until at length He shall destroy thee, because thou hast not hearkened to His word. And the heavens which are above thee shall become brass, and the earth which is beneath thee shall become iron; and God shall make the rain [which should fall upon] thy land to be darkness only, and dust shall descend from heaven upon thee until it shall cover thee up and destroy thee. And thou shalt be smitten in battle before thine enemies. Thou shalt go forth to attack them by one road, and by seven ways shalt thou take to flight before their faces, and thou shalt be routed; and thy dead body shall become food for the fowl of the heavens, and there shall be none to bury thee. And God shall punish thee with sores (or, leprosy), and with the wasting disease, and with the fever that destroyeth, and with the punishments (i.e., plagues) of EGYPT, and with blindness and terror of heart; and thou shalt grope about by day like a blind man in the darkness, and thou shalt find none to help thee in [thy] trouble. Thou shalt marry a wife, and another man shall carry her away from thee by force. Thou shalt build a house, and shalt not dwell therein. And thou shalt plant a vineyard and shalt not harvest the grapes thereof. Men shall slay thy fat oxen before thine eyes, and thou shalt not eat of their flesh. Men shall snatch away thine ass, and shall not bring him back to thee. Thy sheep shall run to the slaves and to thine enemy, and thou shalt find none to help thee. And thy sons and thy daughters shall follow other people, and thou shalt see with thine own eyes how they are smitten, and shalt be able to do nothing. An enemy whom thou knowest not shall devour the food of thy land and thy labour, and thou shalt not be able to prevent him; and thou shalt become a man of suffering and calamity. When the day dawneth thou shalt say, 'Would that the evening had come!' and when the evening cometh thou shalt say, 'Would that the morning had come!' through the greatness of thy fear. - [All these things shall come upon thee] if thou wilt not hearken to the word of the Lord. But if thou wilt truly hearken unto the word of the Lord - hear thou - the goodness of God shall find thee, and thou shalt rule the countries of the enemy, and thou shalt inherit everlasting glory from the Lord God of ISRAEL, Who ruleth everything. For He honoureth him that honoureth Him, and He loveth him that loveth Him, for He is the Lord of death and of life, and He directeth and ruleth all the world with His wisdom, and His power, and His [mighty] arm."

41. Concerning the blessing of Kings

"Hearken thou now to the blessing that shall come upon thee, if thou wilt do the Will of God. Thou shalt be blessed in all thy ways, blessed shalt thou be in the city, blessed shalt thou be in the field, blessed shalt thou be in thy house, blessed shalt thou be outside it, and blessed shall be the fruit of thy belly. And those who were gathered together said, Amen. Blessed shall be the fruit of thy land. Amen. Blessed shall be the fountains of thy waters. Amen. Blessed shall be the fruit that thou hast planted. Amen. Blessed shall be thy cattle-runs and the flocks of thy sheep. Amen. Blessed shall be thy granaries and thy barns. Amen. Blessed shalt thou be in thy coming in. Amen. Blessed shalt thou be in thy going forth. Amen.

"And God shall bring to thee thine enemies who have risen up against thee, and they shall be trodden small beneath thy feet. Amen. And God shall send His blessing on thy houses and on everything to which thou hast put thine hand. Amen. And God shall multiply for thee good things, namely, children of thy body, produce of thy land, and births among thy flocks and herds. Amen. And in the land which He swore [to give to] thy fathers, He will give thee according to the days of heaven. Amen. And God shall open for thee the storehouse of the blessing of the heavens, and He shall give thee blessed rain, and shall bless the fruit of thy labour. Amen. Thou shalt lend unto many peoples, but thou shalt not borrow. Amen. Thou shalt rule over many nations, but they shall not rule over thee. Amen. And God shall set thee at the head and not at the tail, and thou shalt be at the top and not at the bottom. Amen. And thou shalt gather together of every blessing of the land for thy flocks and herds, and thou shalt take the spoil of the nations for thine army, and they shall bow down to thee to the face of the earth, to thy sovereignty, because of the greatness of thy glory. Thine honour shall rise up like the cedar, and like the Morning Star, the brilliance of thy glory shall be before all the nations of the earth, and before every tribe of thy people ISRAEL.

"For God shall be with thee in all thy ways, and He will perform thy will in everything that thou determinest. And thou shalt inherit the countries of thine enemy, and the greatness of thy people shall be praised because of the greatness of thine awesomeness, and because of the multitude of thy soldiers. And all those who do not perform the Will of God will fear thee because thou dost do His Will, and dost serve Him, and therefore He will give thee great majesty in the sight of those who see thee. Their hearts shall tremble before the bridle of thy horses, and the quiver of thy bow, and the glitter of thy shield, and they shall bow down to the face of the earth, for their hearts shall be terrified at the sight of thy majesty. And when those who are in the mountains see thee afar off they shall come down to the plain, and those who are on the seas and in the deep waters shall come forth, so that the Lord may bring them into thy hand, because they have transgressed the command of God. And thou, when thou doest His Will, shalt receive from Him everything for which thou hast asked; for if thou lovest Him He will love thee, and if thou keepest His commandment He will grant thee the petition of thy heart, and everything that thou seekest thou shalt receive from Him. For He is the Good One to the good, and the Compassionate to the compassionate, and He doeth the will of those who fear Him, and He giveth a reward to those who wait patiently for Him. Be patient in respect of wrath, and at the end He will make thee to rejoice; love righteousness and He will make life to blossom for thee. Be a good man to the good, and a reprover of sinners. And put aside the wickedness of the evil man by rebuking and correcting him, and condemn and disgrace the evil man who doeth violence to his neighbour in the court of law. And do justice to the poor man and to the orphans, and release them from the hand of him that doeth them wrong. And deliver him that is forsaken and the man who is in misery, and release him from the hand of him that causeth him to suffer. Judge not with partiality, and have no respect of persons, but judge righteously. When thou undertakest to judge, love not gifts (i.e., bribes) and accept not persons. And admonish thy governors (or, judges) that they be free from the taking of gifts, and that they accept not the persons of their friends, or of their enemies, or of rich or poor, in giving judgment; and they shall surely judge their neighbours in righteousness, and with a just judgment.

42. Concerning the Ten Commandments

"And hear ye, ISRAEL, that which God commandeth you to keep; He saith, 'I am the Lord thy God Who hath brought thee out of the land of EGYPT and out of the house of bondage. There shall be no other gods besides Me, and thou shalt not make any god that is graven, and no god that is like what is in the heavens above, or in the earth beneath, or in the water which is under the earth. Thou shalt not bow down to them, and thou shalt not serve them, for I the Lord thy God am a jealous God. [I am He] Who visiteth the sin of the father on the children to the third and fourth generation of those who hate Me, and I perform mercy to a thousand (or, ten thousand) generations of those who love Me and keep My commandments.

"Thou shalt not swear a false oath in the Name of the Lord thy God, for the Lord will not hold innocent the man who sweareth a false oath in His Name.

"And observe the day of the Sabbath to sanctify it, even as the Lord thy God commanded. Six days thou shalt do thy work, and on the seventh day, the Sabbath of the Lord thy God, thou shalt do no work at all, neither thyself, nor thy son, nor thy daughter, nor thy nor thine ass, nor any beast, nor the stranger that abideth with thee. For in six days God made the heavens and the earth, and the sea and all that is in them, and rested on the seventh day, and because of this God blessed the seventh day and declared it free [from work].

"Honour thy father and thy mother so that may be good to thee the many days that thou shalt find in the land which the Lord thy God hath given thee.

"Thou shalt not go with the wife of [another] man.

"Thou shalt not slay a life.

"Thou shalt not commit fornication. Thou shalt not steal.

"Thou shalt not bear false witness against thy neighbour.

"Thou shalt not covet thy neighbour's wife, nor his house, nor his land, nor his manservant, nor his maidservant, nor his ox, nor his cattle, nor his ass, nor any of the beasts that thy neighbour hath acquired."

This is the word which God hath spoken, His Law and His Ordinance. And those who sin He rebuketh, so that they may not be confirmed in error, and may restrain themselves from the pollution wherewith God is not pleased. And this is the thing with which God is not pleased, and it is right that men should abstain from it.

"No man shall uncover the shame of one with whom he hath kinship; for I am the Lord your God. The shame of thy father and mother thou shalt not uncover, for it is thy mother. Thou shalt not uncover the shame of thy father's wife, for it is the shame of thy mother. Thou shalt not uncover the shame of thy sister who was begotten by thy father or thy mother. Whether she was born unto him from outside or whether she is a kinswoman of thine thou shalt not uncover her shame. Thou shalt not uncover the shame either of thy son's daughter, or the shame of the daughter of thy daughter, for it is thine own shame. Thou shalt not uncover the shame of the daughter of thy father's wife, for she is thy sister, the daughter of thy mother, and thou shalt not uncover her shame. Thou shalt not uncover the shame of thy father's sister, for she is of thy father's house. Thou shalt not uncover the shame of thy mother's sister, for she is of thy mother's house. Thou shalt not uncover the shame of the wife of thy father's brother, for she is thy kin[swoman]. Thou shalt not uncover the shame of thy son's wife, for she is thy son's wife. Thou shalt not uncover the shame of thy daughter and the wife of thy brother's son, for it is thine own shame. Thou shalt not uncover the shame of thy brother's wife, for it is thy brother's shame as long as thy brother liveth. Thou shalt not uncover the shame of a woman and that of her daughter, nor that of the daughter of her son, nor that of the daughter of her daughter. Thou shalt not cause their shame to be uncovered; it is thy house and it is sin.

"And thou shalt not take to wife a maiden and her sister so as to make them jealous each of the other, and thou shalt not uncover their shame, nor the shame of the one or the other as long as the first sister is alive. Thou shalt not go to a menstruous woman, until she is purified, to uncover her shame whilst she is still unclean. And thou shalt not go to the wife of thy neighbour to lie with her, and thou shalt not let thy seed enter her.

"And thou shalt not vow thy children to MOLOCH to defile the Name of the Holy One, the Name of the Lord.

"And thou shalt not lie with a man as with a woman, for it is pollution.

"And thou shalt not go to a beast and thou shalt not lie with it so as to make thy seed go out upon it, that thou mayest not be polluted thereby. And a woman shall not go to a beast to lie with it, for it is pollution. And ye shall not pollute yourselves with any of these things, for with them the nations whom I have driven out before you have polluted themselves, and with them ye shall not pollute your bodies.

"And sanctify ye your souls and your bodies to God, for He is the Holy One, and He loveth those who sanctify their souls and their bodies to Him. For He is holy, and to be feared, and He is high, and merciful, and compassionate. And to Him praise is meet for ever and ever. Amen."

43. How the men of the Army of ISRAEL received [their] orders
And the city rejoiced because the King had made his son King, and had appointed him King from his own territory to that of another. But the city sorrowed also because the King had commanded that they should give their children who were called "firstborn". And those who were on the right hand should sit in the

same way as their fathers sat with King SOLOMON, even so should they sit at the right hand of his son DAVID, the King of ETHIOPIA; and those who were on the left hand should sit as their fathers sat with King SOLOMON, even so should they sit on the left hand of his son DAVID, the King of ETHIOPIA; and their rank should be like that of their fathers, and their names should be like those of their fathers. And each should be according to his ordinance, and each according to his greatness, and each according to his position of authority, and each according to his wages, and each according to his rank; in this wise shall they be. As SOLOMON did to his nobles so shall DAVID do to his nobles; and as SOLOMON ordained for his governors so shall DAVID order the direction of his house.

And the names of those who were appointed to be sent away were these: -

'AZÂRYÂS (AZARIAH), the son of ZÂDÔK, the priest, who was the high priest.

'ÊLYÂS, the son of 'ARNÎ the Archdeacon; now the father of 'ARNÎ was the Archdeacon of NATHAN the prophet.

'ADRÂM, the son of 'ARDĔRÔNES, leader of the peoples.

FANKÊRÂ, the son of SÔBÂ, scribe of the oxen.

'AKÔNHÊL, the son of TÔFÊL, the youth.

SÂMNĔYÂS, the son of 'AKÎTÂLAM, the recorder.

FIKÂRÔS, the son of NĔYÂ, commander of the armed men, that is to say, chief of the troops.

LÊWÂNDÔS, the son of 'AKÎRÊ, commander of the recruits (?).

FÂKÛTÊN, the son of 'ADRÂY, commander on the sea.

MÂTÂN, the son of BENYÂS, chief of the house.

ADʿARAZ, the son of KÎRÊM, servant of decorations.

DALAKĔM, the son of MÂTRÊM, chief of the horse-soldiers.

'ADARYÔS, the son of NÊDRÔS, chief of the foot-soldiers.

'AWSTĔRÂN, the son of YÔDÂD, bearer of the "glory".

'ASTAR'AYÔN, the son of 'ASÂ, messenger of the palace (?).

ÎMÎ, the son of MATÂTYÂS, commander of the host (?)

MÂKRÎ, the son of 'ABÎSÂ, judge of the palace.

'ABÎS, the son of KÂRYÔS, assessor of taxes (tithes ?).

LÎK WENDEYÔS, the son of NÊLENTEYÔS, judge of assembly.

KÂRMÎ, the son of HAḌNĔYÂS, chief of the royal workmen.

SERÂNYÂS, the son of 'AKÂZ'ÊL, administrator of the King's house.

These are all those who were given to DAVID, king of ETHIOPIA, the son of SOLOMON, King of ISRAEL. And SOLOMON also gave him horses, and chariots, and riding-camels, and mules, and wagons for carrying loads, and gold, and silver, and splendid apparel, and byssus, and purple, and gems, and pearls and precious stones; and he gave his son everything that would be wished for in the country of ETHIOPIA.

And then they made ready to set out, and [though] there was great joy with the nobles of the King of ETHIOPIA, there was sadness with the nobles of the King of ISRAEL, because through the firstborn son of SOLOMON, King of ISRAEL, that is to say, the King of ETHIOPIA, the firstborn sons of the nobles of ISRAEL were given to rule over the country of ETHIOPIA with the son of SOLOMON the King. Then they assembled together and wept, together with their fathers, and their mothers, and their relations, and their kinsfolk, and their peoples, and their countrymen. And they cursed the King secretly and reviled him because he had seized their sons against their will. But unto the King they said, "Because of this thou hast done well. Thy wisdom is so good that the kingdom of ISRAEL, by the Will of God and by thy wisdom, extendeth to the country of ETHIOPIA. And God will gather together the other kingdoms [of the world] into thy hand, for thou hast a right mind towards God, and thou wishest that they shall serve the God of ISRAEL, and that idols may be destroyed out of the world."

And they praised him and said unto him, "Now know we that God spake concerning thee to our father ABRAHAM [when He said], 'In thy seed shall all the nations of the earth be blessed.'" And they made their faces to appear happy, and they jested before him, and they praised him exceedingly (i.e., fulsomely) because of his wisdom. And when they said these things unto him, he understood them in [his] wisdom, and bore with them patiently; now God beareth with us patiently knowing well all our sins. And the whole earth, and the heavens, and the ends of the world, and the sea, and the dry land, are the kingdom of God. He judgeth. And He hath given the earth to the king to be subject unto him, that he may judge (or, rule), as He doth, those who do evil so that he may requite them with evil, and those who do good so that he may reward them with good. For the Spirit of God resteth in the heart of the king, and His hands are in his mind, and His knowledge is in his understanding.

44. How it is not a seemly thing to revile the King

Now it is not a seemly thing to revile the king, for he is the anointed of God. It is neither seemly nor good. If he doeth that which is good he will not suffer loss in three kingdoms: FIRST, God shall overthrow for him his enemy, and he shall not be seized by the hand of his enemy. SECONDLY, God shall make him reign with Him and with His righteousness, and shall make him to sit on His right hand. THIRDLY, God shall make him to reign upon earth with glory and joy, and shall direct his kingdom for him, and shall bring down the nations under his feet. And if he treateth God lightly, and doth not do that which is good, and doth not himself walk in the path of uprightness, God shall work as He pleaseth against him; on earth He will make his days to be few, and in heaven (sic) his place of abode shall be the habitation of SHEÔL with the Devil. And on earth he shall enjoy neither health nor gladness [and he shall live] in fear and terror, without peace and with perturbation.

It is not a good thing for any of those who are under the dominion of a king to revile him, for retribution belongeth to God. Now the priests are like the prophets, only better than the prophets, for the mysteries are given unto them, so that they may lay hold upon the sun of righteousness, whilst the Seraphim, who were created out of fire, are only able to lay hold upon the mysteries with tongs. As for the priests He named them "salt", and moreover, He named the priests "lamp" and also "light of the world", and also "the sun that lighteneth the darkness", CHRIST, the Sun of righteousness, being in their hearts. And a priest, who hath in him understanding, rebuketh the king concerning that he hath seen; and that which he hath not seen God will enquire into, and there is none who can call Him to account. Moreover, the people must not revile the bishops and the priests, for they are the children of God and the men of His house, for which reason they must rebuke [men] for their sins and errors. And thou, O priest, if thou seest sin in a well-known man, shalt not hesitate to rebuke him; let neither sword nor exile make thee afraid. And hear how angry God was with ISAIAH because he did not rebuke King 'ÛZYÂN (UZZIAH). And hearken also concerning SAMUEL the Prophet, how he rebuked SAUL[37] the king, being in no way afraid of him, and how he rent his kingdom [from him] by his word; and [hearken also] how ELIJAH [rebuked] AHAB.[38] Do thou then fear not, and rebuke and teach him that transgresseth.

And ISRAEL from of old reviled their kings and provoked their prophets to wrath, and in later times they crucified their Saviour. But believing Christian folk dwell in peace, without sickness and suffering, without hatred and offence, with our king . . .[39] who loveth God and who removeth not from his heart the thing of righteousness, and faith in the Churches and in the believers. And his enemies shall be scattered by the might of the Cross of JESUS CHRIST.

Footnotes
37. See 1 Samuel, chap. xv.
38. 1 Kings, chap. xvii.
39. The name of the reigning king to be added by the copyist.

45. How those who were sent away wept and made a plan
And the children of the nobles of ISRAEL, who were commanded to depart with the son of the king, took counsel together, saying, "What shall we do? For we have left our country and our birth place, and our kinsfolk and the people of our city. Now, come ye, let us establish a covenant between us only, whereof our kinsfolk shall know nothing, that we will love each other in that country: none shall hasten or tarry here, and we will neither fear nor have any doubt. For God is here, and God is there, and may God's Will be done! And to Him be praise for ever and ever! Amen." And 'AZÂRYÂS and 'ÊLMÎYÂS, sons of the priests, answered, "Let not the other matter - that our kinsfolk hate us - cause us sorrow, but let us sorrow on account of our Lady ZION, because they are making us to leave her. For in her they have committed us to God, and we have served her

to this day; and let us be sorrowful because they have made us to leave her. It is because of her and because of this that they have specially made us to weep." And the others answered and said unto them, "Verily she is our Lady and our hope, and our object of boasting, and we have grown up under her blessedness. And how is it possible for us to forsake ZION our mistress? For we have been given to her. And what shall we do? If we resist his command the king will kill us, and we are unable to transgress the word of our fathers or the king's command. And what shall we do concerning ZION our Lady?"

And 'AZÂRYÂS, the son of ZADOK the priest, answered and said, "I will counsel you what we shall do. But make a covenant with me to the end of your lives; and swear to me that ye will not repeat it whether we live or whether we die, or whether we be taken captive or whether we go forth [unhindered]." And they swore an oath to him in the Name of the Lord God of ISRAEL, and by the heavenly ZION, the Tabernacle of the Law of God, and by what God had promised unto ABRAHAM, and by the purity and excellence of ISAAC, and by His making JACOB to arrive in and inherit a land whereto he was a stranger, and his seed after him.

And when they had sworn thus to him, he answered and said unto them, "Come now, let us take [with us] our Lady ZION; but how are we to take her? I will show you. And carry ye out my plan and if God willeth we shall be able to take our Lady with us. And if they should gain knowledge of our doings and slay us, that shall not trouble us, because we shall die for our Lady ZION." And they all rose up, and kissed his head, and his face, and his eyes, and they said unto him, "We will do everything that thou hast counselled us to do; whether we die or whether we live, we are with thee for the sake of our Lady ZION. If we die it will not cause us sorrow, and if we live - the Will of God be done!" And one of them, the son of YÔAS (BENAIAH), whose name was ZECHARIAH, said, "I cannot sit down because of the great gladness that is in my heart. Tell me, moreover, canst thou indeed carry her off, and is it not a lie? Thou canst go into the House of God in the place of thy father ZADOK, and the keys are continually in thy hand. But ponder well what we counsel thee before they take the keys out of thy hand. Thou knowest the hidden openings (or, windows) which King SOLOMON made; but none of the priests may enter therein except thy father once each year in order to offer up sacrifice in the Holy of Holies on behalf of himself and on behalf of the people. Ponder, consider, and sleep not in the matter of thy wish to carry away ZION. And we will depart with her as soon as she hath been committed to our care, and we shall have joy and our fathers sorrow when she arriveth with us in the country of ETHIOPIA."

And AZÂRYÂS said unto them, "Do ye what I tell you, and we shall succeed. Give ye to me each of you ten dîdrachmas,[40] and I will give them to a carpenter so that he will make haste to prepare for me good planks of wood - now because of his love of money he will fasten them together very quickly - of the height, and breadth, and length and size of our Lady [ZION]. And I will give him the dimensions of myself, and I will say unto him, "Prepare for me pieces of wood for a framework (?) so that I may make a raft therefrom; for we are going to travel over the sea, and in the event of the ship sinking I shall be able to get up on the raft, and we shall be saved from the sea. And I will take the framework without the pieces of wood thereof being fixed together, and I will have them put together in ETHIOPIA. And I will set them down in the habitation of ZION, and will drape them with the draperies of ZION, and I will take ZION, and will dig a hole in the ground, and will set ZION there, until we journey and take it away with us thither. And I will not tell the matter to the king until we have travelled far."

And they each gave him ten dîdrachmas, and this money amounted to one hundred and forty dîdrachmas, and he took them and gave them to a carpenter, who straightway fashioned a good piece of work from the remains of the wood of the house of the sanctuary, and AZÂRYÂS rejoiced and showed it to his brethren.

Footnotes
40. i.e., double drachmas.

46. How they made a plan concerning ZION

And while AZÂRYÂS was asleep at night the Angel of the Lord appeared unto him, and said unto him, "Take to thee four goats, each a yearling - now they shall be for your sins, thyself, and 'ÊLMEYÂS, and 'ABÎS, and MÂKRÎ - and four pure sheep, yearlings also, and an ox whereon no yoke hath ever been laid. And thou shalt offer up the ox as a sacrifice on the east side of her (i.e., ZION), and the sheep and the goats to the right, and left thereof, and at the west of it, which is close to its exit. And your Lord DAVID shall speak to SOLOMON the King and shall say unto him, 'One thing I ask from thee, O father, I would offer up a sacrifice to the holy city JERUSALEM, and to my Lady ZION, the holy and heavenly Tabernacle of the Law of God.' And SOLOMON shall say unto him, 'Do so.' And DAVID shall say unto him, 'Let the son of the priest offer up sacrifice on my behalf, even as he knoweth'; and he will give thee the command, and thou shalt offer up the sacrifice. And thou shalt bring forth the Tabernacle of the Law of God after thou hast offered up the sacrifice, and I will again show thee what thou shalt do in respect of it as to bringing it out; for this is from God. For ISRAEL hath provoked God to wrath, and for this reason He will make the Tabernacle of the Law of God to depart from him."

And when AZÂRYÂS awoke from his dream he rejoiced greatly, and his heart and his mind were clear, and he remembered everything that the Angel of the Lord had shown him in the night, and how he had sealed him [with the sign of the Cross], and given him strength and heartened him. And he went to his brethren, and when they were gathered together he told them everything that the Angel of God had shown him: how the Tabernacle of the Law of God had been given to them, and how God had made blind His eye in respect of the kingdom of

ISRAEL, and how its glory had been given to others, and they themselves were to take away the Tabernacle of the Law of God, and how the kingdom of SOLOMON was to be seized by them - with the exception of two "rods", and how it was not to be left to ÎYÔRBĔʿÂM (REHOBOAM) his son, and how the kingdom of ISRAEL was to be divided. And [AZÂRYÂS said], "Rejoice with me. I rejoice because it hath been shown unto me thus; for the grace of their priesthood and kingdom shall depart with us, and it shall be by the Will of God. Thus said he (i.e., the Angel) unto me. And now come ye, and let us go and tell DAVID our Lord so that he may say to his father, 'I will offer up a sacrifice.'"

And they went and told [DAVID, the son of SOLOMON] and he rejoiced, and he sent to YÔʿAS (BENAIAH), the son of YÔDÂHĒ, to come to him, that he might send him to his father, and he came. And DAVID sent him to his father SOLOMON, and he said unto him, "Send me away, for I will depart to my own country, together with everything that thy goodness hath given me; and may thy prayers accompany me always whithersoever I shall go. But now there is one petition which I would make unto thee, if peradventure I have found grace with thee, and turn not away thy face from me. For I thy servant am going to depart, and I wish to offer up a sacrifice of propitiation (or, salvation) for my sins in this thy holy city of JERUSALEM and of ZION, the Tabernacle of the Law of God. And peace [be] with thy majesty."

47. Concerning the offering of AZÂRYÂS (AZARIAH) and the King

And YÔʿÂS (BENAIAH), the son of YÔDÂHĒ, went and told King SOLOMON, and the King rejoiced over it and commanded them to make ready the altar of offering so that his son might sacrifice. And he brought and gave unto him that which he had vowed to God, one hundred bulls, one hundred oxen, ten thousand sheep, ten thousand goats, and ten of every kind of animal that may be eaten, and ten of every kind of clean bird, so that he might offer libations and sacrifices to the God of ISRAEL; and twenty silver sâHal of fine white flour, each weighing twelve shekels, and forty baskets of bread. All these things did SOLOMON the King give unto his son DAVID. And again DAVID sent a message saying, "Let AZÂRYÂS the priest offer up sacrifice on my behalf"; and SOLOMON said unto him, "Do that which thou wishest." And AZÂRYÂS rejoiced because of this thing, and he went and brought from his father's flock an ox whereon never yoke had been laid, and four yearlings of the goats and four clean yearlings of the sheep. And the king went to offer up sacrifice, and the priests made themselves ready, and the poor folk were gathered together, and the birds of the heavens rejoiced, and they were all united in their great gladness that day. And AZÂRYÂS mingled [his offerings] with the offerings of the king, and he made an offering with his vessels, even as the Angel of God had commanded him to do by night. And then, after they had offered up their sacrifices, they went back to their houses and slept.

48. *How they carried away ZION*

And behold, the Angel of the Lord appeared again to AZÂRYÂS and he stood up above him like a pillar of fire, and he filled the house with his light. And he raised up AZÂRYÂS and said unto him, "Stand up, be strong, and rouse up thy brother ÊLMĔYÂS, and 'ABĔSÂ, and MÂKARÎ, and take the pieces of wood and I will open for thee the doors of the sanctuary. And take thou the Tabernacle of the Law of God, and thou shalt carry it without trouble and discomfort. And I, inasmuch as I have been commanded by God to be with it for ever, will be thy guide when thou shalt carry it away."

And AZÂRYÂS rose up straightway, and woke up the three men his brethren, and they took the pieces of wood, and went into the house of God - now they found all the doors open, both those that were outside and those that were inside - to the actual place where AZÂRYÂS found ZION, the Tabernacle of the Law of God; and it was taken away by them forthwith, in the twinkling of an eye, the Angel of the Lord being present and directing. And had it not been that God willed it ZION could not have been taken away forthwith. And the four of them carried ZION away, and they brought it into the house of AZÂRYÂS, and they went back into the house of God, and they set the pieces of wood on the place where ZION had been, and they covered them over with the covering of ZION, and they shut the doors, and went back to their houses. And they took lamps and set them in the place where [ZION] was hidden, and they sacrificed the sheep thereto, and burned offerings of incense thereto, and they spread purple cloths over it and set it in a secret place for seven days and seven nights.

49. *How his Father blessed his Son*

And then the King of ETHIOPIA rose up to depart to his country, and he came to his father that he might pray on his behalf, and he said unto him, "Bless me, father"; and he made obeisance unto him. And the King raised him up, and blessed him, and embraced his head, and said, "Blessed be the Lord my God Who blessed my father DAVID, and Who blessed our father ABRAHAM. May He be with thee always, and bless thy seed even as He blessed JACOB, and made his seed to be as many as the stars of heaven and the sand of the sea. And as ABRAHAM blessed ISAAC my father even so shall thy blessing be - the dew of heaven and the spaciousness of the earth - and may all animals and all the birds of the heavens, and all the beasts of the field, and the fish of the sea, be in subjection unto thee. Be thou full, and not lacking in fullness; be thou perfect, and not lacking in perfection; be gracious, and not obstinate; be in good health, and not suffering; be generous, and not vindictive; be pure, and not defiled; be righteous, and not a sinner; be merciful, and not oppressive; be sincere, and not perverse; be long-suffering, and not prone to wrath. And the enemy shall be afraid of thee, and thine adversaries shall cast themselves under the sole of thy foot. And my Lady ZION, the holy and heavenly, the Tabernacle of the Law of God, shall be a guide unto thee at all times, a guide in respect of what thou shouldst think in thy heart and shouldst do with thy fingers, whether it be far or near to thee, whether it be low or high to thee, whether it be strong or weak to thee, whether it be outside or inside thee, whether it be to thee in the house or in the field, whether it be visible or invisible to thee, whether it be away from or near to thee, whether it be hidden from or revealed to thee, whether it be secret or published abroad to thee - unto thee our Lady ZION, the holy and heavenly, the pure Tabernacle of the Law of God, shall be a guide." And DAVID was blessed, and he made obeisance, and departed.

50. How they bade farewell to his Father and how the city mourned

And they bade [the king] farewell and departed. And first of all they set ZION by night upon a wagon together with a mass of worthless stuff, and dirty clothes, and stores of every sort and kind. And [when] all the wagons were loaded, and the masters of the caravan rose up, and the horn was blown, and the city became excited, and the youths shouted loudly, awesomeness crowned it and grace surrounded it (i.e., ZION). And the old men wailed, and the children cried out, and the widows wept, and the virgins lamented, because the sons of their nobles, the mighty men of ISRAEL, had risen up to depart. But the city did not weep for them alone, but because the majesty of the city had been carried off with them. And although they did not know actually that ZION had been taken from them, they made no mistake in their hearts and they wept bitterly; and they were then even as they were when God slew the firstborn of EGYPT. There was not a house wherein there was not wailing, from man even to the beast; the dogs howled, and the asses screamed, and all those who were left there mingled their tears together. It was as though the generals of a mighty army had besieged the great city, and had captured it by assault, and looted it, and taken its people prisoners and slain them with the edge of the sword; even thus was that city of ZION - JERUSALEM.

And King SOLOMON was dismayed at the weeping and outcry of the city, and he looked out from the roof of the palace, the fort of the king's house, and saw the whole city weeping and following them. And as a child, whom his mother hath removed from her breast and left, followeth in her footsteps crying out and weeping, even so did the people cry out and weep; and they cast dust upon their heads, and they shed tears with their eyes. And when SOLOMON saw the majesty of those who had departed, he was deeply moved and he trembled, and his bowels quaked, and his tears fell drop by drop upon his apparel, and he said, "Woe is me! for my glory hath departed, and the crown of my splendour hath fallen, and my belly is burned up because this my son hath departed, and the majesty of my city and the freemen, the children of my might, are removed. From this moment our glory hath passed away, and our kingdom hath been carried off unto a strange people who know not God, even as the prophet saith, 'The people who have not sought Me have found Me.'[41] From this time forth the law, and wisdom, and understanding shall be given unto them. And my father prophesied concerning them, saying, 'ETHIOPIA shall bow before Him, and His enemies shall eat the dust.'[42] And in another [place] he saith, 'ETHIOPIA shall stretch out her hands to God, and He shall receive her with honour, and the kings of the earth shall praise God.'[43] And in a third [place] he saith, 'Behold, the PHILISTINES,[44] and the Tyrians, and the people of ETHIOPIA, who were born without the Law. The Law shall be given unto them, and they shall say unto ZION, 'our mother[45] because of a man who shall be born.' Will this man then be my son who is begotten of me?"

Footnotes
41. Isaiah lxv. 1.
42. Psalm lxxii. 9, 10.
43. Psalm lxviii. 31.
44. Psalm lxxxiii. 7 (?).
45. Compare Psalm lxxxvii. 2-4; Isaiah li. 16.

51. How he said unto ZADOK the Priest, "Go and bring the Covering (or, Clothing) which is upon it (i.e., ZION)"

And he said unto ZADOK the priest, "Go, bring that covering which is upon ZION, and take thee this covering which is better than that, and lay it over the two [coverings] which are below it." (Now this covering was made of threads of the finest gold wirework twisted together and hammered out into a pattern, and they were not woven like the threads of purple.) "And the five mice[46] which were given to ZION, and the ten[47] figures of their shame (i.e., the emerods) which the nobles of the PHILISTINES made for their redemption - now on the fringes are figures of gold that came forth from the land of KÂDÊS, which MOSES in SINAI commanded should be made (or, worked) in the fringe of the apparel of AARON his brother - gather [all these] together in the covering of ZION and give [them] to my son DAVID. For his mother said in [her] message by TÂMRÎN her servant, 'Give us some of the fringe of the covering of ZION, so that we may worship it, we and those who are in subjection unto us and all our kingdom.' And now, give it to him, and say unto him, 'Take [and] worship this covering of ZION, for thy mother sent a message concerning this, and hath said unto thee thyself, 'Give us some of the fringe of its covering, which we can worship, so that we may not, like the heathen, worship another [god].' And ZION, the Tabernacle of the Law of God, shall be unto thee a guide wheresoever thou art. But it must remain with us perpetually, although we have not paid it all the honour which is its due; and you, although it be not with you, must honour it, and revere it according to what is due to it and what is meet. For God said unto ELI by the mouth of SAMUEL the Prophet, 'I wished you to remain, thou and thy father's house, to offer up incense to the Tabernacle of My Law, and to dwell before Me for ever, but now I have repented. I will turn My face away from thee because thou hast treated

My offerings with contempt, and hast preferred thy sons to Me. And now, him that honoureth Me I will honour, and him that esteemeth Me lightly I will esteem lightly; and I will destroy all thy seed.'[48] This He said because the LEVITES had esteemed Him lightly. And say unto him: Take this covering of ZION, and this votive gift shall be in the place of it, and place it in thy sanctuary. And when thou takest an oath and makest another to take an oath, swear thou and make him to swear by it, so that thou dost not make mention of the names of other gods of the heathen. And when thou sacrificest let thy face be towards us, and sacrifice to JERUSALEM and the holy ZION; and when thou prayest let thy face be towards JERUSALEM, and pray towards us."

Footnotes
46. 1 Samuel vi. 4.
47. The text of Samuel (vi. 4) gives "five emerods."
48. 1 Samuel ii. 29-34.

52. How ZADOK the Priest Departed

And ZADOK the priest went and gave DAVID the covering of ZION, and he delivered unto him all the commands which SOLOMON had spoken. And DAVID, the son of SOLOMON, rejoiced because of this, and he marvelled and held himself to be blessed exceedingly, and said, when the covering of the Tabernacle of the Law of God was committed to his charge, "This shall be to me my Lady." And AZÂRYÂS answered and said before his father, "Thou rejoicest over the covering, but how very much more wilt thou rejoice over the Lady of the covering!" And his father said unto him, "Verily he rejoiceth over the Lady of the covering, and he might subjugate all of us if he were not going to his own country." And he said unto the king, "Make now a covenant with me that thou wilt give to this my son this possession for his Lady and his sponsor and his protection, that he may guard it all the days of his life, for himself and for his seed after him; and that thou wilt give him tithe, and that thou wilt give him a city of refuge in thy kingdom, and also the tenth of the cities in all thy kingdom; and that he shall be unto thee priest, and seer, and prophet, and teacher to thee and to thy seed after thee, and the anointer with oil of thy kingdom for thy children and thy children's children." And he said, "I agree." And they struck (i.e., made) a covenant, and he received from his father the votive offering, and the covering of ZION, and a chain of gold.

And they loaded the wagons, and the horses, and the mules in order to depart, and they set out on their journey prosperously, and they continued to travel on. And MICHAEL the [Arch] Angel marched in front, and he spread out [his wings] and made them to march through the sea as upon dry land, and upon the dry land he cut a path for them and spreading himself out like a cloud over them he hid them from the fiery heat of the sun. And as for their wagons, no man hauled his wagon, but he himself (i.e., MICHAEL) marched with the wagons, and whether it was men, or horses, or mules, or loaded camels, each was raised above the ground to the height of a cubit; and all those who rode upon beasts were lifted up above their backs to the height of one span of a man, and all the various kinds of baggage which were loaded on the beasts, as well as those who were mounted on them, were raised up to the height of one span of a man, and the beasts were lifted up to the height of one span of a man. And every one travelled in the wagons like a ship on the sea when the wind bloweth, and like a bat through the air when the desire of his belly urgeth him to devour his companions, and like an eagle when his body glideth above the wind. Thus did they travel; there was none in front and none behind, and they were disturbed neither on the right hand nor on the left.

53. How the Wagon was given to ETHIOPIA

And they halted by GÂZÂ, the city of the mother of the king, which SOLOMON the king had given to the Queen of ETHIOPIA when she came to him. And from there they came in one day to the border of GĚBĚS. (EGYPT), the name of which is "MESRÎN". And when the sons of the warriors of ISRAEL saw that they had come in one day a distance of thirteen days' march, and that they were not tired, or hungry, or thirsty, neither man nor beast, and that they all [felt] that they had eaten and drunk their fill, these sons of the warriors of ISRAEL knew and believed that this thing was from God. And they said unto their king, "Let us let down the wagons, for we have come to the water of ETHIOPIA. This is the TAKKAZÎ which floweth down from ETHIOPIA, and watereth the Valley of EGYPT"; and they let down their wagons there, and set up their tents.

And the sons of the warriors of ISRAEL went and drove away all the people, and they said unto [DAVID] their king, "Shall we tell thee a matter? Canst thou hold it [secret]?" And the King said unto them, "Yes, I can [hold it secret]. And if ye will tell it to me I will never let it go forth or repeat it to the day of my death." And they said unto him, "The sun descended from heaven, and was given on SINAI to ISRAEL, and it became the salvation of the race of ADAM, from MOSES to the seed of JESSE, and behold, it is with thee by the Will of God. It is not through us that this hath been done, but by the Will of God; it is not through us that this hath been done, but by the Will of Him that fashioned it and made it hath this happened. We wished, and God hath fulfilled [our wish]; we agreed concerning it, and God made it good; we held converse [concerning it], and God performed; we meditated [upon it], and God devised the plan; we spoke, and God was well pleased; we directed our gaze, and God directed it rightly; we meditated, and God hath justified. And now God hath chosen thee, and is well pleased with thy city, to be the servant of the holy and heavenly ZION, the Tabernacle of the Law of God; and it shall be to thee a guide for ever, to thee and thy seed after thee if thou wilt keep His command and perform the Will of the Lord thy God. For thou wilt not be able to take it back, even if thou wishest, and thy father cannot seize it, even if he wisheth, for it goeth of its own free will whithersoever it wisheth, and it cannot be removed from its seat if it doth not desire it. And behold, it is our Lady, our Mother and our salvation, our fortress and our place of refuge, our glory and the haven of our safety, to those who lean upon it."

And AZÂRYÂS made a sign to ÊLMEYÂS, and he said unto him, "Go, beautify, and dress our Lady, so that our King may see her." And when AZÂRYÂS had said this, King DAVID was perturbed and he laid both hands upon his breast, and he drew breath three times and said, "Hast thou in truth, O Lord, remembered us in Thy mercy, the castaways, the people whom Thou hast rejected, so that I may see Thy pure habitation, which is in heaven, the holy and heavenly ZION? With what shall we requite the Lord in return for all the good things which He hath done for us? there being with Him no glory and praise! He hath crowned us with His grace, so that we may know upon earth His praise and may all serve Him according to His greatness. For He is the Good One to His chosen ones, and unto Him belongeth praise for ever."

And King [DAVID] rose up and skipped about like a young sheep and like a kid of the goats that hath sucked milk in abundance from his mother, even as his grandfather DAVID rejoiced before the Tabernacle of the Law of God. He smote the ground with his feet, and rejoiced in his heart, and uttered cries of joy with his mouth. And what shall I say of the great joy and gladness that were in the camp of the King of ETHIOPIA? One man told his neighbour, and they smote the ground with their feet like young bulls, and they clapped their hands together, and marvelled, and stretched out their hands to heaven, and they cast themselves down with their faces to the ground, and they gave thanks unto God in their hearts.

54. How DAVID [the King of ETHIOPIA] Prophesied and Saluted ZION

And King [DAVID] came and stood up before ZION, and he saluted it, and made obeisance thereto, and said, "O Lord God of ISRAEL, to Thee be praise, because Thou doest Thy Will and not the will of men. Thou makest the wise man to forget his wisdom, and Thou destroyest the counsel of the counsellor, and Thou raisest the poor man from the depth, and Thou settest the sole of his foot upon a strong rock. For a full cup of glory is in Thy hand for those who love Thee, and a full cup of shame for those who hate Thee. As for us, our salvation shall go forth out of ZION, and He shall remove sin from His people, and goodness and mercy shall be poured out in all the world. For we are the work of His hands, and who shall rebuke us if He loveth us as ISRAEL His people? And who shall reprove Him if He raiseth us up to heaven His throne? For death and life are from Him, and glory and dishonour are in His hand, He hath the power to punish and to multiply His compassion, and He can be wroth and multiply His mercy, for it is He who trieth the heart and the reins. He giveth and He taketh away, He planteth and He uprooteth. He buildeth up and He throweth down. He beautifieth and He deformeth; for everything belongeth to Him, and everything is from Him, and everything existeth in Him. And as for thee, O Tabernacle of the Law of God, salvation be whither thou goest, and from the place whence thou goest forth; salvation be in the house and in the field, salvation be here and be there, salvation be in the palace and in the lowly place, salvation be on the sea and on the dry land, salvation be in the mountains and in the hills, salvation be in the heavens and on the earth, salvation be in the firm grounds and in the abysses, salvation be in death and in life, salvation be in thy coming and in thy going forth, salvation be to our children and to the tribe of thy people, salvation be in thy countries and in thy cities, salvation be to the kings and to the nobles, salvation be to the plants and to the fruits, salvation be to men and to beasts, salvation be to the birds and to the creeping things of the earth; be salvation, be an intercessor, and a merciful one, and have regard for thy people. Be unto us a wall, and we will be unto thee a fence; be thou a king unto us and we will be thy people; be thou a guide unto us and we will follow after thee. And be not impatient, and mark not closely, and be not angry at the multitude of our sins, for we are a people who have not the Law, and who have not learned Thy praise. And from this time forward guide us, and teach us, and make us to have understanding, and make us to have wisdom that we may learn Thy praise. And Thy name shall be praised by us at all times, and all the day, and every day, and every night, and every hour, and all the length of time. Give us power that we may serve Thee. Rise up, ZION, and put on thy strength, and conquer thine enemies, and give us strength, our queen, and put thou to shame those who hate thee, and make to rejoice those who love thee."

And then he made a circuit and said, "Behold ZION, behold salvation, behold the one who rejoiceth, behold the splendour like the sun, behold the one adorned with praise, behold the one who is decorated like a bride, not with the apparel of fleeting glory, but the one who is decorated with the glory and praise which are from God, whom it is meet that [men] shall look upon with desire and shall not forsake; whom [men] shall desire above all things and shall not reject; whom [men] shall love willingly and shall not hate; whom [men] shall approach willingly and shall not keep afar off. We will draw nigh unto thee, and do not thou withdraw far from us; we will support ourselves upon thee, and do not thou let us slip away; we will supplicate thee, and do not thou be deaf to us; we will cry out to thee; hear thou our cry in all that we ask of thee, and desire not to withdraw thyself from us, until thy Lord cometh and reigneth over thee; for thou art the habitation of the God of heaven."

Thus spake DAVID the King, the son of SOLOMON, King of ISRAEL. For the spirit of prophecy descended upon him because of his joy, and he knew not what he said and he was like PETER and JOHN on the top of Mount TÂBÔR.[49] And they all marvelled and said, "This, the son of a prophet, is he to be numbered among the prophets?"

Footnotes
49. Matthew xvii. 4; Luke ix. 33.

55. *How the People of ETHIOPIA Rejoiced*

And [the people of ETHIOPIA] took flutes, and blew horns, and [beat] drums, and [played on] pipes, and the Brook of EGYPT was moved and astonished at the noise of their songs and their rejoicings; and with them were mingled outcries and shouts of gladness. And their idols, which they had made with their hands and which were in the forms of men, and dogs, and cats, fell down, and the high towers (pylons or obelisks ?), and also the figures of birds, [made] of gold and silver, fell down also and were broken in pieces. For ZION shone like the sun, and at the majesty thereof they were dismayed. And they arrayed ZION in her apparel, and they bore the gifts to her before her, and they set her upon a wagon, and they spread out purple beneath her, and they draped her with draperies of purple, and they sang songs before her and behind her.

Then the wagons rose up (i.e., resumed their journey) as before, and they set out early in the morning, and the people sang songs to ZION, and they were all raised up the space of a cubit, and as the people of the country of EGYPT bade them farewell, they passed before them like shadows, and the people of the country of EGYPT worshipped them, for they saw ZION moving in the heavens like the sun, and they all ran with the wagon of ZION, some in front of her and some behind her. And they came to the sea AL-AHMAR, which is the Sea of ERITREA (i.e., the RED SEA), which was divided by the hand of MOSES, and the children of ISRAEL marched in the depths thereof, going up and down. Now at that time the Tabernacle of the Law of God had not been given unto MOSES, and therefore the water only gathered itself together, a wall on the right hand and a wall on the left, and allowed ISRAEL to pass with their beasts and their children and their wives. And after they had crossed the sea God spake to MOSES and gave him the Tabernacle of the Covenant with the Book of the Law. And when the holy ZION crossed over with those who were in attendance on her, and who sang songs to the accompaniment of harps and flutes, the sea received them and its waves leaped up as do the high mountains when they are split asunder, and it roared even as a lion roareth when he is enraged, and it thundered as doth the winter thunder of DAMASCUS and ETHIOPIA when the lightning smiteth the clouds, and the sound thereof mingled with the sounds of the musical instruments. And the sea worshipped ZION. And whilst its billows were tossing about like the mountains their wagons were raised above the waves for a space of three cubits, and among the sound of the songs the [noise of the] breaking of the waves of the sea was wonderful. The breaking of the waves of the sea was exceedingly majestic and stupefying, and it was mighty and strong. And the creatures that were in the sea, those that could be recognized, and those that were invisible, came forth and worshipped ZION; and the birds that were on it flapped their pinions and overshadowed it. And there was joy to the Sea of ERITREA, and to the people of ETHIOPIA, who went forth to the sea and rejoiced exceedingly, and with a greater joy than did ISRAEL when they came out of EGYPT. And they arrived opposite Mount SINAI, and dwelt in KÂDÊS, and they remained there whilst the angels sang praises; and the creatures of the spirit mingled their praises with [those] of the children of earth, with songs, and psalms, and tambourines joyfully.

And then they loaded their wagons, and they rose up, and departed, and journeyed on to the land of MEDYÂM, and they came to the country of BÊLÔNTÔS, which is a country of ETHIOPIA. And they rejoiced there, and they encamped there, because they had reached the border of their country with glory and joy, without tribulation on the road, in a wagon of the spirit, by the might of heaven and of MICHAEL the Archangel. And all the provinces of ETHIOPIA rejoiced, for ZION sent forth a light like that of the sun into the darkness wheresoever she came.

56. Of the Return of ZADOK the Priest, and the giving of the Gift

And when ZADOK the priest returned to SOLOMON the King he found him sorrowful. And the King answered and said unto ZADOK the priest, "When the Queen came there appeared to me by night this vision: It seemed as if I were standing in the chamber of JERUSALEM, and the sun came down from heaven into the land of JUDAH, and lighted it up with great splendour. And having tarried a time it went down and lighted up the Country of ETHIOPIA, and it did not return to the land of JUDAH. And again the sun came down from heaven to the country of JUDAH, and lighted it up more brilliantly than it did the first time; but the ISRAELITES paid no heed to it, and they wished to extinguish its light. And it rose below the earth in a place where it was not expected, and it illumined the country of RÔM, and the country of ETHIOPIA, and afterwards all those who believed on it."

And ZADOK the priest answered and said unto him, "O my lord, why didst thou not tell me before that thou hadst seen a vision of this kind? Thou makest my knees to tremble. Woe be unto us, if our sons have carried off our Lady, the holy, heavenly ZION, the Tabernacle of the Law of God!" And the King answered and said unto him, "Our wisdom is forgotten and our understanding is buried. Verily the sun that appeared unto me long ago when I was sleeping with the Queen of ETHIOPIA was the symbol of the holy ZION. But tell me: yesterday when thou didst take off the splendid covering that was lying upon ZION, didst thou not make certain that ZION was [there]?" And ZADOK the priest answered and said, "I did not, lord; it had three coverings over it, and I took off the outermost, and dressed ZION in the covering which thou didst give me, and I brought [the other] to thee." And the King said unto ZADOK, "Go quickly and look at our Lady and examine her closely." And ZADOK the priest took the keys, and went and opened the house of the sanctuary, and he examined [the place] quickly, and he found there nothing except the wooden boards which AZÂRYÂS had fastened together and had made to resemble the sides of the pedestal of ZION.

110

57. *Concerning the Fall of ZADOK the Priest*

And when ZADOK saw this he fell forward on his face flat upon the ground, and his spirit was poured out over him, for he was terrified; and he became like a dead man. And when he tarried in coming out SOLOMON sent to him ÎYÔAS (BENAIAH), the son of YÔDÂHÊ, and he found ZADOK like one dead. And he lifted up the head of ZADOK, and felt his heart and his nose to find out whether there was any sign of breath being in him; and he fanned him, and lifted him up, and rubbed him and laid him out upon the table. And he rose up and looked at the place where ZION had been set, and he found her not, and he fell down upon the ground. And he cast dust upon his head, and [then] rose up and went out and wailed at the doors of the house of God; and the sound of his cries was heard as far as the King's house. And the King rose up and commanded the crier to go round, and the soldiers to blow the trumpets, so that the people might go forth and pursue the men of the land of ETHIOPIA, and if they overtook them they were to seize his son and bring him back with ZION, and slay the [other] men with the sword. For with his mouth he spake and said, "As the Lord God of ISRAEL liveth, they are men of death and not of life; for verily they deserve death because they have robbed the house of the sanctuary of God, and have desired to pollute the habitation of His Name in a land wherein there is not the Law."

58. *How SOLOMON Rose up to Slay them*

Thus spake King SOLOMON. And the King rose up in wrath and set out to pursue [the men of ETHIOPIA]. And when the King, and his nobles, and his mighty men of war rose up (i.e., had set out), the elders of ISRAEL, and the widows, and the virgins gathered together in the house of God, and they wept for ZION, for the Tabernacle of the Law of God had been taken away from them. Now after ZADOK had remained [senseless] for a season, his heart returned to him. And then the King commanded that the soldiers should go forth on the right hand and on the left, on the chance that some of the [fugitives] might turn aside through fear of the theft. And the King himself rose up and followed the track of the road of the men of ETHIOPIA, and he sent out mounted horsemen, so that they might [ride on before him and] find out where they were, and might return and bring him news [of them]. And the horsemen journeyed on and came to the country of MESR (EGYPT), where the men of ETHIOPIA had encamped with their king, and where they had made peace with ZION, and they rejoiced. And the soldiers of King SOLOMON questioned the people, and the men of the country of EGYPT said unto them, "Some days ago certain men of ETHIOPIA passed here; and they travelled swiftly in wagons, like the angels, and they were swifter than the eagles of the heavens." And the King's soldiers said unto them, "How many days ago is it since they left you?" And the men of EGYPT said unto them, "This day is the ninth day since they left us." And some of the King's horsemen who returned said unto King SOLOMON, "Nine days have passed since they left EGYPT. Some of our companions have gone to seek for them at the Sea of ERITREA, but we came back that we might report this to thee. Bethink thyself, O King, I beseech thee. On the second day they went forth from thee, and they arrived on the third day at the river TAKKAZÎ [of] the land of MESR (EGYPT). And we being sent forth by thee from JERUSALEM, arrived on the day of the Sabbath. And we came back to thee to-day [which is] the fourth day of the week. Consider in thy wisdom the distance which those men traversed." And the King was wroth and said, "Seize the five of them, until we find out the truth of their words."

And the King and his soldiers marched quickly, and they came to GÂZÂ. And the King asked the people, saying, "When did my son leave you?" And they answered and said unto him, "He left us three days ago. And having loaded their wagons none of them travelled on the ground, but in wagons that were suspended in the air; and they were swifter than the eagles that are in the sky, and all their baggage travelled with them in wagons above the winds. As for us, we thought that thou hadst, in thy wisdom, made them to travel in wagons above the winds." And the King said unto them, "Was ZION, the Tabernacle of the Law of God, with them?" And they said unto him, "We did not see anything."

59. How the King Questioned an Egyptian, the Servant of PHARAOH

And SOLOMON left that place, and he met a noble of the nobles of EGYPT, whom King PHARAOH had sent unto him with a gift; and there was an abundance of treasures with him, and he came and made obeisance to the King. And SOLOMON the King made haste to question him, even before he had presented his gift and embassy, and said unto him, "Hast thou seen men of ETHIOPIA fleeing by this road?" And the ambassador of PHARAOH answered and said unto the King, "O King, live for ever! My lord, King PHARAOH, sent me unto thee from ALEXANDRIA. And behold, I will inform thee how I have come. Having set out from ALEXANDRIA I came to KÂHĔRÂ (CAIRO), the city of the King, and on my arrival these men of ETHIOPIA of whom thou speakest arrived there also. They reached there after a passage of three days on the TAKKAZÎ, the river of EGYPT, and they were blowing flutes, and they travelled on wagons like the host of the heavenly beings. And those who saw them said concerning them, 'These, having once been creatures of earth, have become beings of heaven.' Who then is wiser than SOLOMON the King of JUDAH? But he never travelled in this wise in a wagon of the winds. And those who were in the cities and towns were witnesses that, when these men came into the land of EGYPT, our gods and the gods of the King fell down, and were dashed in pieces, and the towers of the idols were likewise broken into fragments. And they asked the priests of the gods, the diviners of EGYPT, the reason why our gods had fallen down, and they said unto us, 'The Tabernacle of the God of ISRAEL, which came down from heaven, is with them, and will abide in their country for ever.' And it was because of this that, when they came into the land of EGYPT, our gods were broken into fragments. And thou, O King, whose wisdom hath no counterpart under the heavens, why hast thou given away the Tabernacle of the Law of the Lord thy God, which thy fathers kept pure for thee? For, according to what we hear, that Tabernacle used to deliver you out of the hand of your enemies, and the spirit of prophecy, which was therein, used to hold converse with you, and the God of heaven used to dwell in it in His Holy Spirit, and ye are called men of the house of God. Why have ye given your glory to another?" And SOLOMON answered in wisdom and said, "How was he (i.e., DAVID) able to carry away our Lady, for she is with us?"

60. How SOLOMON Lamented for ZION

And SOLOMON entered into his tent, and wept bitterly, and said, "O God, willest Thou to take away the Tabernacle of Thy Covenant from us in my days? If only Thou hadst taken away my life before this which Thou hast taken away in my days! For Thou canst not make Thy word to be a lie, and Thou canst not break Thy Covenant which Thou didst make with our fathers, with NOAH Thy servant who kept righteousness, and with ABRAHAM who did not transgress Thy commandment, and with ISAAC Thy servant who kept his body pure from the pollution of sin, and with ISRAEL, Thy holy one, whom Thou didst make many by the Holy Spirit, and didst call 'Thy trace' [sic], ISRAEL, and with MOSES and AARON Thy priests, in whose days Thou didst make the Tabernacle of the Law to come down from heaven upon earth, to the children of JACOB Thine inheritance, with Thy Law and Thy Commandment, in the form of the constitution of the angels. For Thou hadst already founded ZION as the habitation of Thy glory upon the mountain of Thy sanctuary. And again Thou didst give it to MOSES that he might serve it nobly upon the earth, and might make it to dwell in the 'Tent of Witness', so that Thou Thyself mightest come there from the mountain of Thy sanctuary, and mightest make the people to hear Thy voice, so that they might walk in Thy Commandments."

"Now I know that Thou esteemest Thine inheritance more lightly than Thy people ISRAEL. And until this present it was with us, and we did not minister unto it rightly, and for this reason Thou art angry with us, and Thou hast turned Thy face from us. O Lord, look not upon our evil deeds, but consider Thou the goodness of our forefathers. My father DAVID, Thy servant, wished to build a house to Thy Name, for he had heard the word of Thy prophet, who said, 'Which is the house for My habitation, and which is the place for Me to rest in? Is it not My hands that have made all this, saith the Lord,[50] Who ruleth everything?' And when he had meditated upon this Thou didst say unto him, 'It is impossible for thee to build this, but he who hath gone forth from thy loins shall build a house for me.'[51] And now, O Lord, Thy word hath not been made a lie, and I have built Thy house, Thou being my helper. And when I had finished building Thy house, I brought the Tabernacle of the Covenant into it, and I offered up sacrifices to Thy thrice-holy Name, and Thou didst look on these [benevolently]. And the house was full of Thy glory, the whole world being filled with Thy Godhead, and we Thy people rejoiced at the sight of Thy glory therein. And this day it is three years since that time, and Thou hast snatched away Thy light from us that Thou mayest illumine those that are in darkness. Thou hast removed our honour that Thou mayest honour those who are unworthy; Thou hast blotted out our majesty that Thou mayest make majestic him that is not majestic; Thou hast taken away our life that Thou mayest build up him whose life is far from Thee.

"Woe is me! Woe is me! I weep for myself. Rise up, DAVID, my father, and weep with me for our Lady, for God hath neglected us and hath taken away our Lady from thy son. Woe is me! Woe is me! Woe is me! For the Sun of righteousness hath neglected me. Woe is me! For we have neglected the command of our God, and we have become rejected ones on the earth. As priests we have not acted well, and as Kings we have not done what is right in respect of judgement to the orphans. Woe be unto us! Woe be unto us! What is right hath passed from us, and we are rebuked. Woe be unto us! Our joy hath turned aside to our enemies, and the grace that was ours hath been removed from us. Woe be unto us! Woe be unto us! Our back is turned towards the spears of our enemies. Woe be unto us! Woe be unto us! Our children have become the spoil and captives of those whom we recently had spoiled and made captives. Woe be unto us! Woe be unto us! Our widows weep, and our virgins mourn. Woe be unto us! Woe be unto us! Our old men wail and our young men lament. Woe be unto us! Woe be unto us! Our women shed tears and our city is laid waste. Woe be unto us! Woe be unto us! From this day to the end of our days [we must mourn], and our children likewise. Woe be unto us! Woe be unto us! For the glory of the glorious daughter of ZION is removed, and the glory of the daughter of ETHIOPIA, the vile,[52] hath increased.

"God is wroth, and who shall show compassion? God hath made unclean, and who shall purify? God hath planned, and who shall gainsay His plan? God hath willed, and who shall oppose His intention? God speaketh, and everything shall come to pass. God hath abased, and there is none that shall promote to honour. God hath taken away, and there is none who shall bring back. God hateth, and there is none who shall make Him to love. Woe be unto us! Our name was honoured, to-day it is nothing. Woe be unto us! From being men of the household we have become men of the outside, and from being men of the inner chambers we have been driven out through our sins. For God loveth the pure, but the priests would have none of the pure, and have loved the impure. And the prophets rebuked us, but we would not accept rebuke, and they [wished to] make us hear, but we would not hear. Woe be unto us! Through our sins we are rejected, and because of our defection we shall be punished. Sovereignty profiteth nothing without purity, and judgement profiteth nothing without justice, and riches profit nothing without the fear of God. The priests love the words of fables more than the words of the Scriptures; and they love the sound of the harp more than the sound of the Psalter; and they love the service of the world more than prayer; and they love the disputing of the world more than the voice of the Godhead; and they love laughter and fornication more than the weeping of life; and they love the food that passeth away more than the fasting to God; and they love wine and sweet drink more than sacrificing to God; and they love idleness more than prayer; and they love possessions more than [the giving of] alms; and they love sleeping more than praising; and they love dozing more than watching. Woe be unto us! Woe be unto us!

"O Queen, we have been negligent in respect of the Commandment of God. We have loved the words of the fablemongers more than the word of the priests. We have wished to gaze upon the face of our women rather than upon the face of God in repentance. We have loved to look upon our children rather than to hear the word of God. We have consoled ourselves more with the sardius stone than with the administering right judgement to the orphans. We have loved to look upon our honour rather than to hear the voice of God. We have loved the word of foolishness more than the words of the wise. We have loved the words of fools more than hearing the words of the Prophets. Woe be unto us! Of our own free will we have polluted our life. Woe be unto us! Woe be unto us! The repentance and mercy which God loveth we have not done. Woe be unto us! He gave us glory, and we have thrown it away. He made us very wise, and of our own free will we have made ourselves more foolish than the beasts. He gave us riches, and we have beggared ourselves even [to asking for] alms. We looked upon our horses, and forgot our coming back. We have loved fleeting things, and we have not recognized those that abide. We have made our days to deride our life, we have preferred the luxuriousness of food, which becometh dung, to the food of life which endureth for ever. [We have put on] the garments of apparel which benefit not the soul, and have put off the apparel of glory which is for ever. Our governors and the people do what God hateth, and they love not what God loveth, love of their neighbours, and lowliness, and graciousness, and mercy for the poor, and patient endurance, and love of the house of God, and the adoration of the Son. But what God hateth is, augury by birds, and idolatry, and enquiry of witches, and divination, and magic, and flies, and 'aKarînô,[53] the animal that hath been torn, and the dead body of a beast, and theft, and oppression, and fornication, and envy, fraud, drink and drunkenness, false swearing [against] neighbours, and the bearing of false testimony [against] neighbours.

"All these things which God hateth they do. And it is because of them that God hath taken the Tabernacle of His Covenant away from us and hath given it to the people who do His Will and His Law, and His Ordinance. He hath turned His face from us and hath made His face to shine upon them. He hath despised us and hath loved them. He hath shown mercy unto them and hath blotted us out, because He hath taken away the Tabernacle of His Covenant from us. For He hath sworn an oath by Himself that He will not abrogate winter and summer, seed time and harvest, fruit and work, sun and moon, as long as ZION is on the earth, and that He will not in wrath destroy heaven and earth, either by flood or fire, and that He will not blot out man, and beast, and reptiles and creeping things, but will show mercy

115

to the work of His hands, and will multiply His mercy on what He hath formed. And when God taketh away the Tabernacle of His Covenant He will destroy the heavens, and the earth, and all His work; and this day hath God despised us and taken from us the Tabernacle of His Law." And whilst SOLOMON was saying these things he ceased not to weep, and the tears ran down his cheeks continually.

And the Spirit of Prophecy answered and said unto him, "Why art thou thus sorrowful? For this hath happened by the Will of God. And [ZION] hath not been given to an alien, but to thy firstborn son who shall sit upon the throne of DAVID thy Father. For God swore unto DAVID in truth, and He repenteth not, that of the fruit of his body He would make to sit upon his throne for ever, in the Tabernacle of His Covenant, the Holy ZION. And I will set him above the kings of the earth, and his throne shall be like the days of heaven and like the ordinance of the moon for ever.[54] And He who sitteth upon the throne of the Godhead in the heavens shall rule the living and the dead in the flesh for ever. And angels and men shall serve Him, and every tongue shall praise Him, and every knee shall bow to Him in the abysses and in the rivers. Comfort thyself with this [word], and get thee back to thy house, and let not thy heart be wholly sad."

And the King was comforted by this [word], and he said, "The Will of God be done, and not the will of man." And again the Angel of God appeared unto him openly, and said unto him, "As for thyself, thou shalt build the house of God, and it shall be glory and as a support for thee; and if thou wilt keep His Commandment and wilt not serve other gods thou shalt be beloved by God, even as DAVID thy father."

Footnotes

1 Isaiah lxvi. 1.

2 1 Chronicles xxii. 8, 9.

1 Or, cringing, or, degraded. The ancient Egyptians often spoke of "Kesh, the vile."

1 Probably a corruption of the name Ekron (2 Kings i. 2), the city-god of which was Baal-zebub.

1 Psalms lxxii. 11; lxxxix. 3, 4, 27, 29; cxxxii. 11-13.

61. How SOLOMON Returned to JERUSALEM

And then SOLOMON came back to the city of JERUSALEM, and he wept there with the elders of JERUSALEM a great weeping in the house of God. And after this the King and ZADOK the priest embraced each other, and they wept bitterly in the habitation of ZION, and they remained silent for a long time. And the elders rose up and spake unto the King, saying, "Be not thou sorrowful concerning this thing, O our Lord, for we know, from first to last, that without the Will of God ZION will not dwell [in any place], and that nothing happeneth without the Will of God. And as concerning ZION in olden time, in the days of ELI the priest, before our fathers had asked for a king, the PHILISTINES carried ZION away captive into [their] camp - God having neglected ISRAEL in the battle, and its priests 'AFNÎ (HOPHNI) and PÎNÂHAS (PHINEHAS) having fallen by the edge of the sword. And the PHILISTINES carried away the Tabernacle of the Law of God, and brought it into their city, and set it in the house of their god DAGON. And DAGON was broken to pieces and destroyed, and became like dust, and their land became a desert through mice, and they ate up all the fruit of their land, and their persons became sores and boils. And they gathered together their priests, and magicians, and star-gazers, and they entreated them and said unto them, 'How can we relieve ourselves of these sores and the tribulation which have come upon us, and upon our country?' And those magicians meditated and withdrew themselves to be alone, and they brought their magical instruments, and pondered, and considered, and planned how they could relieve them from tribulation of their city and their persons. And they discovered that this punishment had come upon them and their city because of ZION. And they went to their kings and their governors, and they said unto them, 'All these things have befallen you through the heavenly ZION, the Tabernacle of the Law of God. And now, know ye how ye will take her back into her city, and her country, and her house. And we must by no means send her away empty, but must give her an offering, so that she may forgive you your sins, and do away your tribulation when she hath returned to her city. And if ye will not send her to her city, no good will come of making her to live with you, but ye shall continue to be punished until ye are destroyed.'

"And their kings and governors said unto their priests, 'What gift now say ye that we ought to give her, and how shall we send her back? Find out, and tell us what we must do.' And the priests of the PHILISTINES took counsel together again, and they said unto their kings and governors, 'Make for her according to the heads of your houses, sixty figures of mice in gold, since mice have destroyed your land, and sixty figures of the member of a man, since your own persons have suffered from sores and boils on your members.'[55] And the PHILISTINES made as they commanded them one hundred and twenty offerings of gold, and gave them to ZION. And again they said unto the priests, 'How shall we send her away? And whom do ye say shall set her in her city?' And again the magicians of the PHILISTINES said unto them, 'Let them bring two she-camels[56] that brought forth their firstborn at the same time, and let them attach a wagon[57] to them - and they must keep back their young ones and shut them up in the house - and they must yoke the two she-camels together, and then set them free and let them go where they will. And if they march straight for JERUSALEM we shall know that peradventure God hath had compassion on our land; but if they wander about, and go hither and thither, and wish to turn back to the place whence they started, then we shall know that God is [still] wroth with us, and that He will not remove His punishment until He hath blotted out ourselves and our city.'

"And the PHILISTINES did as the priests commanded their governors, and they sent away ZION, and prostrated themselves before her. And those camels made their way straight to the country of JUDAH, and they came to the threshing floor and the house of thy kinsfolk received them. And those who did not receive them were the men of the house of DÂN, and they did not do homage to ZION, for they regarded her in anger as their destroyed (?) God. And they cut up the pieces of wood of the wagon, and they made those camels to be sacrifices, and ZION returned to her place. And whilst ZION was in [her] house SAMUEL the Prophet ministered unto her, and vision and prophecy were revealed unto him, and he pleased God in all his actions, and he ruled ISRAEL for forty-eight years.

"And after him our people entreated God to give them a king like the nations that were round about them. And SAMUEL the Prophet anointed SAUL king, and he reigned forty years. And he was of the tribe of BENJAMIN, which was the youngest branch of the peoples of ISRAEL. And SAMUEL the Prophet also anointed thy father DAVID. And when the PHILISTINES fought with SAUL the King, SAUL was conquered and died with [YÔ]NÂTHÂN his son. And those of his sons who were left wished to carry away ZION, when they knew that their father and their brother were dead. And then when they wished to hide her and to transfer her to the Valley of GÊLÂBÛHÊ (GILBOA) in order that thy father DAVID might not carry them off, she would not let them carry her away until thy father came and carried her away from their city, but not with offerings, and not with incense and burnt offerings. For it was impossible to carry ZION away unless she wished it and God wished it. And again, when thy father reigned rightly over ISRAEL he took her from the city of SAMARIA and brought her here to JERUSALEM, dancing on his feet before her, and clapping his hands because of joy for her; for she was taken by him that she might come to the city of DAVID thy father. And as for that which thou sayest concerning the going of ZION to their city, to the country of ETHIOPIA, if God willed it and she herself willed it, there is no one who could prevent her; for of her own will she went, and of her own will she will return if God pleaseth. And if she doth not return it will be God's good pleasure. And as for us, if God hath willed it JERUSALEM shall remain to us wherein thou hast built for us a house of God. And now, let not thine heart be sad, but comfort thou thyself with what we have said unto thee. And the wisdom, which the Lord God of ISRAEL hath given thee, hath sprouted from thee. For wisdom is a strange thing. As a lamp is not the sun, and as vinegar and aloes are neither profitable nor useful additions to honey, even so the words of fools are not beneficial to the wise man. And as smoke is to the eye, and unripe fruit to the tooth, even so the words of fools are not beneficial to the wise."

Footnotes
55. Five mice and five emerods; see 1 Samuel vi. 4.
56. "Two milch kine," 1 Samuel vi. 7.
57. "A new cart," 1 Samuel vi. 7.

62. Concerning the answer which SOLOMON made to them

And SOLOMON the King answered and said unto them, "Hearken ye unto me and to what I shall say unto you. Supposing He had taken me away whilst I was carrying ZION - what is impossible to God? And supposing He had taken you away whilst ye were carrying her - what is impossible to God? And supposing He were to make them to inherit our city, and destroy us - what is impossible to God? For everything is His, and none can gainsay His Will, and there is none who can transgress His command in heaven above or on earth below. He is the King Whose kingdom shall never, never pass away, Amen. But now let us go and kneel in the House of God."

And the elders of ISRAEL together with their King went into the House of God, and they entered the Holy of Holies, and they made supplication, and prostrated themselves, and ascribed blessing to God. And SOLOMON wept in the habitation of the heavenly ZION, the Tabernacle of the Law of God, and they all wept with him, and after a little while they held their peace. And SOLOMON answered and said unto them, "Cease ye, so that the uncircumcised people may not boast themselves over us, and may not say unto us, 'Their glory is taken away, and God hath forsaken them.' Reveal ye not anything else to alien folk. Let us set up these boards, which are lying here nailed together, and let us cover them over with gold, and let us decorate them after the manner of our Lady ZION, and let us lay the Book of the Law inside it. JERUSALEM the free that is in the heavens above us, which JACOB our father saw, is with us, and below it is the Gate of Heaven, this JERUSALEM on the earth. If we do the Will of God and His good pleasure, God will be with us, and will deliver us out of the hand of our enemy, and out of the hand of all those who hate us; God's Will, and not our will, be done, and God's good pleasure, and not our good pleasure, be done. Through this He hath made us sorrowful. Henceforward His wrath will cool in respect of us, and He will not abandon us to our enemies, and He will not remove His mercy far from us, and He will remember the covenant with our fathers ABRAHAM, and ISAAC, and JACOB. He will not make His word to be a lie, and will not break His covenant so that our fathers' seed shall be destroyed."

63. How the Nobles of ISRAEL agreed [with the King]

And then the elders of ISRAEL made answer and said unto him, "May thy good pleasure be done, and the good pleasure of the Lord God! As for us, none of us will transgress thy word, and we will not inform any other people that ZION hath been taken away from us." And they established this covenant in the House of God - the elders of ISRAEL with their King SOLOMON unto this day. And SOLOMON lived [thus] for eleven years after the taking away of ZION from him, and then his heart turned aside from the love of God, and he forgot his wisdom, through his excessive love of women. And he loved very greatly the daughter of PHARAOH, the king of EGYPT, whose name was MÂKSHÂRÂ, and he brought

119

her into the house which he had made; and there were figures of the sun, moon, and stars in the roof thereof, and it was illumined by night as brightly as by day. Its beams were made of brass, and its roof of silver, and its panels (?) of lead, and its walls of stone, red with black, and brown with white [and] green; and its floor was of blocks of sapphire stone and sardius. And he used to go and dwell therein through his love for his house and his wife MÂKSHÂRÂ, the daughter of PHARAOH the king of EGYPT.

Now the queen possessed certain idols which her father had given her to bow down before, and because, when SOLOMON saw her sacrificing to them and worshipping them, he did not rebuke her or forsake her, God was wroth with him, and made him to forget his wisdom. And she multiplied her sacrifices, and her worship, and her folly, according to the stupidity of the EGYPTIANS, and all the people of her house worshipped the idols, and learned the foolish service of idols. And enjoying the pleasure of their foolish service they worshipped with the daughter of PHARAOH, and the children of ISRAEL joined themselves to her, and the women and their handmaidens joined themselves unto her in the worship and foolish service of idols. And SOLOMON himself found pleasure in hearing their foolish service and folly. And when she saw that he loved her, and hearkened, and held his peace, and asked many questions about the foolish service of the gods of the EGYPTIANS, she made herself exceedingly agreeable to him, and she spoke to him with honeyed words, and with the tender speech of women, and with the sweet smile that accompanieth the presentment of an evil deed, and with the turning of the face and the assumption of a look of good intent, and with the nodding of the head. With actions of this kind she caused his heart to turn away from his good intent, and she enticed him to the evil of her work, wishing to drag him down into the folly of the foolish service of idols through carelessness. And as the deep sea draweth down into its depths the man who cannot swim, until the water overwhelmeth him and destroyeth his life, even so did that woman wish to submerge SOLOMON the King.

64. How the Daughter of PHARAOH Seduced SOLOMON

And then the daughter of PHARAOH appeared before SOLOMON, and said unto him, "It is good to worship the gods like my father and all the kings of EGYPT who were before my father." And SOLOMON answered and said unto her, "They call gods the things which have been made by the hands of the worker in metal, and the carpenter, and the potter, and the painter, and the hewer in stone, and the sculptor; these are not gods, but the work of the hand of man, in gold, and silver, in brass and lead, in iron and earthenware, and in stone, and ye call 'our gods' the things that are not your gods. But we worship none else than the Holy God of ISRAEL and our Lady, the holy and heavenly ZION, the Tabernacle of the Law of God, whom He hath given us to worship, us and our seed after us."

And she answered and said unto him, "Thy son hath carried away thy Lady ZION, thy son whom thou hast begotten, who springeth from an alien people into which God hath not commanded you to marry, that is to say, from an ETHIOPIAN woman, who is not of thy colour, and is not akin to thy country, and who is, moreover, black." And SOLOMON answered and said unto her, "Though thou speakest thus art thou not thyself of [that race] concerning which God hath not commanded us that we should take wives from it? And thy kin is her kin, for ye are all the children of HAM. And God, having destroyed of the seed of HAM seven kings, hath made us to inherit this city, that we and our seed after us may dwell therein for ever. And as concerning ZION, the will of God hath been performed, and He hath given her unto them so that they may worship her. And as for me, I will neither sacrifice to nor worship thine idols, and I will not perform thy wish."

And though she spake in this wise unto him, and though she shewed herself gracious unto him evening and morning, and night and day, he continued to refuse her [request]. And one day she beautified and scented herself for him, and she behaved herself haughtily towards him, and treated him disdainfully. And he said unto her, "What shall I do? Thou hast made thy face evil towards me, and thy regard towards me is not as it was formerly, and thy beautiful form is not as enticing as usual. Ask me, and I will give thee whatsoever thou wishest, and I will perform it for thee, so that thou mayest make thy face (or, attitude) gracious towards me as formerly"; but she held her peace and answered him never a word. And he repeated to her the words that he would do whatsoever she wished, and she said unto him, "Swear to me by the God of ISRAEL that thou wilt not play me false." And he swore to her that he would give her whatsoever she asked for, and that he would do for her everything that she told him. And she tied a scarlet thread on the middle of the door of [the house of] her gods, and she brought three locusts and set them in the house of her gods. And she said unto SOLOMON, "Come to me without breaking the scarlet thread, bend thyself and kill these locusts before me and pull out their necks"; and he did so. And she said unto him, "I will henceforward do thy will, for thou hast sacrificed to my gods and hast worshipped them." Now he had done thus because of his oath, so that he might not break his oath which she had made him to swear, even though he knew that it was an offence (or, sin) to enter into the house of her gods.

Now God had commanded the children of ISRAEL, saying, "Ye shall not marry strange women that ye may not be corrupted by them through their gods, and through the wickedness of their works and the sweetness of their voices; for they make soft the hearts of simple young men by the sweetness of their gentle voices, and by the beauty of their forms they destroy the wisdom of the foolish man." Who was wiser than SOLOMON? yet he was seduced by a woman. Who was more righteous than DAVID? yet he was seduced by a woman. Who was stronger than SAMSON? yet he was seduced by a woman. Who was handsomer than 'AMNÔN? yet he was seduced by TAMAR the daughter of DAVID his father. And ADAM was the first creation of God, yet he was seduced by EVE his wife. And through that seduction death was created for every created thing. And this seduction of men by women was caused by EVE, for we are all the children of EVE.

65. Concerning the sin of SOLOMON

Now SOLOMON sinned an exceedingly great sin through the worship of idols, and from being a wise man he became a fool, and his sin is written down in the Book of the Prophets. And the Archbishops who were there answered and said, "Hath God had mercy on SOLOMON for this error which is written down [as] his sin?" Yea, God hath had mercy upon him, and his name is numbered with [the names of] ABRAHAM, ISAAC, and JACOB, and DAVID his father in the Book of Life in heaven. For God is a forgiver of those who have sinned. Come now, and consider, which was the greater of the two, the sin of his father DAVID or the sin of his son SOLOMON? DAVID caused URIAH to be slain in battle by means of a plan of deceit so that he might take his wife BÊRSÂBÊH (BATHSHEBA), the mother of SOLOMON; and he repented, and God had compassion on him. And when he was dying he advised his son SOLOMON, saying, "Kill JOAB as he killed 'AMÊR (ABNER), and kill SHIMEI because he cursed me";[58] and he performed the will of his father and slew them after the death of DAVID his father. And SOLOMON killed no one except his brother when he wished to marry the Samênâwît,[59] the wife of his father DAVID whose name was 'ABÎS (ABISHAG). And as concerning the error of SOLOMON which is written down I will reveal it to you, even as God hath revealed it to me.

Footnotes
58. 1 Kings ii. 5 ff.
59. i.e., the "Shunammite woman" (see 1 Kings i. 3).

66. Concerning the prophecy of CHRIST

Now, according to the interpretation of prophecy, the name SOLOMON signifieth in the secret speech "CHRIST". And as SOLOMON built the house of God, so CHRIST raised up His Body and made it into the Church. And when He said unto the JEWS, "Throw down this house, and in three days I will build it up [again],"[60] He spake to them of the house of His Body. And as SOLOMON multiplied wives from alien peoples because of their beauty and winsomeness, and desires [arose] in him in his feigning love [for them], so CHRIST gathered together from alien peoples those who had not the Law, but who believed on Him. And there was no uncircumcised man to Him, and no pagan; and there was no slave, and no JEW, and no servant and no free man;[61] but He gathered them all into His heavenly kingdom by His Flesh and Blood. And in the Song of Songs SOLOMON himself sang and said, "There are sixty mighty men round about the bed of SOLOMON, all of them trained in war and holding swords, each man with his sword upon his thigh."[62] The number sixty indicateth the number of the righteous Patriarchs, and the Prophets, and the Apostles, and the Martyrs, and the Believers, and the Saints, and the Monks who have resisted the evil thought and the war of SATAN. And the word "sword" is, being interpreted, the word of the

Scriptures. The word of the Lord cutteth like a straight sharp razor, and in like manner the Scriptures cut from men's hearts the danger caused by lying dreams by night. And the words "bed of SOLOMON" are, being interpreted, the Church of CHRIST.

And again SOLOMON sang, saying, "King SOLOMON hath made a litter for himself,"[63] and these words are to be interpreted that CHRIST hath put on our body. The name SOLOMON in the language of the HEBREWS is, being interpreted, "CHRIST". And the foolish JEWS imagine that the words of DAVID, "The Lord said unto me, 'Thou art my son and I this day have begotten thee,'"[64] were spoken concerning SOLOMON his son. "O God, give Thy judgment to the king, and Thy righteousness to the son of the king, so that he may judge thy people with righteousness and thy needy ones with justice. And he shall live and they shall give him of the gold of ARABIA, and shall pray for him continually, and shall follow him [with good words], and he shall be a support for the whole earth on the tops of the mountains, and his fruit shall be greater than the cedar, and he shall flourish in the city like the grass of the earth, and his name shall be blessed for ever, and his name shall be before the sun. I have brought thee forth from the belly before the Morning Star. God hath sworn, and He will not repent, thou art His priest for ever, after the appointment of MELCHIZEDEK."[65]

And concerning this prophecy and others like thereunto, which DAVID prophesied concerning CHRIST, the foolish JEWS, who are blind of heart, say that what DAVID said in the beginning of his book was spoken concerning his son SOLOMON; this do the JEWS say, and they make CHRIST to be SOLOMON because of the similarity of name, and the wisdom, and because He was the Son of DAVID in the flesh. And although those who came after DAVID and SOLOMON, namely ELIJAH and ELISHA, knew this, they ascribed SOLOMON'S sin to him in the Book of KINGS in order that they might put to shame the JEWS, who are blinded in heart and the enemies of righteousness. And SOLOMON the King, the son of DAVID the King and Prophet, was himself also King and Prophet, and he prophesied many similitudes concerning CHRIST and concerning the Church, and he wrote four books of prophecy, and is numbered with ABRAHAM, ISAAC, and JACOB, and DAVID his father in the kingdom of the heavens.

Footnotes
60. John ii. 19.
61. Galatians iii. 28.
62. Song of Solomon iii. 7 ff.
63. Song of Solomon iii. 9.
64. Psalm ii.
65. Psalms lxxii. 1 ff.; cx. 4.

67. Concerning the lamentation of SOLOMON

And now I will tell you how he died. His days were sixty [years], when a sickness attacked him. And his days were not as the days of DAVID his father, but they were twenty [years] shorter than his, because he was under the sway of women and worshipped idols. And the angel of death came and smote him [in] the foot, and he wept and said, "O Lord God of ISRAEL, I am conquered by the terrestrial law, for there is no one free from blemish before Thee, O Lord, and there is no one righteous and wise before Thee, O Lord. For Thou dost scrutinize and try the heart. Nothing is hidden from Thee. Thou lookest upon the hidden things [as if they were] revealed, and Thou searchest out the heart. Have mercy upon me, Lord. Thou examinest the heart of man and dost try the reins. Have mercy upon me, Lord. Thou hearest both the whisper and the thunderclap. Have mercy upon me, Lord. And if Thou hast mercy upon the righteous who have not transgressed Thy commandments, what is there wonderful in Thy mercy? Have mercy upon me, Lord. But if Thou shouldest show mercy upon me, a sinner, Thy mercy would be a marvellous and gracious thing. Have mercy upon me, Lord. And although I have sinned remember ABRAHAM, and ISAAC, and JACOB, my fathers who did not transgress Thy commandment. Have mercy upon me, Lord, for Thou art merciful and forgiving; for the sake of DAVID Thy servant have mercy upon me, Lord. O Master of the world, and of kings and governors, have mercy upon me, Lord. O Thou who makest fools to be wise, and the wise to be fools, have mercy upon me, Lord. O Turner of sinners and Rewarder of the righteous, have mercy upon me, Lord." And as he spake these words tears streamed down his face, and he searched for his napkin.

And the Angel of God went down to him and said unto him, "Hearken thou unto what I shall say unto thee, for the sake of which God hath sent me. From being a wise man thou hast turned thyself into a fool, and from being a rich man thou hast turned thyself into a poor man, and from being a king thou hast turned thyself into a man of no account, through transgressing the commandment of God. And the beginning of thy evil was the taking of many wives by thee, for through this thou didst transgress His Law, and His decree, and the ordinance of God which MOSES wrote and gave to you, to ISRAEL, that ye should not marry wives from alien peoples but only from your kinsfolk and the house of your fathers, that your seed might be pure and holy and that God might dwell with you. But thou didst hold lightly the Law of God, thinking that thou wast wiser than God, and that thou wouldst get very many male children. But the foolishness of God is wiser than the wisdom of men, and He hath only given thee three sons: the one who carried off thy glory into an alien land, and made the habitation of God to be in ETHIOPIA; the one who is lame of foot, who shall sit upon thy throne for the people of ISRAEL, the son of the kin of thy kin from TARBÂNA, of the house of JUDAH; and the one who is the son of a Greek woman, a handmaiden, who in the last days shall destroy REHOBOAM and all thy kin of ISRAEL; and this land shall be his because he believeth in Him that shall come, the Saviour. And the tribe of REHOBOAM, and those who are left of ISRAEL, shall crucify Him that shall come, the Redeemer, and the memory of you shall be blotted out from the earth. For they shall think out a plan which they shall not be able to establish, and He will be wroth with them and blot out the memorial of them.

"And as for thee, JOSEPH, the son of JACOB, shall be a symbol of thee. For his brethren sold him into the land of EGYPT from SYRIA, the country of LÂBÂ (LABAN), and on his going down into the land of EGYPT there arose a famine in SYRIA and in all the world. And through his going down he called his kinsfolk and delivered them from famine and gave them a habitation in the land of EGYPT, the name whereof is GÊSHÊN (GOSHEN). For he himself was King under PHARAOH, King of EGYPT. Similarly the Saviour Who shall come from thy seed shall set thee free by His coming, and shall bring thee out of SHEÔL, where until the Saviour cometh thou shalt suffer pain, together with thy fathers; and He will bring thee forth. For from thy seed shall come forth a Saviour Who shall deliver thee, thee and those who were before thee, and those who shall [come] after thee, from ADAM to His coming in the kin of your kin, and He shall make thee to go forth from SHEÔL as JOSEPH brought out his kinsfolk from the famine, that is to say the first SHEÔL in the land of famine, so also shall the Saviour bring out of SHEÔL you who are His kinsfolk. And as afterwards the EGYPTIANS made [the kinsmen of JOSEPH] slaves, so also have the devils made you slaves through the error of idols.

"And as MOSES brought his kinsmen out of the servitude [of EGYPT], so shall the Saviour bring you out of the servitude of SHEÔL. And as MOSES wrought ten miracles and punishments (or, plagues) before PHARAOH the King, so the Saviour Who shall come from thy seed shall work ten miracles for life before thy people. And as MOSES, after he had wrought the miracles, smote the sea and made the people to pass over as it were on dry land, so the Saviour Who shall come shall overthrow the walls of SHEÔL and bring thee out. And as MOSES drowned PHARAOH with the EGYPTIANS in the Sea of ERITREA, so also shall the Saviour drown SATAN and his devils in SHEÔL; for the sea is to be interpreted by SHEÔL, and PHARAOH by SATAN, and his hosts of EGYPTIANS by devils. And as MOSES fed them [with] manna in the desert without toil, so shall the Saviour feed you with the food of the Garden (i.e., Paradise) for ever, after He hath brought you out from SHEÔL. And as MOSES made them to dwell in the desert for forty years, without their apparel becoming worn out, or the soles of their feet becoming torn, so the Saviour shall make you to dwell without toil after the Resurrection. And as JOSHUA brought them into the Land of Promise, so shall the Saviour bring you into the Garden of Delight. And as JOSHUA slew the seven Kings of CANAAN, so shall the Saviour slay the seven heads of 'IBLÎS.[66] And as JOSHUA destroyed the people of CANAAN, so shall the Saviour destroy sinners and shut them up in the fortress of SHEÔL. And as thou hast built the house of God, so shall churches be built upon the tops of the mountains."

Footnotes
66. i.e., SATAN, the Devil.

68. *Concerning MARY, Our Lady of Salvation*

"And again, there shall be unto thee a sign that the Saviour shall come from thy seed, and that He shall deliver thee with thy fathers and thy seed after thee by His coming. Your salvation was created in the belly of ADAM in the form of a Pearl before EVE. And when He created EVE out of the rib He brought her to ADAM, and said unto them, 'Multiply you from the belly of ADAM.' The Pearl did not go out into CAIN or ABEL, but into the third that went forth from the belly of ADAM, and it entered into the belly of SETH. And then passing from him that Pearl went into those who were the firstborn, and came to ABRAHAM. And it did not go from ABRAHAM into his firstborn ISHMAEL, but it tarried and came into ISAAC the pure. And it did not go into his firstborn, the arrogant ESAU, but it went into JACOB the lowly one. And it did not enter from him into his firstborn, the erring REUBEN, but into JUDAH, the innocent one. And it did not go forth from JUDAH until four sinners had been born, but it came to FÂRÊS (PEREZ), the patient one, And from him this Pearl went to the firstborn until it came into the belly of JESSE, the father of thy father. And then it waited until six men of wrath had been born, and after that it came to the seventh, DAVID,[67] thy innocent and humble father; for God hateth the arrogant and proud, and loveth the innocent and humble. And then it waited in the loins of thy father until five erring fools had been born, when it came into thy loins because of thy wisdom and understanding. And then the Pearl waited, and it did not go forth into thy firstborn. For those good men of his country neither denied Him nor crucified Him, like ISRAEL thy people; when they saw Him Who wrought miracles, Who was to be born from the Pearl, they believed on Him when they heard the report of Him. And the Pearl did not go forth into thy youngest son 'ADRÂMÎ. For those good men neither crucified Him nor denied Him when they saw the working of miracles, and wonders by Him that was to be born from the Pearl, and afterwards they believed in Him through His disciples.

"Now the Pearl, which is to be your salvation, went forth from thy belly and entered into the belly of 'ÎYÔRBĔ'ÂM (REHOBOAM) thy son, because of the wickedness of ISRAEL thy people, who in their denial and in their wickedness crucified Him. But if He had not been crucified He could not have been your salvation. For He was crucified without sin, and He rose [again] without corruption. And for the sake of this He went down to you into SHEÔL, and tore down its walls, that He might deliver you and bring you out, and show mercy upon all of you. Ye in whose bellies the Pearl shall be carried shall be saved with your wives, and none of you shall be destroyed, from your father ADAM unto him that shall come, thy kinsman 'ÊYÂKÊM (JOACHIM), and from EVE thy mother, the wife of ADAM, to NOAH and his wife TARMÎZÂ, to TÂRÂ (TERAH) and his wife 'AMÎNYÂ, and to ABRAHAM and his wife SÂRÂ (SARAH), and to ISAAC and his wife RĔBKÂ (REBECCA), and to JACOB and his wife LĔYÂ (LEAH), and to YAHÛDÂ and his bride TĔ'EMÂR (TAMAR), and to thy father and his wife BÊRSÂBÊH (BATHSHEBA), and to thyself and TARBÂNÂ thy

126

wife, and to REHOBOAM thy son and his wife 'AMÎSÂ, and to ÎYÔ'AKÊM (JOACHIM) thy kinsman, who is to come, and his wife HANNÂ.

"None of you who shall have carried the Pearl shall be destroyed, and whether it be your men or your women, those who shall have carried the Pearl shall not be destroyed. For the Pearl shall be carried by the men who shall be righteous, and the women who have carried the Pearl shall not be destroyed, for they shall become pure through that Pearl, for it is holy and pure, and by it they shall be made holy and pure; and for its sake and for the sake of ZION He hath created the whole world. ZION hath taken up her abode with thy firstborn and she shall be the salvation of the people of ETHIOPIA for ever; and the Pearl shall be carried in the belly of 'AYÔRBĔ'ÂM (REHOBOAM) thy son, and shall be the saviour of all the world. And when the appointed time hath come this Pearl shall be born of thy seed, for it is exceedingly pure, seven times purer than the sun. And the Redeemer shall come from the seat of His Godhead, and shall dwell upon her, and shall put on her flesh, and straightway thou thyself shalt announce to her what my Lord and thy Lord speaketh to me.

"I am GABRIEL the Angel, the protector of those who shall carry the Pearl from the body of ADAM even to the belly of HANNÂ, so that I may keep from servitude and pollution you wherein the Pearl shall dwell. And MICHAEL hath been commanded to direct and keep ZION wheresoever she goeth, and URIEL shall direct and keep the wood of the thicket[68] which shall be the Cross of the Saviour. And when thy people in their envy have crucified Him, they shall rush upon His Cross because of the multitude of miracles that shall take place through it, and they shall be put to shame when they see its wonders. And in the last times a descendant of thy son 'ADRÂMÎS shall take the wood of the Cross, the third [means of] salvation that shall be sent upon the earth. The Angel MICHAEL is with ZION, with DAVID thy firstborn, who hath taken the throne of DAVID thy father. And I am with the pure Pearl for him that shall reign for ever, with REHOBOAM thy second son; and the Angel URIEL is with thy youngest son 'ADRÂMÎ[S]. This have I told thee, and thou shalt not make thy heart to be sad because of thine own salvation and that of thy son."

And when SOLOMON had heard these words, his strength came [back] to him on his bed, and he prostrated himself before the Angel of God, and said, "I give thanks unto the Lord, my Lord and thy Lord, O thou radiant being of the spirit, because thou hast made me to hear a word which filleth me with gladness, and because He doth not cut off my soul from the inheritance of my father because of my sin, and because my repentance hath been accepted after mine affliction, and because He hath regarded my tears, and hath heard my cry of grief, and hath looked upon my affliction, and hath not let me die in my grief, but hath made me to rejoice before my soul shall go forth from my body. Henceforward [the thought of] dying shall not make me sorrowful, and I will love death as I love life. Henceforward I will drink of the bitter cup of death as if it were honey, and henceforward I will love the grave as if it were an abode of costly gems. And when I have descended and have been thrust down deep into SHEÔL, because of my sins, I shall not suffer grief, because I have heard the word which hath made me glad. And when I have gone down into the lowest depth of the deepest deep of SHEÔL, because of my sins, what will it matter to me? And if He crush me to powder in His hand and scatter me to the ends of the earth and to the winds because of my sins, it will not make me sorrowful, because I have heard the word that hath made me to rejoice, and God hath not cut my soul off from the inheritance of my fathers. And my soul shall be with the soul of DAVID my father, and with the soul of ABRAHAM, and ISAAC, and JACOB my fathers. And the Saviour shall come and shall bring us out from SHEÔL with all my fathers, and my kinsmen, old and young. And as for my children, they shall have upon earth three mighty angels to protect them. I have found the kingdom of the heavens, and the kingdom of the earth. Who is like unto God, the Merciful, Who showeth mercy to His handiwork and glorifieth it, Who forgiveth the sins of the sinners and Who doth not blot out the memorial of the penitent? For His whole Person is forgiveness, and His whole Person is mercy, and to Him belongeth praise." Amen.

Footnotes
67. David was the eighth of Jesse's sons.
68. Compare Genesis xxii. 13.

69. Concerning the Question of SOLOMON

And SOLOMON turned and looked at the Angel and stretched out both his hands, and said, "My lord, is the coming of the Saviour of which thou speakest near or far off?" And the Angel answered and said unto him, "He will come three and thirty generations from thy kin and from thy seed and will deliver you. But ISRAEL will hate their Saviour, and will be envious of Him because He will work signs and miracles before them. And they will crucify Him, and will kill Him, and He shall rise up again and deliver them, for He is merciful to the penitent and good to those who are His chosen ones. And behold, I tell you plainly that He will not leave in SHEÔL His kinsmen of ISRAEL by whom the Pearl hath been carried."

And when the Angel of God had spoken these words unto SOLOMON, he said unto him, "Peace be unto thee." And SOLOMON answered and said unto him, "My lord, I beseech thee, I would ask thee one question; be not unheedful of my cry." And the Angel said unto him, "Speak, ask me thy question, and I will make thee to know what I have heard and seen." And SOLOMON said unto him, "Now I am grieved because of ISRAEL, His people, whom He hath chosen as His firstborn from among all the ancient tribes of His inheritance; tell me, will they be blotted out after the coming of the Saviour?" And the Angel of God answered him again and said unto him, "Yea, I have told thee that they will crucify the Saviour. And when they have poured out His blood on the wood of the Cross they shall be scattered all over the world." And SOLOMON said, "I weep for my people. Woe to my people! who from first to last have always provoked their Creator to wrath. I and those who have been before me are unworthy to have mercy shown unto us because of the evil of our works, for we are a faithless generation. Woe unto those who shall pour out innocent blood, and calumniate the righteous man, and divide his spoil, and who neither believe on His word nor walk in His Commandment! Their judgement is waiting, and their error abideth; great is their punishment. And their sin is waiting, and it shall never be forgiven to them, and the sin of their fathers shall be remembered; for their work was sin, and they shall be destroyed by that which they themselves have imagined. And woe also unto my soul! for I who have been honoured shall on my death be treated with contempt; and I who have been renowned for wisdom upon the earth shall become dust. In what way is the king superior if he hath not done good upon the earth to the poor? Their falling into the grave is the same, and their path in the deep is the same. Of what benefit (or, use) are we who are men? We are created in vain, and after a little time we become as if we had never been created. As for the breath which we breathe, if it cease for a short time, our soul passeth away, and if the beat of the spark of our heart which moveth in our mind passeth away we become dust, and our friends and acquaintances hold us to be a loathsome thing. And the understanding of our mind which is above [in] our heads [is destroyed] when our soul is poured out, and we become worms and filth; and when the heat of our body hath passed away we become nothingness and we pass away like the dissolving of a cloud. What then? To multiply speech is useless, and the goodliness of the stature is destroyed, and the strength of kings is blotted out, and the might of governors is destroyed and is no more found. And we all pass away like shadows, and when we have passed away in death our name is forgotten, and the trace of us cannot be found; after three generations of our children there is none who will remember our name."

And straightway he turned his face to REHOBOAM his son, and he said unto him, "O my son, withhold thyself from evil and do the things that are good, so that thou mayest find many days upon earth. And do not bow down to strange gods, and do not worship them, but fear and honour God only, so that thou mayest conquer thy foes and thy adversaries, and mayest inherit the habitation of thy father in the heavens, and also eternal life."

And he said unto him, "Write me in the roll of the Book, and lay it in the chest." And he said unto ZADOK the priest, "Anoint my son and make him king. As my father DAVID, my lord, made me king whilst he was alive, even so do I make my son REHOBOAM king. And his seed shall be the salvation of myself and of my fathers for ever, according to what the Angel of the Lord spake unto me."

70. How REHOBOAM reigned

Then ZADOK the priest took REHOBOAM and made him king, and he anointed him and performed for him whatsoever the Law demanded. And

REHOBOAM laid a tablet of wood upon the Tabernacle, and he found it with the name of his father SOLOMON [written upon] it, and then they set him upon the king's mule, and said unto him, "All hail! Long live the royal father!" and the city resounded with cries, and the trumpet was blown. And before REHOBOAM could return to his father SOLOMON died. And they laid SOLOMON in the tomb of his father DAVID, and they mourned for him with great mourning, for there was not found his like in wisdom in those days.

And when seven days had passed REHOBOAM made the mourning for his father to cease. And the people of ISRAEL gathered themselves together to REHOBOAM, and they said unto him, "Lighten for us [our] labour, for thy father made it very heavy in the hewing of wood, and in the dressing of stone, and in making wagons for bringing down cedarwood." And REHOBOAM took counsel with the councillors and the elders of the house of the king, and they said unto him, "Answer them graciously. For at this present thou art like a young animal and thy loins are not able to bear the yoke. And now, speak unto them graciously, and say unto them, 'I will do for you everything ye wish.' And when thy hand hath gotten power over them thou canst do with thy people what thou wishest." And REHOBOAM drove out the elders and brought in the foolish young men who had been brought up with him. And he took counsel with them, and told them of the message which the house of ISRAEL had sent to him and what the elders of the house of the king had counselled him to do. And those foolish young men said unto him, "An aged man giveth the counsel of an aged man, and the elder giveth the counsel of an elder, and a man stricken in years giveth the counsel of the man who is stricken in years, and a young man like thyself giveth the counsel which appertaineth to youth. As for these men who are stricken in years, their loins are as tender as those of a young animal that cannot walk. And as concerning this matter of which thou speakest, who can dispute the command of our Lord the King?" And one of them leaped up into the air before REHOBOAM, and another drew his sword, and another brandished his spear, and another seized his bow and quiver. And when they had made an end of their playing they counselled him, saying, "O our lord, may we be with thee, and thou with us! Now thy father in wisdom gave us, the sons of men of ISRAEL who are learned in the art of war, to grow up with thee that thy kingdom might be strong after him. O our lord, show not a timid face to those men, lest they think that thou art weak and art not able to make war against them and against thine enemies. For if they see in us an attitude of weakness in word and in deed, we shall be held in contempt by them, and they will not give us gifts, or presents, or slaves, or tribute, and thy kingdom will be destroyed. But address them with bold words, and speak unto them haughtily, saying, 'In respect of my father ye say in wood and in stone, but I will make you to serve me with chains of iron and with scorpion-whips. For my thin flank shall be stronger than the thickest part of my father's body, and my counsel is greater than the counsel of my father who begot me. None shall diminish for you the labour and the forced service, nay it shall be increased for you in every particular. And if ye will not do my command, I will make your cattle my plunder, and your children shall be captives, and my knife of slaughter shall consume you. And I will seize your cities and your fields, and your plantations, and your wells, and your gardens, and your lands, and your fruit (or, crops), and I will bind your honourable ones in chains of iron, and your riches shall [provide] food for my servants, and your women shall be for the adornment of the house of my nobles. And I will not alter this my decision, and will not diminish it, and I will neither make it to be a lie nor to have no effect; and I will carry it out quickly, and will write it down for ever. For the whole of this land was given to DAVID my grandfather for his kingdom, and to my father SOLOMON after him. And [God] hath given it to me after my fathers as to them, and I will make you to serve me as ye served them; and now take counsel and obey me.'"

And thus also did REHOBOAM speak unto the elders of ISRAEL. And the people all rose up together in their full number, and they said, "Get back to [your] house[s], O ISRAEL. Have we none else whom we can make king save in the house of JUDAH and in the house of BENJAMIN? We will reject their houses and the men of both of them, and we will make as our king and governor the man whom we wish for and in whom our soul delighteth." And they took up their weapons of war, and fled in a body, and came to the city of SAMARIA of BÊTH ÊFRÂTÂ, where they took counsel and were gathered together in a body. And the house of ISRAEL cast lots among themselves so that they might make king the man whom they chose from the house of the father of the man wherein the lot fell. And the lot fell on the house of EPHRAIM, on the son of NÂBÂT, and they chose a man from the house of his father, and made JEROBOAM king. And thus was the kingdom separated from REHOBOAM, the son of SOLOMON, and there were left to it only the house of BENJAMIN and the house of JUDAH his father.

And the word which God spake unto DAVID His servant was not made a lie, "Of the fruit of thy body I will make to sit upon thy throne";[69] and again He said, "Ordained like the moon for ever";[70] and again He said, "God sware unto DAVID truly and will not repent."[71] He Who reigned on the throne of DAVID His father was JESUS CHRIST, his kinsman in the flesh by a virgin, Who sat upon the throne of His Godhead; and upon earth He granted to reign upon His throne the King of ETHIOPIA, SOLOMON'S firstborn. To REHOBOAM God gave only two stems (or, roots); and the King of RÔMÊ is the youngest son of SOLOMON. And God did this in order that foolish people might not call us JEWS, because of SOLOMON and because of REHOBOAM his son - now God knoweth the heart - and He did this that they might not imagine such a thing. They called REHOBOAM "King of JUDAH", and they called the King of SAMARIA "King of ISRAEL". And of the generations of REHOBOAM, from REHOBOAM to 'ÎYÂKÊM (JOACHIM) were forty-one generations. And there were born to MALKÎ two children, LEVI and SHEM, the begetter of HÔNÂSÊ. And HÔNÂSÊ begat KALÂMYÔS, and KALÂMYÔS begat JOACHIM, and JOACHIM begat MARY, the daughter of DAVID. And again 'ÎLÎ begat MALKÎ, and MALKÎ begat MÂTÎ, and MÂTÎ begat 'ÊLÎ and JACOB, and HANNA, the wife of JOACHIM. And 'ÊLÎ took a wife and died without children. And JACOB took to wife YÔHADÂ, the wife of 'ÊLÎ, and he begat by her JOSEPH the carpenter, who was the betrothed of MARY. And JOSEPH was the son of JACOB in the flesh and the son of 'ÊLÎ according to the Law; now God had commanded MOSES that the ISRAELITES were to marry their kinsfolk, each in the house of his fathers, and that they were not to marry alien women.

Footnotes
69. 2 Samuel vii. 12; Psalm cxxxii. 11.
70. Psalm lxxxix. 37.
71. Psalm lxxxix. 35.

71. Concerning MARY, the daughter of DAVID

And from this it is evident that MARY was the daughter of DAVID, and that JOSEPH was the son of DAVID. Therefore was MARY betrothed to JOSEPH her kinsman, as it is said in the Gospel, "O JOSEPH, son of DAVID, fear thou not to take to wife MARY thy betrothed, for that which is to be born of her is of the Holy Spirit, the Word of God."[72] And there was born of her God, the Word, Light of Light, God of God, Son of the Father, Who came and delivered His creation; from the hand of SHEÔL, and from SATAN, and from death He hath delivered all of us who have believed in Him, He hath drawn us to His Father and hath raised us up into heaven His throne to become His heirs; for He is a lover of man, and unto Him praise belongeth for ever. Amen.

Footnotes
72. Matthew i. 20.

72. Concerning the King of RÔMÊ (CONSTANTINOPLE)

And we will begin to tell you what we have heard, and what we have found written, and what we have seen concerning the King of RÔMÊ. The kingdom of RÔMÊ was the portion and dominion of JAPHET, the son of NOAH. And sitting down they made twelve great cities, and DARIUS built the greatest cities of their kingdoms: 'ANTÔKYÂ (ANTIOCH), DÎRESYÂ (TYRE ?), and BÂRTONYÂ (PARTHIA ?), and RÂMYÂ (ROMA ?), and those who reigned dwelt there; and King CONSTANTINE built CONSTANTINOPLE after his own name. Now the sign of the Cross having appeared to him during the battle in the form of stars cut in the heavens, he was delivered out of the hands of his enemy; and from that time onwards the Kings of RÔMÊ made their habitation there. And that DARIUS had many descendants; and from DARIUS to the days of SOLOMON were eighteen generations. And of his seed was born a man whose name was ZANBARÊS, and he made in wisdom a drawing of the astrolabe, and placed stars therein, and [he made also] a balance (i.e., clock) for the sun. And he [fore]saw what would come after, and that the kingdom would not remain to the children of JAPHET, but would depart to the seed of DAVID, of the tribe of SHEM. And when he thus saw, he sent a message to DAVID the King, saying, "Take my daughter for thy son"; and DAVID the King took her and gave her to SOLOMON his son, and SOLOMON begat a son by her and called his name "'ADRÂMÎ". And ZANBARÊS died before [this] and BALTASÔR, who was of his kinsmen, became king. And he lacked male offspring to reign after him upon his throne, and he was jealous lest the children of his father should reign after him. And he sent a written message to SOLOMON the King, saying, "Hail to the greatness of thy kingdom, and to thine honourable wisdom! And now, give me thy son, whom I will make king over the city of RÔMÊ. For I have not been able to beget male children, but only three daughters. And I will give him whichever of my daughters he pleaseth, and I will give him my throne, and he shall be king, he and his seed after him in the city of RÔMÊ for ever."

And when King SOLOMON had read this letter, he meditated, saying, "If I keep back my son he will send to the King of the East, who will give him his son, and that which I have planned will be made void; therefore I will give him my son." And he took counsel with his counsellors of the house of ISRAEL, and he said unto them, "We have already given our son and our children to the country of ETHIOPIA, and ISRAEL hath a kingdom there. And now, so that we may have a third kingdom, the country of RÔMÊ, I will send thither 'ADRÂMÎS my youngest son. Hold ye not it against me as an evil thing that formerly I took away your sons, for it is a pleasing thing to God that the men of ETHIOPIA have learned His Name, and have become His people. In like manner, the men of RÔMÊ, if we give them our children, will become the people of God, and unto us moreover shall be given the name of 'People of God', being spoken of thus and called thus: The people of ISRAEL have taken the kingdom of ETHIOPIA and the kingdom of RÔMÊ. Give ye your youngest sons as before [ye gave the eldest], and let those of middle age stay in our city."

And they rose up, and took counsel, and returned, and said unto him, "We will speak this matter unto the King, and he shall do his will." And he said unto them, "Make me hear what ye would say." And they said unto him, "Thou hast already taken the eldest of our houses, and now take the youngest of their children." And he was pleased with this counsel, and he did for them as they wished. And he set forward 'ADRÂMÎ his son, who took some of the nobles of the lower grades of the house of ISRAEL, and the lot fell upon him in the name of his father SOLOMON; and they gave him a priest of the tribe of the LEVITES whose name was 'AKÎMÎHÊL, and they set 'ADRÂMÎ upon the king's mule, and cried out to him, "Hail! [Long] live the royal father!" And all the people said, "It is right and proper." And they anointed him with the oil of kingship, and commanded him to keep all the laws of the kingdom, and they made him to swear that he would worship no other god except the God of ISRAEL. And they blessed him as they had blessed DAVID his brother, and admonished 'ADRÂMÎ even as they had admonished DAVID, and they accompanied him on his way as far as the sea coast.

And SOLOMON the King wrote and sent a letter, saying, "Peace be to BALTASÔR, the King of RÔMÊ! Take my son 'ADRÂMÎ, and give him thy daughter, and make him king in the city of RÔMÊ. Thou didst wish for a king of the seed of DAVID my father, and I have done thy will. And I have sent unto thee his nobles, fourteen on his right hand and fourteen on his left, who shall keep the Law with him and be subject unto thee according to thy will."

And they arrived there with the ambassadors of the King of RÔMÊ, together with much splendour and all the equipment that was requisite for the country of RÔMÊ. And they came to the city of RÔMÊ, to BALTÂSÂR the King, and they repeated all that SOLOMON had sent them to say, and delivered over to him his son. And BALTÂSÂR rejoiced exceedingly, and gave him his eldest daughter, whose name was 'ADLÔNYÂ; and he made a great marriage feast according to the greatness of his kingdom, and established him over all his city of RÔMÊ. And he blessed him, for he was noble in stature, and his wisdom was marvellous, and he was exceedingly mighty in his strength.

And one day BALTÂSÂR wished to test his knowledge in the trying of cases, a man, the possessor of a vineyard, having come to him and appealed to him, saying, "My lord, 'ARSÂNÎ, the son of YÔDÂD, hath transgressed thy word, and hath laid waste my vineyard with his sheep. And behold, I have seized his sheep and they are in my house; what decision wilt thou come to in respect of me?" And the owner of the sheep came to the King and made an appeal to him, saying, "Give me back my sheep, for he hath carried them off because they went into his vineyard." And the King said unto them, "Go ye and argue your case before your King 'ADRÂMÎ, and whatsoever he shall say unto you that do." And they went and argued their case before him. And 'ADRÂMÎ asked him, saying, "How much of the vineyard have the sheep eaten? The leaves, or the tendrils, or the young grapes, or the shoots by the roots?" And the owner of the vineyard answered and said unto him, "They have eaten the tendrils and the branches that had grapes upon them, and there is nothing left of the vines except the twigs by the root." And 'ADRÂMÎ asked the owner of the sheep, saying, "Is this true?" And the owner of the sheep answered and said unto him, "My lord, they ate [only] the tendrils with leaves on them." And 'ADRÂMÎ answered and said, "This man saith that they ate the grapes: is this true?" And the owner of the sheep answered and said, "No, my lord, but they ate the blossoms before they had formed into grapes."

73. Concerning the first judgment of 'ADRÂMÎ, King of RÔMÊ

And 'ADRÂMÎ said unto them, "Hearken ye to the judgment which I will declare unto you. If the sheep have destroyed all the shoots from the root of the vine, then they all belong to thee. And if they have eaten the leaves of the branches, and the blossoms of the grapes, take the sheep, shear their wool, and [take also] the young of those which have not yet brought forth. But the sheep which have already brought forth young for the first time leave to the owner of the sheep." And all those who heard the judgment which he pronounced marvelled, and BALTÂSÂR said, "Verily, this judgment is a judgment of the people of the God of ISRAEL. Henceforward judge him that hath a case at law, wage war with him that would wage war, rule him that would be ruled, keep alive him that should be kept alive, and pass the judgment that ought to be passed according as men would be judged, and take this city to thyself and to thy seed after thee." And all the men of the city of RÔMÊ were well pleased, and they made 'ADRÂMÎ king over them, and they rejoiced in him with a great joy; for it happened thus by their will and by the Will of God. And [then] a fever seized BALTÂSÂR, and thereupon he sent 'ADRÂMÎ to the war, and into everything that he wished, whilst he himself remained in the city; and after this BALTÂSÂR died, and 'ADRÂMÎ directed the kingdom. And the city of RÔMÊ became the possession of 'ADRÂMÎ and of his generations after him, for by the Will of God the whole of the kingdom of the world was given to the seed of SHEM, and slavery to the seed of HAM, and the handicrafts to the seed of JAPHET.

74. Concerning the King of MEDYÂM

The king of MEDYÂM was of the seed of SHEM. For of the seed of ISAAC was ESAU, who went forth from his mother's womb with JACOB clinging to the sole of his foot; and JACOB carried away the right of the firstborn from ESAU for the sake of a mess of pottage. And the name of ESAU'S kingdom was called, according to his name of contempt, "EDOM", for the interpretation of "EDOM" is "lentiles"; and because of this the seed of ESAU were called "EDOMITES". For through the greed of his belly he forsook and lost the right of the firstborn of the seed of SHEM. For unless the soul be restrained by temperance, it will bring down into a net the whole of the lust of the belly which is of the body. For the body is greedy, but temperance restraineth the soul, and therefore PAUL said, "That which the soul doth not wish the body wisheth; and that which the body doth not wish the soul wisheth, and each contendeth against the other."[73] If a man willeth a thing, and his soul bandeth itself with the desire of his body he becometh like the Devil; but if he restraineth his body, and his soul bandeth itself with his desire he becometh like CHRIST. For the Apostles say that CHRIST is the Head of every man who travelleth upon the straight road. And our Lord said unto His disciples, "Walk in the Spirit, and perform ye not the lust of your bodies."[74] And when they heard this they forsook all the lust of the flesh, and they said unto our Lord, "Behold now, we have forsaken everything and followed Thee; what is our reward?" And our Saviour said unto them, "Ye have made your bodies like unto those of the angels, and shall do mighty deeds even as do I. And behold, I have given you authority to raise the dead, and I have given you power to heal the sick, and ye shall trample upon all the power of the Enemy. And at My second coming ye shall judge and shall put to shame the Twelve Tribes of ISRAEL, because they have not believed on Me, and have treated My glory with contempt. And as for those who believe in Me, ye shall magnify them and shall make them to rejoice with you in My kingdom."[75]

Footnotes
73. Galatians v. 17.
74. Galatians v. 16.
75. Compare Matthew x. 8; xix. 28; Luke x. 19.

75. *Concerning the King of BABYLON*

Now the King of BABYLON is of the seed of SHEM, and we will show you clearly that the King of BABYLON is of the seed of SHEM. It came to pass in days of old that there lived in the kingdom of MANASSEH, the King of ISRAEL, a certain man whose name was KARMÎN, and he was a fearer of God, and he gave many alms and oblations to the poor of ISRAEL. And when he made offerings to the house of God, he did so with sincerity, and his tithe he gave twofold; and he was good in all his ways, and there was no evil whatsoever before him. And SATAN, the enemy of all good, became envious of him, for he saw that his course of life was good. And that man was exceedingly rich in camels and horses, and flocks of sheep, and herds of cattle, and gold and silver, and fine apparel, and he used to feed the mule of the king in 'ARMÂTÊM, a city of ISRAEL. Now his native place was the country of JUDAH, his fathers' portion, but because of [his] love for wealth he departed into 'ARMÂTÊM to dwell there, and ISRAEL allowed him to settle there because of his riches; for he was exceedingly rich and had many possessions, and the governors [of JUDAH] were afraid of him.

76. *Concerning lying witnesses*

And there was a certain depraved man of the seed of BENJAMIN, whose name was BENYÂS, who used to lead the mule of the King of ISRAEL, and KARMÎN used to feed him, together with the mule of King MANASSEH. And among the neighbours of KARMÎN there were certain men who were envious of him because of [his] pastures and wells, and because of the multitude of his flocks and herds and servants, for the region [where he had settled] was the inheritance of their fathers, and for this reason they wished to drive him away from their country. And they kept watch upon BENYÂS, the leader of the king's mule, with evil intent, and they abused KARMÎN, and said unto BENYÂS, "This KARMÎN blasphemeth, and he hath blasphemed the King of ISRAEL, the anointed of God, saying, 'This king is not the son of a free woman, but the son of an old woman servant whom [a certain man] bought for two Kôr-measures [of grain] to work at the mill and brick-making.' Do thou take thy case against him to the king and accuse him, for we will be thy witnesses before the king, and we will not let thee be put to shame." And they made a covenant together, and they swore to him that they would bear false witness against KARMÎN, by whose tongue such a word had never been uttered, and into whose mind such a thought had never entered.

And BENYÂS went to his lord, the King, and told him all this matter. And the King said unto him, "Is there any man who hath heard this with thee?" And BENYÂS answered and said unto him, "Yea, there are some who have heard - two of the nobles of ISRAEL who belong to 'ARMÂTÊM." And the King said unto him, "Go now and bring them hither secretly so that we may find out whether they agree with thy words; [and if they do] we will cut off the head of KARMÎN." And BENYÂS departed and brought ZARYÔS and KÂRMÊLÔS, of the tribe of MANASSEH, for it had been agreed between them that they would not put him to shame before the King in the matter of their lying testimony. And these two men agreed together and planned when they were on [their] way, saying, "When we have spoken to the King if he shall ask us afterwards separately (so that he may find out the truth of our words), saying, 'Where did you hear these words?' we will each of us answer and say unto him, 'When we were drinking wine with him.' And when he shall say unto us, 'What day [was this]?' we will say, 'Five days after the new moon.' And when he saith unto us, 'What time [of the day]?' we will say unto him, 'At the ninth hour, when he was sitting with us, and we were drinking wine together.' And when he shall ask us, saying, 'What did ye drink out of? and where were ye sitting?' we will say unto him, 'Out of cups of gold, and our seats were in the hall of his house where the cushions for reclining upon were placed.'" And they agreed together on this evil plot [whilst they were] on their way.

And when they arrived in the presence of the King BENYÂS brought them forward, and the King questioned them, and they repeated to him all their lying counsel. And he asked them - according as they had surmised on the road - the occasion, and the day, and the hour of their drinking [wine] and their sitting [in the hall], and they told him. Now, God hath commanded that kings, and governors, and all those who occupy a high position shall investigate an accusation, even as God commanded MOSES.

And when the King had enquired into all this matter, he called the captain of his host who stood before him, and said unto him, "Go at dawn of day to-morrow and surround the house of KARMÎN and let not anyone of his people escape thee, neither man nor woman, and slay [them all] with the sword. And as for KARMÎN, cut off his head, and bring hither all his possessions, and his goods, and all his flocks and herds, and his gold and silver."

And those liars rejoiced and returned to their district, and they went into the house of KARMÎN and held converse with him with words of peace, and they paid him compliments, and they made jests before his face, evil being in their hearts. And then was fulfilled on them the prophecy of DAVID, who said, "Those who speak words of peace with their neighbour, and [have] evil in their hearts, reward them according to the evil of their works and according to the evil of their thoughts."[76] And they drank themselves drunk in the house of KARMÎN, and they slept together with him. And when they had fallen asleep, behold, the Angel of God was sent to KARMÎN, and he awoke him and said unto him, "Leave all thy possessions and save thyself, for men have been commanded by MANASSEH the King to cut off thy head. Take as much of thy riches as thou canst carry, and flee into another country, for this MANASSEH is a slayer of the prophets, and a seeker after the blood of innocent men."

Then KARMÎN rose up straightway, and sought out his treasure in gold and took it, and he awoke his wife and his two sons, and he also awoke his chosen servants, and loaded them with possessions of great value, and went forth by night. And he sent off his wife and his sons with two servants to go to JERUSALEM, and departed with two of his servants to a remote country - a distance of three months' journey - and he arrived at BABYLON. And he came to BALÂ'ÔN, the King of BABYLON, and gave him a gift, and related unto him what had happened to him. And BALÂ'ÔN loved KARMÎN, and gave him a habitation near the house of his merchant, who had departed to a far country for a period of three years.

And those men who had borne lying testimony they killed in bed in KARMÎN'S house.

And the wife of the merchant loved KARMÎN, and she was seduced by him, and became with child; now the behaviour of women is bad. And the husband of the woman had left her when she was with child, and she brought forth and gave the child to a nurse who brought it up. And in the second year she went astray and became with child by KARMÎN, for the person of KARMÎN was exceeding goodly in ISRAEL. And the woman wished to throw the child whom she had conceived into the river when he was born and to wait for the merchant her husband as if she had not gone astray, and had not done anything [wrong]. Even as SOLOMON the wise man saith, "There are three things which are difficult to me in my mind, and the fourth of these I cannot comprehend: - The track of the eagle in the heavens, the path of the serpent on the rock, the track of a ship on the sea."[77] Now the fourth of them of which he speaks concerneth the wicked woman, who, having wronged her husband, and washed herself, sitteth down like a woman who hath done nothing, and she sweareth an oath falsely.

And at that time the wife of BALÂ'ÔN, the King of BABYLON, conceived and brought forth something which was like unto an eagle, a perfect bird but altogether without wings. And she called a handmaiden who was a favourite, and sent the thing away in a wicker-basket and commanded her to cast it into the sea (i.e., river), without letting anyone know about it. And the time for the bringing forth of the wife of the merchant arrived, and she brought forth a man child, comely in form [and worthy of] compassion. And without suckling it she called to a handmaiden who was a favourite, and put it into the inner part of a box and commanded her to throw him into the sea (i.e., river), without anyone knowing about it; for she was afraid of her husband. And in the same night two women brought forth, [the merchant's wife] and the wife of the King, and at daybreak the two women sent their handmaidens to cast their children into the river.

And by the Will of God these two handmaidens met each other before they had thrown the children into the river, and they talked together. And the handmaiden of the King asked the handmaiden of the merchant, saying, "What is in thy box?" and she showed her the beautiful child. And the King's handmaiden said unto her,

"Why hast thou brought him here?" And the merchant's handmaiden said unto her, "Because the wife of my lord hath gone astray with a certain ISRAELITE, and she conceived and brought forth a child, and she hath commanded me to throw him into the river." And the King's handmaiden said unto her, "Why doth she not bring up a child who is so beautiful?" And the merchant's handmaiden said unto her, "Her husband left her with child, and she brought forth a child, and is rearing him; how then can she rear this child who is of strange and alien seed?" And the merchant's handmaiden asked the King's handmaiden, saying, "What hast thou in thy box?" And the King's handmaiden said unto her, "My lady hath brought forth a child that hath not the appearance of a man but of a wingless eagle, and she hath commanded me to throw it into the river. And now, give me this child of thine that I may give it to my mistress, and do thou take this bird, and cast it into the river"; and they did so. And the handmaiden of the King took the child [of KARMÎN] to her mistress, and the Queen rejoiced, and it was reported to the King that the Queen had borne a son. And the Queen gave the boy to the nurses, and he grew up in the house of the King, and she called his name "NÂBÛKĔDNÂSAR" (NEBUCHADNEZZAR), which is, being interpreted, "By the luck of the bird."

And through this it is well known that the King of BABYLON is the seed of SHEM. And he came and overthrew JERUSALEM by the Will of God, and he carried away captive the children of ISRAEL, and he made them to wander in the town of BABYLON with the grandchildren of MANASSEH. And he was so very rich that he set up a pillar of gold on the plain of BABYLON sixty cubits high, and he was very arrogant, and he used to say, "I make the sun to shine in the heavens"; and he worshipped idols. And God abased him so that he might know Him, and He set his portion with the beasts of the field. And when he knew the Name of the Lord after seven years He had compassion upon him, and brought him back in repentance. And the kingdom of BABYLON was his, and it belonged to those who were of his seed for ever.

Footnotes
76. Psalm xxviii. 3, 4
77. Proverbs xxx. 18.

77. Concerning the King of PERSIA

And the King of PERSIA is likewise of the seed of SHEM, and we will inform you concerning the matters that relate to him. JUDAH begot two sons, and he brought in TĔ'MÂR (TAMAR) for his eldest son, and he died. And JUDAH sent his younger son to her that he might raise up seed to his brother by his brother's wife. And he did that which God hated, and he did not wish to raise up seed to his brother as his father JUDAH had commanded him. Now when he lay with TAMAR he made his seed to go into the ground, so that it might not germinate in her womb and be called the seed of his brother, but he wished to raise up seed by his own wife

139

in his own name. And when God saw his evil act He turned His face away from him and slew him. And JUDAH, the father-in-law of TAMAR, brought her back, and set her in the house of her father, and said unto her kinsfolk, "Keep carefully this Israelitish woman, and let her not defile herself with an alien. For I have a little son, and if God will let him grow up I will give him to her." And whilst TAMAR was living as a widow in her father's house, behold, JUDAH her father-in-law came to the place where his sheepfolds were to shear wool with great satisfaction and pleasure. And when TAMAR heard that her father-in-law had come, she cast away from her the apparel of widowhood, and she put herself in splendid apparel, and she veiled herself after the manner of a harlot, and she followed him and sat down. And he sent a message to her, saying, "I wish to company with thee." And she said unto him, "What wilt thou give me for my hire?" And he said unto her, "I will send to thee in the morning early a sucking lamb"; and she said unto him, "Give me a pledge until thou givest me the lamb." And he gave her [his] staff, and ring, and the close-fitting cap that was under his headdress. And he companied with her, and she took [the things] and departed unto her house. And he sent the lamb unto her early in the morning. And his servants enquired and said, "Where is the house of the harlot?" And they said unto him, "There is no harlot in our town"; and they returned into their city and told him that there was no harlot in their town. And JUDAH said, "Leave ye [it]; the Will of God be done."

Then TAMAR conceived and they told her father-in-law that she had conceived. And he went and took the elders of ISRAEL to the father of TAMAR, and he said unto him, "Bring to me thy daughter who hath conceived that we may stone her with stones even as MOSES commanded, for she hath brought reproach upon the house of ISRAEL." And the father and kinsfolk of TAMAR told her that her father-in-law spake thus. And she brought out the ring, and the staff, and the cap, and gave [them] to her father and her kinsfolk, and she said unto them, "The owner of these things hath seduced me; let them stone me with him with stones." And when JUDAH saw his possessions he recognized [them] and he said, "TAMAR is more righteous than I"; and he left her and came to his house. And TAMAR brought forth twins, two nations, FÂRÊS (PEREZ) and ZÂRÂ. And FÂRS (PERSIA) was founded in the name of FÂRÊS, and he ruled over it and his seed after him, and they were called "FARASÂWÎYÂN" (PERSIANS). Behold now, it is proved that the King of PERSIA is of the seed of SHEM.

78. Concerning the King of MOAB

And the King of MOAB is of the seed of SHEM, and we will inform you how this hath come to pass. When God made ABRAHAM to depart from his father's country into the land of KÂRÂN (HARRAN), He made LOT to pass over into the land of SODOM and GOMORRAH. And when God wished to blot out the people of SODOM and GOMORRAH, He sent His Angels MICHAEL and GABRIEL to bring out LOT and to burn up the cities of SODOM and GOMORRAH; and they destroyed them and brought out LOT with his children. And his wife turned round so that she might see the city of her father and her mother. Now the wrath of God came down on the city of SODOM [in the form of] a rain of fire from heaven, which burned up mountains, and hills, and stones, and earth. And lightnings, and forked lightnings, and peals of thunder came down mingled with the crashing of the wrath of God, and a cloud of fire which made the heat to emit smoke. And when all this uproar was being heard the Angels said unto LOT, "Turn not round after ye have gone forth from the city, turn not round that ye die not the death." But when 'AKMÂBÂ, the wife of LOT, heard this, she turned round, and she became a pillar of salt, and she existeth to this day, to this very day. And as for LOT, God made him to dwell in the mountains of ARARAT. And he planted a new vineyard, and his daughters made their father to drink wine, and they plotted a wicked plot, and they said, "How (i.e., why) shall the possession of our father be wasted (or, blotted out)? Our mother hath been destroyed on the road, and there is no one to marry us here." And they made their father drunk, and his elder daughter lay with him whilst his mind was clouded with wine, and LOT the righteous man did not know when his daughter lay with him and when she rose up from him, for his mind was clouded with strong drink. And NOAH was drunk and naked before his wife and children, and he cursed his son who laughed at him; and [the act of lying with his daughter] was not reckoned against LOT as sin, for he did it unknowingly. And his elder daughter conceived and brought forth a child, and she called him "MOAB", which is, being interpreted, "From my father on my knee". And he was the father of the MOABITES and the AGARENES. Behold now, it is clear that the King of MOAB is of the seed of SHEM.

79. Concerning the King of AMALEK

And it came to pass that when the elder daughter of LOT had brought forth her son, she said unto the younger daughter, "Come now, let us make our father drink wine, so that thou also mayest company with him that, peradventure, thou mayest get offspring." And again they prepared wine, and again they spoke to him the words of foolishness, and said unto him, "Drink wine, O our father, so that thy heart may be comforted"; and he, the simple man, drank and became drunk. And again, when he had drunk and his mind was clouded with wine, the younger daughter came and lay with him, and again he did not know of her lying with him, or of her rising up from him. And she also conceived and gave birth to a son, and she called his name "AMMON", and he is the father of the AMALEKITES. Behold now, it is clear that the King of AMALEK is of the seed of SHEM.

80. Concerning the King of the PHILISTINES

And behold, the seed of SAMSON reigned over the PHILISTINES. And SAMSON was of the seed of DAN, [one] of the twelve sons of JACOB, and he was the son of a handmaiden of JACOB; and we will inform you how this SAMSON came into being. The Angel of the Lord appeared to the mother of SAMSON and said unto her, "Keep thyself from all pollution, and company with no man except thy husband, for he who shall be born of thee shall be a NAZARITE, holy to the Lord, and he shall be the deliverer of ISRAEL from the hand of the PHILISTINES." And then she brought forth SAMSON. And again the Angel appeared unto her and said unto her, "Thou shalt not let a razor go upon his head, and he shall neither eat flesh nor [drink] wine, and he shall marry no strange woman but only a woman of his own kin and from the house of his father." And how God gave him strength ye have heard in the Book of JUDGES.[78] But he transgressed the commandment of God, and came and married a daughter of the uncircumcised PHILISTINES. And because of this God was wroth, and He delivered him into the hands of men of the uncircumcised PHILISTINES, and they blinded his eyes, and they made him act the buffoon in the house of their king. And he pulled the roof down upon them, and slew seven hundred thousand of them, and during his life he slew seven hundred thousand of them with iron, and stone, and [his] staff, and the jaw-bone of an ass. For their number was as that of the locusts, until he released ISRAEL from the service of the PHILISTINES.

And then DALÎLÂ (DELILAH) conceived by SAMSON, and whilst she was with child SAMSON died with the PHILISTINES; and DELILAH brought forth a son and she called his name "MENAHEM", which is, being interpreted, "Seed of the strong man". Now DELILAH was the sister of MAKSÂBÂ, the wife of the King of the PHILISTINES, and when SAMSON slew the King of the PHILISTINES in the house with his people and his household, and he died with him, DELILAH went to her sister MAKSÂBÂ, the Queen of the PHILISTINES. Now both women were beautiful, and they had no children, but both had conceived; MAKSÂBÂ had been with child six months by KWÔLÂSÔN, the King of the PHILISTINES, and DELILAH had been with child four months by SAMSON; and the husbands of both were dead. And the two women loved each other exceedingly. And their love for each other was not like the love of sisters, but like that of the mother for the child, and of the child for the mother; even so was their love. And they lived together. And the dominion over those who were left of the slaughter [made] by SAMSON in the house of the king was in the hands of MAKSÂBÂ, for none of the mighty men of war of the kingdom of the PHILISTINES were left, and therefore MAKSÂBÂ ruled over those that were left. And they spake unto her morning and evening, saying, "We have no other king except thyself, and except that one that shall go forth from thy belly. If our Lord DÂGÔN will do a favour unto us that which is in thy belly shall be a son, who shall reverence our god DÂGÔN and shall reign over us. And if it be a daughter we will make her to reign over us, so that thy name and the name of KWÔLÂSÔN our lord shall be your memorial over us."

And then MAKSÂBÂ brought forth a man-child and all the men of the PHILISTINES rejoiced, and they did homage to her and sang, saying, "DÂGÔN and BÊL have honoured her and loved MAKSÂBÂ, and the seed of KWÔLÂSÔN is found again from MAKSÂBÂ." And DELILAH also bore a son, and the two women brought up the children in great state and dignity. And when the children were five years old they ate and played together before them, and the mothers made garments of costly stuff for them, and [set] daggers above their loins, and chains on their necks. And the people seated the son of MAKSÂBÂ on the throne of his father, and made him king over the PHILISTINES.

Footnotes
78. See chapters xv. xvi.

81. *How the son of SAMSON slew the son of the King of the PHILISTINES*

Now that other son AKAMHÊL, the son of SAMSON, spake unto his mother DELILAH, saying, "Why am I not reigning and sitting upon this throne?" And his mother said unto him, "Cease, my son. This throne did not belong to thy father, and this city was not thy father's city; when the God of thy father hath let thee grow up thou shalt go to thy father's throne." And her son said unto her, "Nay, I will neither forsake thee, my mother, nor MAKSÂBÂ my mother, and I will be king here."

And one day the two youths were drunk after [their] meal was ended, and the doors were shut. And the two women were sitting together about to eat flesh, and the two youths were playing before them, and they ate with them, and a maidservant held the dish between them. And 'AKÊMÊHÊL, the son of DELILAH, took from the dish [a piece of] flesh, which would fill both his hands, and put it to his mouth, and TEBRÊLÊS, the son of MAKSÂBÂ, the King of the PHILISTINES, snatched away that part of the flesh that was outside his mouth. And 'AKÊMÊHÊL drew his sword and cut off his head, and it fell into the dish before he could swallow what he had seized; and his body fell upon the paving of the house; and his hands and his feet twitched convulsively, and he died straightway. And fear and dismay laid hold upon their two mothers, and they spake never a word to anyone because they were afraid, but they swallowed the food which was in their mouths, and they looked at each other, not knowing what to do.

And that handmaiden rose up from them, and she took the head of TEBRÊLÊS out of the dish, and put it back on its neck and covered it over with her garment. And DELILAH rose up and seized the sword of the dead son of her sister, and went to kill 'AKÊMÊHÊL, but he saved himself by hiding behind a pillar. And he made ready to kill his mother. And her sister rose up and seized her, saying, "Why should we be destroyed through their [quarrel?]. This [youth] is [sprung] from a bad root, and cannot [bear] good fruit; come, my sister, let him not destroy thee also." And she took the sword from her hand, and drew up from her pillow (?) rich purple clothing which kings wear, and she gave it to him, and she spake kindly words unto him, saying, "Take the apparel, my son, and thou thyself shalt sit upon the throne of the kingdom of the PHILISTINES." And 'AKÊMÊHÊL raged like a savage bear, for he wished to slay both women until he made them to leave the house. And they went out, and when he had made them leave the house he took the purple apparel, and went out. And the two women came back, and made the dead body ready for burial, and they buried it secretly.

And when the time for the evening meal had come, the young men and the stewards sought for [their king] and found him not, and they asked about him, and his mother said unto them, "Your king is sick, and this man will sit in place of him." And they took him and set him on the throne, and they prepared a feast, and rejoiced. And from that time onward the son of SAMSON reigned over them, and there was none who transgressed his commandment - now he committed this act [of murder] fif[teen] winters after he was born - and the kingdom of the PHILISTINES became his and his seed's after him. Therefore, beloved, it is well known that the kingdom of the PHILISTINES belongeth to the seed of SHEM.

82. Concerning the going down of ABRAHAM into EGYPT

And we could also inform you that when God had given unto ABRAHAM glory and riches, he lacked a son. And SÂRÂH and ABRAHAM talked together on their bed, and he said unto her, "Thou art barren," and she said unto him, "It is not I who am barren but thyself"; and they continued to discuss the matter and to dispute together about it. And there came a famine in the land of CANAAN, and ABRAHAM heard that there was some food in the land of EGYPT, the country of PHARAOH. And when he had spent all his possessions in charity to the poor during the days of the famine, without providing for the morrow, the famine waxed strong in the land of CANAAN, and he lacked food to eat. And he said, "I give thanks unto God that what He hath given unto me I have expended on my servants. But as for thee, my sister SÂRÂH, come, let us go into the land of EGYPT in order to save ourselves from death by famine." And she said unto him, "Thy will be done, O my lord, and if thou die I will die with thee, and if thou live I will live with thee; it is not for me to gainsay thy word for ever." And then they rose up and set out on their journey.

And when they drew nigh [to EGYPT] ABRAHAM said unto SÂRÂH, "One thing I must ask of thee, and do thou what I ask of thee"; and SÂRÂH said, "Speak, my lord." And he said unto her, "I have heard that the habits of the EGYPTIANS are lawless, and that they live in idolatry and fornication. And when they have seen thee they will plot evil against me, and slay me because of the goodliness of thy beautiful form; for there is among them no one that can be compared unto thee. And now, in order that thou mayest save my life, do thou say, if they happen to ask thee questions about me, 'I am his sister,' so that thou mayest save my soul from death by the hand of the strangers." And SÂRÂH said, "Thy will shall be done. The word which thou tellest me I will speak, and what thou tellest me to do I will do." And they wept and worshipped God, and they came into the great city of the King of EGYPT.

144

And when the EGYPTIANS saw ABRAHAM and SÂRÂH they marvelled at the beauty of their appearance, for they imagined that they had been brought forth by the same mother. And they said unto ABRAHAM, "What is this woman to thee?" And ABRAHAM said unto them, "She is my sister." And they also asked SÂRÂH "What is this man to thee?" And she said unto them, "He is my brother." Therefore did the people make a report to PHARAOH that a pair of goodly form had arrived, one a woman and the other a young man, and that there was no one like unto them in all the land. And PHARAOH rejoiced, and he sent a message to ABRAHAM, saying, "Give me thy sister that I may betroth her to myself." And ABRAHAM pondered in his mind, saying, "If I keep her back he will kill me and take her"; and he said, "Do so, provided that thou dost make me well content." And PHARAOH gave him one thousand, silver taflâHet,[79] and took SÂRÂH to make her his wife. And he brought her into his house, and set her upon his bed and PHARAOH the King of EGYPT would have companied with her. But the Angel of the Lord appeared unto him by night carrying a sword of fire, and he drew nigh unto him, and he lighted up the whole chamber with his fiery flame, and he wished to slay PHARAOH. And PHARAOH fled from one wall of the chamber to the other, and from one corner of the chamber to the other; wheresoever he went the Angel followed him; and there was no place left whereto he could flee and hide himself. Then PHARAOH stretched out his hands and said unto the Angel, "O lord, forgive me this my sin." And the Angel said unto him, "Why dost thou attack the wife of [another] man?" And PHARAOH said unto him, "O lord, slay thou not innocent blood. For he said unto me 'She is my sister,' and therefore I took her to myself innocently. What shall I do to deliver myself from thy hands?" And the Angel said unto him, "Give ABRAHAM'S wife back to him, and give him a gift, and send him away to his own country." And straightway PHARAOH called ABRAHAM, and gave unto him his wife SÂRÂH, together with a handmaiden whose name was 'AGÂR (HAGAR), and he gave unto him gold, and silver, and costly apparel, and sent him away in peace.

And ABRAHAM and his wife returned to their country in peace. And SÂRÂH said unto ABRAHAM, "I know that I am barren. Go thou in to this my handmaiden whom PHARAOH gave unto me; peradventure God will give thee seed in her. As for me, my person is shrunk and withered, and the flower of my body hath dried up." And she gave 'AGÂR unto him. And ABRAHAM went in to 'AGÂR, and she conceived by him, and she brought forth a son and called his name ISHMAEL, which is, being interpreted, "God hath heard me." And afterwards God gave ABRAHAM seed from his wife SÂRÂH and he begat ISAAC. And afterwards SÂRÂH became jealous of ISHMAEL, the son of her handmaiden, because he would reach manhood before her son, and she said, "Peradventure he will slay my son and inherit his father's house." And ABRAHAM offered up offerings to God and said, "Lord, what shall I do in respect of ISHMAEL, my son, my firstborn? I wish him to live for me before Thee, but SÂRÂH, my sister, is jealous because Thou hast given me seed in her old age." Now ISHMAEL was fourteen years old before ISAAC was born. And God said unto ABRAHAM, "What SÂRÂH saith is true; cast out the handmaiden with her son ISHMAEL. Let ISHMAEL live before Me, and I will make him a great nation, and he shall beget twelve nations and shall reign over them. And I will establish My covenant with ISAAC My servant, the son of SÂRÂH, and in him I will bless all the nations of the earth, and I will make for him a great kingdom over all the nations of the earth, and in the heavens also I will make him king."[80]

Footnotes
79. Pieces of money in silver.
80. Genesis xii ff.

83. Concerning the King of the ISHMAELITES

And therefore the children of ISHMAEL became kings over TEREB, and over KEBET, and over NÔBÂ, and SÔBA, and KUERGUE, and KÎFÎ, and MÂKÂ, and MÔRNÂ, and FÎNKÂNÂ, and 'ARSÎBÂNÂ, and LÎBÂ, and MASE'A, for they were the seed of SHEM. And ISAAC reigned over JUDAH and over 'AMÔRÊWÔN, and over KÊTÊWÔN, and 'ÎYÂBÛSÊWÔN, and FÊRZÊWÔN, and 'EÊWÊWÔN, and KÊKÊDÊWÔN, and RÔMYÂ, and 'ANSÔKYÂ (ANTIOCHIA), and SÔRYÂ (SYRIA), and ARMENIA, and FELESTEÊM (PALESTINE), and ETHIOPIA, and EDOM, and PHILISTIA, and ÎYÔÂB, and AMALEK, and PHRYGIA, and BABYLON, and YÔNÂNEST, and 'EBRÂYAST. For as God sware He gave all kingdoms to the seed of SHEM, and an exalted throne and dominion to the seed of SHEM, even as his father NOAH, by the word of God, blessed his son SHEM, saying, "Be lord to thy brethren and reign over them." And this that he said had reference to the Redeemer, the King of us all, JESUS CHRIST the King of heaven and earth, Who magnifieth kings, and Who when He pleaseth abrogateth their power; for unto Him belong power and dominion over all created things for ever and ever. Amen.

84. Concerning the King of ETHIOPIA and how he returned to his country

And the King of ETHIOPIA returned to his country with great joy and gladness; and marching along with their songs, and their pipes, and their wagons, like an army of heavenly beings, the ETHIOPIANS arrived from JERUSALEM at the city of WAKÊRÔM in a single day. And they sent messengers in ships to announce [their arrival] to MÂKĔDÂ, the Queen of ETHIOPIA, and to report to her how they had found every good thing, and how her son had become king, and how they had brought the heavenly ZION. And she caused all this glorious news to be spread abroad, and she made a herald to go round about in all the country that was subject unto her, ordering the people to meet her son and more particularly the heavenly ZION, the Tabernacle of the God of ISRAEL. And they blew horns before her, and all the people of ETHIOPIA rejoiced, from the least to the greatest, men as well as women; and the soldiers rose up with her to meet their King. And she came to the city of the Government, which is the chief city of the kingdom of ETHIOPIA; now in later times this [city] became the chief city of the Christians of ETHIOPIA. And in it she caused to be prepared perfumes innumerable from INDIA, and from BÂLTÊ to GÂLTÊT, and from 'ALSÂFU to 'AZAZAT, and had them brought together there. And her son came by the 'AZYÂBÂ road to WAKÊRÔM, and he came forth to MASAS, and ascended to BÛR, and arrived at the city of the Government, the capital [city] of ETHIOPIA, which the Queen herself had built and called "DABRA MÂKĔDÂ", after her own name.

85. Concerning the rejoicing of Queen MÂKĔDÂ

And DAVID the King came with great pomp unto his mother's city, and then he saw in the height the heavenly ZION sending forth light like the sun. And when the Queen saw this she gave thanks unto the God of ISRAEL, and praised Him. And she bowed low, and smote her breast, and [then] threw up her head and gazed into the heavens, and thanked her Creator; and she clapped her hands together, and sent forth shouts of laughter from her mouth, and danced on the ground with her feet; and she adorned her whole body with joy and gladness with the fullest will of her inward mind. And what shall I say of the rejoicing which took place then in the country of ETHIOPIA, and of the joy of the people, both of man and beast, from the least to the greatest, and of both women and men? And pavilions and tents were placed at the foot of DABRA MÂKĔDÂ on the flat plain by the side of good water, and they slaughtered thirty-two thousand stalled oxen and bulls. And they set ZION upon the fortress of DABRA MÂKĔDÂ, and made ready for her three hundred guards who wielded swords to watch over the pavilion of ZION, together with her own men and her nobles, the mighty men of ISRAEL. And her own guards were three hundred men who bore swords, and in addition to these her son DAVID had seven hundred [guards]. And they rejoiced exceedingly with great glory and pleasure [being arrayed] in fine apparel, for the kingdom was directed by her from the Sea of 'ALÊBÂ to the Sea of 'ÔSÊKÂ, and everyone obeyed her command. And she had exceedingly great honour and riches; none before her ever had the like, and none after her shall ever have the like. In those days SOLOMON was King in JERUSALEM, and MÂKĔDÂ was Queen in ETHIOPIA. Unto both of them were given wisdom, and glory, and riches, and graciousness, and understanding, and beauty of voice (or, eloquence of speech), and intelligence. And gold and silver were held as cheaply as brass, and rich stuffs wherein gold was woven were as common as linen garments, and the cattle and the horses were innumerable.

86. How Queen MÂKĔDÂ made her son King

And on the third day MÂKĔDÂ delivered over to her son seventeen thousand and seven hundred chosen horses, which were to watch the army of the enemy, and would again plunder the cities of the enemy, and seven thousand and seven hundred mares that had borne foals, and one thousand female mules, and seven hundred chosen mules, and apparel of honour, gold and silver measured by the gômôr, and measured by the Kôr, some six and some seven, and she delivered over to her son everything that was his by law, and all the throne of her kingdom.

87. How the nobles (or governors) of ETHIOPIA took the oath

And the Queen said unto her nobles: "Speak ye now, and swear ye by the heavenly ZION that ye will not make women queens or set them upon the throne of the kingdom of ETHIOPIA, and that no one except the male seed of DAVID, the son of SOLOMON the King, shall ever reign over ETHIOPIA, and that ye will never make women queens." And all the nobles of the king's house swore, and the governors, and the councillors, and the administrators.

And she made ÊLMĔYÂS and 'AZÂRYÂS (AZARIAH) the chief of the priests and the chief of the deacons, and they made the kingdom anew, and the sons of the mighty men of ISRAEL performed the Law, together with their King DAVID, in the Tabernacle of Witness, and the kingdom was made anew. And the hearts of the people shone at the sight of ZION, the Tabernacle of the Law of God, and the people of ETHIOPIA cast aside their idols, and they worshipped their Creator, the God Who had made them. And the men of ETHIOPIA forsook their works, and loved the righteousness and justice that God loveth. They forsook their former fornications, and chose purity in the camp that was in the sight of the heavenly ZION. They forsook divination and magic, and chose repentance and tears for God's sake. They forsook augury by means of birds and the use of omens, and they returned to hearken unto God and to make sacrifice unto Him. They forsook the pleasures of the gods who were devils, and chose the service and praise of God. The daughters of JERUSALEM suffered disgrace, and the daughters of ETHIOPIA were held in honour; the daughter of JUDAH was sad, whilst the daughter of ETHIOPIA rejoiced; the mountains of ETHIOPIA rejoiced, and the mountains of LEBANON mourned. The people of ETHIOPIA were chosen [from] among idols and graven images, and the people of ISRAEL were rejected. The daughters of ZION were rejected, and the daughters of ETHIOPIA were honoured; the old men of ISRAEL became objects of contempt, and the old men of ETHIOPIA were honoured. For God accepted the peoples who had been cast away and rejected ISRAEL, for ZION was taken away from them and she came into the country of ETHIOPIA. For wheresoever God is pleased for her to dwell, there is her habitation, and where He is not pleased that she should dwell she dwelleth not; He is her founder, and Maker, and Builder, the Good God in the temple of His holiness, the habitation of His glory, with His Son and the Holy Spirit, for ever and ever. Amen.

And MÂKĔDÂ, the Queen of ETHIOPIA, gave the kingdom to her son DAVID, the son of SOLOMON, the King of ISRAEL, and she said unto him,

"Take [the kingdom]. I have given [it] unto thee. I have made King him whom God hath made King, and I have chosen him whom God hath chosen as the keeper of His Pavilion. I am well pleased with him whom God hath been Pleased to make the envoy of the Tabernacle of His Covenant and His Law. I have magnified him whom God hath magnified [as] the director of His widows, and I have honoured him whom God hath honoured [as] the giver of food to orphans."

And the King rose up and girded up his apparel, and he bowed low before his mother, and said unto her, "Thou art the Queen, O my Lady, and I will serve thee in every thing which thou commandest me, whether it be to death or whether it be to life. Wheresoever thou sendest me I will be sent, and wheresoever thou orderest me to be there will I be, and whatsoever thou commandest me to do that will I do. For thou are the head and I am the foot, and thou art the Lady and I am thy slave; everything shall be performed according to thy order, and none shall transgress thy commandment, and I will do everything that thou wishest. But pray for me that the God of ISRAEL may deliver me from His wrath. For He will be wroth - according to what they tell us - if we do not make our hearts right to do His Will, and if we do not readily observe all His commands in respect to ZION, the habitation of the glory of God. For the Angel of His host is with us, who directed us and brought us hither, and he shall neither depart from us nor forsake us.

"And now, hearken unto me, O my Lady. If I and those who are after me behave rightly and do His Will, God shall dwell with us, and shall preserve us from all evil and from the hand of our enemy. But if we do not keep our hearts right with Him He will be wroth with us, and will turn away His face from us, and will punish us, and our enemies will plunder us, and fear and trembling shall come to us from the place whence we expect them not, and they will rise up against us, and will overcome us in war, and will destroy us. On the other hand, if we do the Will of God, and do what is right in respect of ZION, we shall become chosen men, and no one shall have the power to treat us evilly in the mountain of His holiness whilst His habitation is with us.

"And behold, we have brought with us the whole Law of the kingdom and the commandment of God, which ZADOK the high priest declared unto us when he anointed me with the oil of sovereignty in the house of the sanctuary of God, the horn of oil, which is the unguent of priesthood and royalty, being in his hand. And he did unto us that which was written in the Law, and we were anointed; AZARIAH to the priesthood and I to the kingdom, and 'ALMĔYÂS, the mouth of God, keeper of the Law, that is to say, keeper of ZION, and the Ear of the King in every path of righteousness. And they commanded me that I should do nothing except under their advice, and they set us before the King and before the elders of ISRAEL, and all the people heard whilst ZADOK the priest was giving us the commands. And the horns and the organs were blown, and the sounds of their harps and musical instruments, and the noise of their outcries which were made at that time were in the gates of JERUSALEM. But what shall I tell unto you, O ye who were present there? It seemed to us that the earth quaked from her very foundations, and that the heavens above our heads thundered, and the heart trembled with the knees."

88. How he himself related to his mother how they made him King

"And when these had become silent there rose up the priest who gave us the Commandments, with the fear of God, and he shed tears whilst our bodies quaked and our tears flowed down. God is indeed, without falsehood, in our hearts, and He dwelleth in His commandment. And His commandment is uttered, and it removeth itself not from those who love Him and who keep His commandment, and He is with them continually. And now, hearken to the judgment and laws which the elders and the sons of the mighty men of ISRAEL brought, which they wrote before King SOLOMON and have given unto us, so that we may not turn aside either to the right hand or to the left from what they have commanded us. And also they told us and made us to understand that we bear death and life, and that we are like unto a man who hath fire in his left hand and water in his right, and who can put his hand into whichever he pleaseth. For punishment and life are written therein; for those who have done evil, punishment, and for those who have done good, life."

And 'ÊLMĔYÂS and AZARIAH brought forth that writing which was written before God and before the King of ISRAEL, and they read it before MÂKĔDÂ and before the great men of ISRAEL. And when they heard these words all those who were round about, both small and great, bowed down and made obeisance, and they glorified God Who had made them hear these words and had given them this commandment, so that they might perform the justice and judgment of God. And moreover, He made them members of His house, for ZION was among them, and she is the habitation of the glory of God, and she delivered them from all evil, and blessed the fruit of their lands, and multiplied their sheep and cattle, and blessed their wells of water, and blessed their labours, and the fruit of their gardens, and made their children to grow up, and protected their aged men, and became the foreguard and rearguard wheresoever they dwelt, and vanquished their enemies wheresoever they went. And all the people of ETHIOPIA rejoiced.

And the Queen said unto her son, "My son, God hath given unto thee the right, walk thou therein and withdraw not thyself from it, neither to the right hand nor the left. And love thou the Lord thy God, for He is merciful unto the simple-minded. For His way is known from His commandment, and His goodness is comprehended through the guidance of His word."

Then she turned towards 'ÊLMĔYÂS and AZARIAH and all the mighty men of ISRAEL [saying], "Do ye protect him and teach him the path of the kingdom of God, and the honour of our Lady ZION. And whatsoever our Lady loveth not let us not do. Tell us [this] truly and carefully for ever and from generation to generation, so that she may not be wroth with us, if we do not perform her service well, so that God may dwell with us. And thou, my son, hearken unto the word of thy fathers, and walk in their counsel. And let not drink make thee foolish, nor women, nor pride of apparel, nor the bridles and trappings of horses, nor the sight of the weapons of war of those who are at the head or at the rear. But let thy confidence be in God and in ZION, the Tabernacle of the Law of God, thy Creator, so that thou mayest vanquish thine enemy, and so that thy seed upon the earth may multiply, and so that thy foes and adversaries, near and far, may be overthrown."

And those sons of mighty men answered and said with one voice, "O our Lady, we are with you always, and we will remember the lord, the King. Behold, what is written and the performance thereof shall take place if the God of ISRAEL shall be unto him a helper, and if he hearkeneth to the word of his mother; and we will inform him about the path of doing good works. For there is no one to be found in these days as wise as thyself, except our lord the King. Thou hast drawn us hither as thy servants with our Lady, the heavenly ZION, the Tabernacle of the Law of the Lord our God just as a man draweth a camel that is loaded with valuable possessions with a little piece of thin, tough cord fastened over his nose. And now, reject us not and treat us not as strange people, but make us like unto thy slaves who wash thy feet, for whether we die or whether we live we are with thee; we have no longer any hope in the country of our birth, but only in thee and in our Lady the heavenly ZION, the habitation of the glory of God."

89. *How the Queen talked to the Children of ISRAEL*

And the Queen answered and said unto them, "Not as servants as ye say but as a father and a teacher will we treat you. For ye are the guardians of the Law of God, and the guides of the commandment of the God of ISRAEL, and the men of the house of God, and the guardians of ZION, the Tabernacle of the Law of God, and we do not wish to transgress your commandments, for ye shall be unto us a guide to the path of God away from all evil. At your words we will withdraw from that wherewith God is not well-pleased, and we will draw nigh unto every good thing wherewith God is well-pleased at your commandment. Only do ye instruct all this people, and teach them the words of knowledge, for never before have they heard such things as they have heard this day. It is only those who have understanding in them that wisdom and understanding illumine like the light of the sun. As for me, up to this present I have not drunk deeply of the water of knowledge. Now it is sweeter than honey, and quencheth the thirst more than wine, and it satisfieth and maketh wisdom to bubble up, and it stimulateth the understanding, and maketh a man to pour forth words like a drunken man, and maketh the unsteady man like one who flieth, and maketh a man as hot as he that carrieth a heavy load on a difficult road in a parched land that is burnt up by a blazing sun. When the hearts of the wise are open to prophecy and to knowledge, they do not fear the king because of the greatness of his glory if he turneth himself aside from the way of God. And mark this: The word of the Law, which hath been uttered, is indeed understanding unto those who wish for it, and who drink it in and soak themselves therein. I pray Thee, O Lord God of ISRAEL, Thou Holiest of the

Holy, grant unto me that I may follow wisdom, and may not become a castaway; grant unto me that I may make her a wall unto myself, and may never fall down; grant that I may make her a foundation for me, and may never be overthrown; grant that I may stand upon her as [firmly as] a pillar, and may never shake; grant that I may hide in her, and never have her stripped from me; grant that I may build myself upon her, and may not topple over; grant that I may become vigorous through her, and not suffer from exhaustion; grant that I may stand through her, and may not fall; grant that I may lay hold upon her, and may not slip away; grant that I may grasp her firmly, and may not slide; grant that I may dwell in her in her peace; [grant that] I may be satisfied at her table, and may not vomit, and drink her and not get drunk upon her, and may be satisfied with her and not spit her out.

"I have drunk of her, but have not tottered; I have tottered through her, but have not fallen; I have fallen because of her, but have not been destroyed. Through her I have dived down into the great sea and have seized in the place of her depths a pearl whereby I am rich. I went down like the great iron anchor whereby men anchor ships for the night on the high seas, and I received a lamp which lighteth me, and I came up by the ropes of the boat of understanding. I went to sleep in the depths of the sea, and not being overwhelmed with the water I dreamed a dream. And it seemed to me that there was a star in my womb, and I marvelled thereat, and I laid hold upon it and made it strong in the splendour of the sun; I laid hold upon it, and I will never let it go. I went in through the doors of the treasury of wisdom and I drew for myself the waters of understanding. I went into the blaze of the flame of the sun, and it lighted me with the splendour thereof, and I made of it a shield for myself, and I saved myself by confidence therein, and not myself only but all those who travel in the footprints of wisdom, and not myself only but all the men of my country, the kingdom of ETHIOPIA, and not those only but those who travel in their ways, the nations that are round about. For the Lord hath given us seed in ZION and a habitation in JERUSALEM[81]. And moreover, there hath come to us a portion with those whom He hath chosen, the seed of JACOB, for He hath set His habitation to abide with us. From this time forth they are set down, and from this time forth we are set upright. From this time forth they are despised and rejected, and from this time forth we shall be honoured and loved for ever and ever and throughout all the generations that are to come.

"And ye, O noble ones, hearken unto me, and learn well what cometh forth from my mouth and my words. Love ye what is right and hate falsehood, for what is right is righteousness and falsehood is the head of iniquity. And ye shall not use fraud and oppression among yourselves, for God dwelleth with you, and the habitation of His glory is among you; for ye have become members of His household. And from this time onward cease ye to observe your former customs, [namely] making auguries from birds, and from signs, and the use of charms, and incantations, and portents, and magic. And if after this day there be found any man who observeth all his former customs, his house shall be plundered, and he and his wife and his children shall be condemned."

And the Queen said unto AZARIAH, "Speak and declare how much thou lovest our Lady with her Heavenly King."

Footnotes
81. Compare the LXX Isaiah xxxi. 9. A mistranslation of the Hebrew text?

90. How AZARIAH praised the Queen and her city
And AZARIAH rose up and said unto the Queen, "O our Lady, verily there is no one like unto thee in wisdom and understanding - the which have been given unto thee by God - except my lord the King, who hath brought us unto this land with our Lady ZION, the holy and heavenly Tabernacle of the Law of God. Now we and our fathers of olden time have said, God hath chosen none except the House of JACOB, us hath He chosen, us hath He multiplied, us hath He held to please Him, and He hath made us kings and made us members of His household, and councillors of His glory and of the Tabernacle of His covenant. And as for a country, we say that He hath chosen no country except ours, but now we see that the country of ETHIOPIA is better than the country of JUDAH. And from the time that we arrived in your country everything that we have seen hath appeared good to us. Your waters are good and they are given without price (or, payment), and [we have] air without fans, and wild honey is as [plentiful as] the dust of the market place, and cattle as the sand of the sea. And as for what we have seen there is nothing detestable, and there is nothing malign in what we hear, and in what we walk upon, and in what we touch, and in what we taste with our mouths. But there is one matter that we would mention: ye are black of face - I only state this [fact] because I can see [that ye are] - but if God illumineth (i.e., maketh white) your hearts, [as far as your colour is concerned] nothing can injure you.

"And withdraw ye yourselves from meat that dieth of itself, and from blood, and from bodies torn by wild animals, and from fornication, and from everything that God hateth, so that we may rejoice in you when we see you fearing God and trembling at His word; even as God commanded our fathers and said unto MOSES, 'Give them commands about everything, and tell them to keep My Law and My Ordinance.'[82] And turn ye not aside, neither to the right hand nor to the left, from that which we command you this day; and now [we command] you that ye worship God, the Holy One of ISRAEL, and do His good pleasure; for He hath rejected our nation even as our prophets prophesied, and hath chosen you. Doth not God your Creator belong to all of you? In what will God find it difficult if He loveth us and hateth them? For everything belongeth to Him, and everything is His handiwork, and there is nothing impossible for the Lord God of ISRAEL.

"And hearken ye unto His command, which I will declare unto you. Let not one overcome his fellow by violence. Plunder not the possessions of your neighbours. Ye shall not revile each other, and ye shall not oppress each other, and ye shall not quarrel with each other. And if by chance an animal belonging to your neighbour come among your property, be not blind to the fact but make it go back to him. And if ye do not know who is the owner of the property, take care of it for him, and as soon as one hath found out to whom it belongeth return his property to him. And if the property of your neighbour hath fallen into a pit, or into a well, or into a hollow or into a ravine, do not pass on and go not by it until ye have told him and helped him to drag out the animal. And if a man hath dug a well or hath built a tower (or, shelter), he shall not leave the well without a cover nor the tower without a roof. And if there is a man who is carrying a heavy load, or if the load hath slipped from the man who is carrying it, ye shall not pass on your way until ye have helped him to lift it up or to lighten it for him; for he is your brother. Ye shall not cook a young animal in the milk of his mother. Ye shall not turn aside the right of the poor and the orphans. Ye shall not accept the person, and ye shall not take bribes to turn aside the right and bear false witness.

"And when ye find a bird in your land with her young ones, ye shall spare her life and shall not take away her young, so that your days may be long upon the earth, and your seed may be blessed with (or, for) length of days. And when ye reap the harvest of your food, ye shall not be careful to reap all of it. Gather not up what falleth from it, and the sheaves which ye have forgotten leave when ye go back, and take them not up, but leave them for the stranger in your city, so that God may bless the fruit of your land. And ye shall not work impurity, and ye shall not judge with partiality, and ye shall not deal oppressively with one another in anything, so that ye may be blessed, and so that the fruit of your land may increase, and so that ye may be saved from the curse of the Law which God hath commanded, saying, 'They shall curse the worker of evil.' And He wrote, saying, 'He who leadeth the blind man out of his path is accursed. And he who addresseth vile words to a deaf (or, dumb) man is accursed. And he who defileth his father's bed is accursed. And he who beateth his neighbour with fraud is accursed. And he who perverteth justice for the alien so that he may slay innocent blood is accursed. And he who treateth his father and his mother lightly is accursed. And he who maketh a filthy graven image of stone or smelted metal, the work of a man's hand, and setteth it up and hideth it in his house, and worshippeth it as a god, not believing that God is the Creator of the heavens and the earth, Who made ADAM in His own image and likeness, and set him over everything which He had created, we all being His work - the man who doth not believe [this] accursed let him be! Amen. And he who lieth with a beast, let him be accursed. And he who lieth with a man as with a woman, let him be accursed. And he who slayeth a life, innocent blood, with fraud and violence, let him be accursed.'[83]

"And over and above all these things ye shall worship no other gods, for God is jealous concerning those who despise Him and do thus, and He setteth His face upon them until He rooteth out their lives from the earth, and blotteth out their memory for ever. Blessed are those who hearken to the voice of God, and perform and keep [His commandments]. And blessed are those who turn aside from those who do evil, so that none of the punishments which shall come upon sinners shall fall upon them. And if it be that thou wilt keep the word of God, withdraw thyself from the way of sinners, so that thou mayest not be beaten with the rod wherewith they shall be beaten. Even as DAVID the grandfather of our lord DAVID saith, 'God will not let the rod of sinners [fall] upon the portion of the righteous,' so that the righteous may not lift up their hands in violence (or, oppression). When a man hath the power to do that which is good, and he watcheth himself and telleth his neighbour, he becometh as it were the owner of two talents,[84] and yet other two talents are added to him, and he getteth abundant reward from God. For he hath done it himself and taught his neighbour to do it, and because of this his reward shall be exceedingly great. And again, blessed shall ye be if ye give your possessions, without usury and not as loans."

Footnotes
82. Compare Deuteronomy iv. 1.
83. Deuteronomy xxvii. 15 ff.
84. Compare Matthew xxv. 22.

91. This is what ye shall eat: the clean and the unclean
 And this is what ye shall eat: the clean and that which is not clean. The ox, the sheep, the goat, the ram, the stag, the gazelle, the buffalo, the deskĕna antelope, the we῾elâ antelope, the oryx, the zĕrât gazelle, and every creature with a cleft hoof and nails eat ye, and the creatures that chew the cud. And these which ye shall not eat among those that chew the cud and have a cleft hoof are the camels and the hare and the kârgĕlyôn (coney ?), for they chew the cud but their hoofs are not cleft. The wolf and the pig ye shall not eat, for their hoofs are cleft but they do not chew the cud: ye shall not eat what is unclean. Whatsoever is in the waters with fins and scales eat ye; whatsoever is unclean therein eat ye not. Among birds everything that is clean eat ye, but ye shall not eat the following: the eagle, the vulture, the 'êlyâtân eagle, the osprey, the hawk, and the like, the raven, ostrich, the owl, the sea-gull, the heron, the swan, the ibis, the pelican, the hawk, the hoopoe, the night raven, the hornbill, the water-piper, the water-hen, and the bat; these are unclean. And ye shall not eat the locust nor anything of his kind, nor the 'aKâtân nor anything of his kind, nor the grasshopper nor anything of his kind, nor the field locust nor anything of his kind. Of the things that fly (or, spring) and have two or four or six feet, their flesh is unclean, ye shall not eat thereof. And ye shall not touch their dead bodies, and whosoever toucheth them shall be unclean until the evening.
 "Now these things we have declared unto you in order that ye may keep and perform the fear of God so that ye may be blessed in this your country, which God hath given unto you because of the heavenly ZION, the Tabernacle of the Law of God, for because of her have ye been chosen. And our fathers have been rejected, because God took from them ZION, the Tabernacle of the Law of God, to keep

you and your seed for ever. And He will bless the fruit of your land, and He will multiply your cattle, and will protect them in everything wherein they are to be protected.

"And as for thee, O my Lady, thy wisdom is good, and it surpasseth the wisdom of men. There is none that can be compared with thee in respect of thy intelligence, not only in the matter of the intuition of the women who have been created up to this present, but the understanding of thine heart is deeper than that of men, and there is none who can be compared with thee in the abundance of thine understanding, except my lord SOLOMON. And thy wisdom so far exceedeth that of SOLOMON that thou hast been able to draw hither the mighty men of ISRAEL, and the Tabernacle of the Law of God, with the ropes of thine understanding, and thou hast overthrown the house of their idols, and destroyed their images, and thou hast cleansed what was unclean among thy people, for thou hast driven away from them that which God hateth.

"And as concerning thy name, God hath prepared it [especially], for He hath called thee 'MÂKĔDÂ', whereof the interpretation is 'Not thus'. Consider thou [the people] of thy nation with whom God was not well pleased, and thou wilt say 'Not thus [is it] good, but it is right that we should worship God'; 'Not thus is it good to worship the sun, but it is right to worship God,' thou wilt say. 'Not thus is it good to enquire of the diviner, but it is better to trust in God,' thou wilt say. 'Not thus is it good to resort to the working of magic, but it is better to lean upon the Holy One of ISRAEL,' thou wilt say. 'Not thus is it good to offer up sacrifices to stones and trees, but it is right to offer up sacrifices to God,' thou wilt say. 'Not thus is it good to seek augury from birds, but it is right to put confidence in the Creator,' thou wilt say.

"And besides, inasmuch as thou hast chosen wisdom she hath become to thee a mother; thou didst seek her, and she hath become unto thee a treasure. Thou hast made her a place of refuge for thyself, and she hath become to thee a wall. Thou hast desired her eagerly, and she hath loved thee above everything. Thou hast placed thy confidence in her, and she hath taken thee to her bosom like a child. Thou hast loved her, and she hath become unto thee as thou didst desire. Thou hast laid hold upon her, and she will not let thee go until the day of thy death. Thou hast been sorrowful on her account, and she hath made thee to rejoice for ever. Thou hast toiled for her sake, and she hath made thee vigorous for ever. Thou hast hungered for her sake, and she hath filled thee with food for ever. Thou hast thirsted for wisdom, and she hath given thee drink in abundance for ever. Thou hast suffered tribulation for the sake of wisdom, and she hath become unto thee a healing for ever. Thou hast made thyself deaf for the sake of wisdom, and she hath made thee to hear for ever. Thou hast made thyself blind for the sake of wisdom, and she hath illumined thee more than the sun for ever. And all this hath happened from God because thou hast loved wisdom for ever. For wisdom, and knowledge, and understanding are from the Lord. Understanding and knowledge, and the beginning of wisdom, and the fear of the Lord, and knowledge, and the perception of good, and sympathy, and compassion that existeth for ever, all these things thou hast found, O my Lady, with the God of ISRAEL, the Holy of the holiest, the Knower of hearts, Who searcheth out what is in the heart of man; from Him everything is. And it came to pass by the Will of God, that ZION hath come unto this country of ETHIOPIA, and it shall be a guide to our King DAVID, the lover of God, the guardian of her pavilion, and the director of the habitation of His glory."

92. How they renewed the kingdom of DAVID

And AZARIAH said, "Bring hither the jubilee trumpets, and let us go to ZION, and there we will make new the kingdom of our lord DAVID." And he took the oil of sovereignty and filled the horn [therewith], and he anointed DAVID with the unguent, that is to say, with the oil of sovereignty. And they blew horns and pipes and trumpets, and beat drums, and sounded all kinds of musical instruments, and there were singing and dancing and games, and [displays] with horses and shield [-men], and all the men and women of the people of the country of ETHIOPIA were present, small and great, and the little Blacks, six thousand in number, and virgin women whom AZARIAH had chosen for the women of ZION by the law, whom DAVID the King had destined for [the service of] the table and banquets in the royal fortress when he should go up thereto [clad in] raiment of fine gold. And in this wise was renewed the kingdom of DAVID, the son of SOLOMON the king of ISRAEL, in the capital city, in Mount MÂKĔDÂ, in the House of ZION, when the Law was established for the first time by the King of ETHIOPIA.

And then when he had completed the stablishing of the Law, they made, according to what they had seen in JERUSALEM, the Law in the House of ZION for the nobles of the kingdom, and for those who were inside, and for those that were outside, and for the people, and for the islands, and for the cities, and for the provinces; and for all the inhabitants and for all their tribal kinsfolk they made ordinances in the same manner. And thus the eastern boundary of the kingdom of the King of ETHIOPIA is the beginning of the city of GÂZÂ in the land of JUDAH, that is, JERUSALEM; and its boundary is the Lake of JERICHO, and it passeth on by the coast of its sea to LÊBÂ and SÂBÂ; and its boundary goeth down to BÎSÎS and 'ASNÊT; and its boundary is the Sea of the Blacks and Naked Men, and goeth up Mount KÊBÊRÊNÊYÔN into the Sea of Darkness, that is to say, the place where the sun setteth; and its boundary extendeth to FÊNÊ'ÊL and LASÎFÂLÂ; and its borders are the lands [near] the Garden (i.e., Paradise), where there is food in plenty and abundance of cattle, and [near] FÊNÊKÊN; and its boundary reacheth as far as ZÂWÊL and passeth on to the Sea of INDIA; and its boundary is as far as the Sea of TARSÎS, and in its remote (?) part lieth the Sea of MEDYÂM, until it cometh to the country of GÂZÂ; and its boundary is the place where [our enumeration] began. And moreover, the dominion of the King of ETHIOPIA belongeth to him and to his seed for ever.

93. How the Men of RÔMÊ destroyed the Faith

And after they had waited for three months - now ZION came into the country of ETHIOPIA at the beginning of the first month in the language of the HEBREWS, and in Greek TÂRMÔN and in GĔ'ĔZ (ETHIOPIC) MÎYÂZYÂ, on the sixth (or, seventh) day - they wrote down the Law and the names, and they deposited [the writing] for a memorial for the later days, so that what was right should be done for the pavilion [of ZION] thereby, and so that the glory of the kings of ETHIOPIA and the glory of the kings of RÔMÊ might be well known. For the kings of ETHIOPIA and the kings of RÔMÊ were brethren and held the Christian Faith. Now first of all they believed in an orthodox manner in the preaching of the Apostles up to [the time of] CONSTANTINE, and 'ĔLÊNÎ (HELENA) the Queen, who brought forth the wood of the Cross, and they (i.e., the kings of RÔMÊ) continued [to believe for] one hundred and thirty years.

And afterwards, SATAN, who hath been the enemy of man from of old, rose up, and seduced the people of the country of RÔMÊ, and they corrupted the Faith of CHRIST, and they introduced heresy into the Church of God by the mouth of NESTORIUS. And NESTORIUS, and ARIUS, and YABÂSÔ (?) were those into whose hearts he cast the same jealousy as he had cast into the heart of CAIN to slay his brother ABEL. In like manner did their father the Devil, the enemy of righteousness and the hater of good, cast jealousy, even as DAVID saith, "They speak violence in the heights of heaven, and set their mouths in the heavens, and their tongue waggeth on the earth."[85] And those same men who know not whence they came, and know not whither they are going, revile their Creator with their tongues, and blaspheme His glory, while He is God, the Word of the Lord. He came down from the throne of His Godhead, and put on the body of ADAM, and He is God the Word. And in that body He was crucified so that He might redeem ADAM in his iniquity, and He went up into the heavens, and sat upon the throne of His Godhead in that body, which He had taken. And He shall come again in glory to judge the living and the dead, and shall reward every man according to his work, for ever and ever. Amen.

And we believe thus and we adore the Holy Trinity. And those who do not believe thus are excommunicated by the Word of God, the King of heaven and earth, both in this world and in that world which is to come. And we are strong in the Orthodox Faith which the Fathers the Apostles have delivered unto us, the Faith of the Church. And thus ETHIOPIA continued to abide in her Faith until the coming of our Lord JESUS CHRIST, to Whom be glory forever and ever. Amen.

Footnotes
85. Psalm lxxiii. 8, 9.

94. The first war of the King of ETHIOPIA

And after three months they (i.e., DAVID and his soldiers) rose up to wage war from the city of the Government, with MÂKĔDÂ his mother and ZION his Lady. And the LEVITES carried the Tabernacle of the Law, together with the things that appertained to their office, and they marched along with great majesty, and as in times of old when God on Mount SINAI made ZION to come down in holiness to MOSES and AARON, even so did AZARIAH and 'ÊLMÎYÂS bear along the Tabernacle of the Law. And the other mighty men of war of ISRAEL, marched on the right side of it and on the left, and close to it, and before it and behind it, and although they were beings made of dust they sang psalms and songs of the spirit like the heavenly hosts. And God gave them beautiful voices and marvellous songs, for He was well pleased to be praised by them.

And they came from the city of the Government, and encamped at MÂYA 'ABAW, and on the following morning they laid waste the district of ZÂWÂ with HADĔYÂ, for enmity had existed between them from olden time; and they blotted out the people and slew them with the edge of the sword. And they passed on from that place and encamped at GÊRRÂ, and here also they laid waste the city of vipers that had the faces of men, and the tails of asses attached to their loins.

And [the Queen] returned and encamped in the city of ZION, and they remained therein three months, then their wagons moved on and came to the city of the Government. And in one day they came to the city of SÂBÂ, and they laid waste NÔBÂ; and from there they camped round about SÂBÂ, and they laid it waste as far as the border of EGYPT. And the majesty (or, awe) of the King of ETHIOPIA was so great that the King of MĔDYÂM and the King of EGYPT caused gifts to be brought unto him, and they came into the city of the Government, and from there they encamped in 'AB'ÂT, and they waged war on the country of INDIA, and the King of INDIA brought a gift and a present (or, tribute), and himself did homage to the King of ETHIOPIA. He (i.e., DAVID) waged war wheresoever he pleased; no man conquered him, on the contrary, whosoever attacked him was conquered. And as for those who would have played the spy in his camp, in order to hear some story and relate it in their city, they were unable to run by the wagons, for ZION herself made the strength of the enemy to be exhausted. But King DAVID, with his soldiers, and the armies of his soldiers, and all those who obeyed his word, ran by the wagons without pain or suffering, and without hunger or thirst, and without sweat or exhaustion, and travelled in one day a distance which [usually] took three months to traverse. And they lacked nothing whatsoever of the things which they asked God through ZION the Tabernacle of the Law of God to give them, for He dwelt with her, and His Angel directed her, and she was His habitation. And as for the king who ministered to His pavilion - if he were travelling on any journey, and wished something to be done, everything that he wished for and thought about in his heart, and indicated with his finger, everything [I say] was performed at his word; and everyone feared him. But he feared no one, for the hand of God was with him, and it protected him by day and by night. And he did His Will, and God worked for him and protected him from all evil for ever and ever. Amen.

This I found among the manuscripts of the Church of SOPHIA in CONSTANTINOPLE. And the Archbishops who were there said unto him [DOMITIUS ?], "This is what is written from the days of SOLOMON the King." And DOMITIUS of ANTIOCH said, "Yea, that which is written up to the day of the death of SOLOMON is to be accepted, and that which hath been written by other prophets after his death is to be accepted likewise."

95. How the honourable estate of the King of ETHIOPIA was universally accepted

Now through the KEBRA NAGAST we know and have learned that of a surety the King of ETHIOPIA is honourable, and that he is the King of ZION, and the firstborn of the seed of SHEM, and that the habitation of God is in ZION, and that He there breaketh the might and power of all his enemies and foes. And after him the King of RÔMÊ was the anointed of the Lord because of the wood of the Cross. And as concerning the kingdom of ISRAEL - when the Pearl was born of them, and of the Pearl again was born the Sun of Righteousness, Who hid Himself in her body - now had He not hidden Himself in the body of a man He could not have been seen by mortal eyes - and having put on our body He became like unto us, and He walked about with [men]. And He wrought signs and wonders in their midst. He raised their dead, and He healed their sick folk, and He made the eyes of their blind to see, and He opened the ears of their deaf folk, and He cleansed the lepers, and He satisfied the hungry with food, and He performed many miracles, some of which are written down and some of which are not, even as saith JOHN the Evangelist, the son of ZEBEDEE, "If everything which JESUS did were written down, the whole world would not be able to hold all the writings that would have to be written."[86]

And when the wicked children of ISRAEL saw all this they thought that He was a man, and they were envious of Him because of what they saw and heard, and they crucified Him upon the wood of the Cross, and they killed Him. And He rose from the dead on the third day, and went up into heaven in glory, [and sat] on the throne of the Godhead. And He received from the Father a kingdom incorruptible for ever and ever over the beings of the spirit, and the beings of earth, and over every created being, so that every tongue shall adore His Name, and every knee bow to Him; and He shall judge the living and the dead and reward every man according to his work. So therefore when the JEWS shall see Him they shall be put to shame, and shall be condemned to the fire which is everlasting. But we who believe in the Orthodox Faith shall be upon our throne, and we shall rejoice with our teachers the Apostles, provided that we have walked in the way of CHRIST and in His commandments. And after the JEWS crucified the Saviour of the world, they were scattered abroad, and their kingdom was destroyed, and they were made an end of and rooted out for ever and ever.

160

And all the saints who were gathered together said, "Assuredly, in very truth the King of ETHIOPIA is more exalted, and more honourable than any other king upon the earth, because of the glory and greatness of the heavenly ZION. And God loveth the people of ETHIOPIA, for without knowing about His Law, they destroyed their idols, whereas those unto whom the Law of God had been given made idols and worshipped the gods which God hateth. And in the later times when He was born to redeem ADAM He wrought signs and wonders before them, but they did not believe in Him, neither in His preaching nor in the preaching of His fathers. But the people of ETHIOPIA believed in one trustworthy disciple, and for this reason God hath loved exceedingly the people of ETHIOPIA."

And the Bishops answered and said unto him (GREGORY), "Well hast thou spoken, and thy word is true, and what thou hast expounded and interpreted to us is clear. Even as PAUL saith, 'Hath not the seed of ABRAHAM exalted the seed of SHEM?' They are all kings of the earth, but the chosen ones of the Lord are the people of ETHIOPIA. For there is the habitation of God, the heavenly ZION, the Tabernacle of His Law and the Tabernacle of His Covenant, which He hath made into a mercy-seat through [His] mercy for the children of men; for the rains and the waters from the sky, for the planted things (or, vegetation) and the fruits, for the peoples and the countries, for the kings and nobles, for men and beasts, for birds and creeping things."

And GREGORY the Bishop, the worker of wonders, answered and said unto them, "Verily, salvation hath been given unto all of us Christian people, unto those who have believed in our Lady MARY, the likeness of the heavenly ZION. For the Lord dwelt in the womb of the Virgin, and was brought forth by her without carnal union. And the Ten Words (Decalogue) of the Law were written by the Finger of God, and made (i.e., placed) in ZION, the Tabernacle of the Law of God. And now, come ye, and we will declare from the Law of MOSES the prophecies of the Prophets our Fathers, the holy men of olden time, and the prophecies concerning CHRIST our Redeemer, so that the generations of posterity may hear the interpretation (or, explanation) of the story, and we will relate unto them the narrative of the interpretation of the Scriptures. We will begin then with the beginning of the Book, and we will make [you] to understand in the Spirit, as DAVID saith, through the Holy Spirit, 'In the beginning the Book was written because of me.'"[87]

And one answered and said, "What is the beginning of the Book?" And they answered and said unto him, "It is the Law which was written concerning CHRIST, the Son of God. And it saith, 'In the beginning God made the heavens and the earth'[88]; and they existed from olden time. Now the earth was formless, but there were mixed together darkness, and winds, and water, and mist, and dust; all of these were mixed together. And the Spirit of God hovered above the waters. This meaneth that by the Word of God the heavens and the earth were created; and these words mean that the Spirit of God dwelt over all creation."

Footnotes
86. John xxi. 25.
87. Psalm xl. 7.
88. Genesis i. 1.

96. *Concerning the Prophecy about CHRIST*

Moreover MOSES proclaimed in the Law and said, "A prophet like myself shall rise up for you from your brethren, and hearken ye unto him; and every soul that will not hearken unto that prophet ye shall root out from among the people."[89] And this he said concerning CHRIST the Son of God. And he also prophesied concerning His Crucifixion, and said, "When the serpents afflicted the children of ISRAEL they cried out to MOSES, and MOSES cried out to God to deliver them from the serpents. And God said unto him, Make an image of brass of a serpent and suspend it in a place where it can be known as a sign, and let every one whom a serpent hath bitten look upon that image of brass, and he shall live. And when they failed to look at it they died, and those who looked on it and believed lived."[90] And in like manner was it with CHRIST; those who paid no heed to Him and did not believe in Him perished in SHEÔL, and those who believed and hearkened unto Him inherited the land of everlasting life, where there will never be pain or suffering.

And now we will make known unto you how they paid no heed to CHRIST, the Word of God. When the children of ISRAEL spake against MOSES, saying, "Is it that God hath spoken to MOSES only? How is it that we also do not hear the Word of God that we may believe on Him?"[91] And God, Who knoweth the hearts of men, heard the murmuring of the children of ISRAEL, and He said unto MOSES, "Thou dost ask forgiveness for thy people, and yet they murmur against thee, saying, Why doth not God speak with us? And now, if they believe in Me, let them come hither to Me with thee. And tell them to purify themselves, and to wash their apparel, and let the great men of ISRAEL go up to hear what commands I will give them, and let them hear My voice and perform the commandments which I shall give them." And MOSES told the children of ISRAEL what he had been commanded, and the people bowed low before God, and they purified themselves on the third day. And the seventy elders of ISRAEL[92] went up into Mount SINAI, and they departed from the encampment and ascended Mount SINAI. And they were distant from each other the space of the flight of an arrow, and they stood still, each facing his neighbour. Now, though there were many of them and they used their endeavours, they were not able to ascend into the cloud with MOSES, and fear and trembling seized upon them, and the shadow of death enveloped them; and they heard the sound of the horn and pipes, and [they felt] the darkness and the winds. And MOSES went into the cloud and held converse with God, and all the great men of ISRAEL heard that Voice of God, and they were afraid and quaked with terror, and because of the overwhelming terror which was in their hearts they were unable to stand up. And when MOSES came forth they said unto him, "We will not hear this word of God so that we may not die of terror. And behold, we know that God holdeth converse with thee. And if there be anything that He would say unto us, do thou hearken thereto and declare it unto us. Be thou unto us a mouth in respect of God, and we will be unto Him His own people." Do ye not see that they denied CHRIST and said, "We will not hearken to that Voice so that we may not die in terror"? Now CHRIST was the Word of God, and therefore when they said, "We will not hearken to that Voice," they meant, "We do not believe in CHRIST."

And again MOSES spake unto God and said, "Shew me Thy Face."[93] And God said unto MOSES, "No one can look upon My Face and live, but only as in a mirror. Turn thy face to the west and thou shalt see in the rock the mirroring of My Face." And when MOSES saw the shadow of the Face of God, his own face shone with a brightness which was seven times brighter than the sun, and the light was so strong that the children of ISRAEL could not look upon his face except through a veil. And thereupon he saw that they did not desire to look upon the Face of God, for they said unto him, "Make unto us a veil so that we may not see thy face."[94] And having said these words it is evident that they hated the hearing of His words and the sight of His Face.

And moreover, when ABRAHAM took his son ISAAC up into Mount KARMĚLĚWÔS (CARMEL), God sent down from heaven a ram for the redemption of ISAAC. And ISAAC was not slaughtered, but the ram which had come down from heaven was slaughtered. Now ABRAHAM is to be interpreted God the Father, and ISAAC is to be interpreted as a symbol of CHRIST the Son. And when He came down from heaven for the salvation of ADAM and his sons, the Godhead which had come down from heaven was not slain, but His body which He had put on for our sakes, that earthly body which He had put on from MARY, was slain. Can ye understand and know that likeness and similitude for the earthly being ISAAC, the son of ABRAHAM, who was an offering of the will of his father? The heavenly ram became a redemption (or, substitute), and the son of ABRAHAM was redeemed. And as for Him Who came down, the Son of God, He became the redemption of the Godhead, His body for the earthly, and He died in His body, the Godhead suffering in no wise and remaining unchanged; and the mortal became living in the Resurrection with the Godhead. And it is clearly manifest: in that CHRIST, the Son of God, hath redeemed us, He hath magnified us men. And we must honour especially, both upon the earth and in heaven, this our Lady MARY the Virgin, the Mother of God.

And, hearken ye to this explanation concerning the first man, who is our father ADAM. EVE was created from a man, from a bone in his side, without carnal embrace and union, and she became his companion. And having heard the word of guile, from being the helpmeet of ADAM she became a murderess by making him to transgress the command. And in His mercy God the Father created the Pearl in the body of ADAM. He cleansed EVE'S body and sanctified it and made for it a dwelling in her for ADAM'S salvation. She [i.e., MARY] was born without blemish, for He made her pure, without pollution, and she redeemed his debt without carnal union and embrace. She brought forth in heavenly flesh a King, and He was born of her, and He renewed his life in the purity of His body. And He slew death with His pure body, and He rose without corruption, and He hath raised us up with Him to immortality, the throne of divinity, and He hath raised us up to Him, and we have exchanged life in our mortal body and found the life which is immortal. Through the seduction of ADAM we suffered affliction, and by the patient endurance of CHRIST we are healed. Through the transgression of EVE we died and were buried, and by the purity of MARY we receive honour, and are exalted to the heights.

And EZEKIEL also prophesied concerning MARY and said, "I saw a door in the east which was sealed with a great and marvellous seal, and there was none who went into it except the Lord of hosts; He went in through it and came forth therefrom."[95] Hear ye now this explanation: When he saith, "I saw a door," it was the door of the gate of heaven, the entrance of the saints into the kingdom of the heavens. And when he saith that it was "in the east" he referreth to her purity and her beauty. Men call her the "Gate of Salvation", and also "the East" whereunto the saints look with joy and gladness. And the "closedness" of which he speaketh referreth to her virginity and her body. And when he saith that she was sealed with "a great, wonderful seal", this showeth plainly that she was sealed by God, the Great and Wonderful, through the Holy Ghost. And when he saith, "None goeth through it except the Lord of hosts, He goeth in and cometh out," [he meaneth] the Creator of the heavens and the earth, the Creator of the angels and men and the lords. The Lord of hosts is the fruit of the Godhead, Who put on our body from her, CHRIST. He went into and came forth from her without polluting her.

And MOSES also prophesied concerning MARY, saying, "I saw a bramble bush on Mount SINAI which the devouring fire consumed not."[96] And the signification of this fire is the Godhood of the Son of God; and the bramble bush, which burned without the leaves thereof being shrivelled, is MARY.

Footnotes
89. Compare Deuteronomy xviii. 15.
90. Numbers xxi. 7.
91. Numbers xii. 2.
92. Numbers xi. 16-24; Exodus xix.
93. Exodus xxxiii. 18-23.
94. Exodus xxxiv. 33.
95. Ezekiel xliii. 1.
96. Exodus iii. 2.

97. Concerning the Murmuring of ISRAEL

And once again the children of ISRAEL murmured concerning the ministration of the priests before the Lord, saying, "Are we not ISRAEL, we the seed of ABRAHAM, and why cannot we also offer up sacrifice like them in the Tent of Witness by the Tabernacle of the Law of God, the holy ZION, with censers and incense and the holy instruments? Why should MOSES, and his brother AARON, and their children alone do this? Are we not people whom God hath chosen as much as they are, and shall we not do His Will?" And when MOSES heard [this] he said unto them, "Do ye whatsoever ye will." And the elders of ISRAEL went and had made seventy censers wherewith to cense ZION and to praise God, and they took incense and coals in the censers, and went and came into the Holy of Holies to offer up incense. And immediately they threw the incense into the censers, at the first swing of them fire came forth from the censers, and they were burned up straightway and melted away. And as wax melteth before the face of the fire, even so did they melt away; and as grass withereth when flame approacheth it, even so were they consumed, together with their instruments, and there was nothing left of them except their censers. And God said, "Sanctify to Me these censers for My Tent" (or, Pavilion), and they shall be used for My offerings, for they are consecrated by the death of those men."[97]

Now the censer is MARY, and CHRIST, the Son of God, the Godhead, is the coals, and the odour of the incense is the perfume of CHRIST, and through the perfume of Him Apostles, and Prophets, and Martyrs, and Monks, have rejected the world and inherited the kingdom of heaven. And the chains of the censers are the ladder which JACOB saw, to which [the angels] clung as they went up and came down; and upon the perfume of the incense the prayers of the pure go up to the throne of God.

And when the flame had burned up the sinners, the people who were kinsmen of these who had been destroyed reviled MOSES and AARON, and said unto them, "Ye have made our elders to perish"; and they took up stones to stone MOSES and AARON.[98] And God was exceedingly wroth with ISRAEL, and He abominated as a filthy rag the counsel of DATHAN and ABIRAM, the sons of KORAH. And the Word of God made a sign to the earth, and the earth opened her mouth and swallowed them up, together with all their companions, and their wives, and their children, and their beasts. They went down into SHEÔL alive, and the earth shut herself up over them. And as for the people who had been associated with them and had heard their revilings [of MOSES] God sent upon them a plague, and they died forthwith. And MOSES and AARON came with incense and censers, and they wept before God, and entreated Him for forgiveness for the people, saying, "Remember, O Lord, ABRAHAM Thy friend, and ISAAC Thy servant, and ISRAEL Thy holy one, for we are their seed, and the children of Thy people. Cool Thy wrath in respect of us, and make haste to hear us, destroy us not, and remove Thy punishment from upon Thy people." And God the Merciful saw the sincerity of MOSES, and had compassion upon them.

And God spake unto MOSES and said unto him, "Speak thou to this people and say unto them, 'Sanctify ye yourselves, and bring ye for each of the houses of your fathers a rod,' and write ye [the name] upon it so that ye may know their rods, thou and thy brother AARON. Now of your houses let AARON write upon his rod, but upon thine own rod make no mark, for it shall be a perfect miracle for the children of thy people, a vindication for the wicked, and a sign of life for all those who believe. If thou didst write [thy name] now with them, they would say unto thee, 'This hath been a worker of miracles from of old by the word of God'; let them say this when I have shown them a miracle by it (i.e., the rod). But for the house of thy father write upon the rod of AARON."[99]

Footnotes
97. See Numbers xvi.
98. Compare Exodus xvii. 4; Numbers xvi. 41.
99. Numbers xvii. 8.

98. Concerning the Rod of MOSES and the Rod of AARON

And MOSES spake these words unto them, and they brought a rod into each of the houses of their fathers which they had chosen for purity, and there were twelve rods. And MOSES wrote upon their rods the names of their fathers: on the rod of AARON was written the name of LEVI, and on the rod of KARMÎN was written the name of JUDAH, and on the rod of ADÔNYÂS was written the name of REUBEN, and on the rod of every man of all the houses of ISRAEL was written in like manner the name of his father. And God said unto MOSES, "Carry [the rods] to ZION, to the Tent of Witness, and shut them up therein until the morning, and [then] take them out before the men and give unto each of them his rod, according to the houses of their fathers whose names are written on the rods, and the man on whose rod a mark shall be found is he whom I have chosen to be priest to Me." And MOSES told the people these words, and they did according as God had commanded them. And then, when the morning had come, MOSES took the rods, and all the elders of ISRAEL and AARON came. And MOSES came before them, and he lifted up the rods and brought them before all the people, and the rod of AARON was found with the fruit and flower of an almond which emitted a fragrant perfume. And MOSES said unto them, "Look ye now. This is the rod which the Lord your God hath chosen, fear ye Him and worship Him"; and all the people bowed down before God.

Now this rod is MARY. And the rod which without water burst into bloom indicateth MARY, from whom was born, without the seed of man, the Word of God. And that He saith "I have chosen, I will make manifest a miracle, and he shall be priest to Me," meaneth that God chose MARY out of all the congregation of ISRAEL, even as DAVID her father prophesied, saying, "The Lord loveth the gates of ZION more than all the habitations of JACOB,"[100] and he further said,

"Marvellous is His speech concerning thee, O city of God."[101] And when he saith, "more than all the habitations of ISRAEL" and "her gates" [he referreth to] the silence of her mouth, and the purity of her lips, and the praise which goeth forth from her mouth, like honey which floweth from her lips, and the purity of her virginity which was without spot or blemish or impurity before she brought forth; and after she had brought forth she was pure and holy, and so shall it be, even as it was, unto all eternity. And in the heavens she goeth about with the angels a pure thing; and she is the rod of AARON. She liveth in ZION with the pot which is filled with manna, and with the two tables that were written with the Finger of God. And the heavenly, spiritual ZION is above them, the ZION, the making and constitution of which are wonderful, of which God Himself is her Maker and Fashioner for the habitation of His glory.

And God spake unto MOSES [saying], "Make a Tabernacle of wood which is indestructible [by worms and rot], and cover it over with plates of fine gold, every part thereof."[102] And the gold is the fineness of the Godhead that came down from heaven, for the Godhead comprehendeth all heaven and earth; and in like manner is plated with gold the Tabernacle, the abode of the heavenly ZION. And the Tabernacle is to be interpreted as MARY, and the wood which is indestructible is to be interpreted as CHRIST our Redeemer. And the Gômôr,[103] which is the pot of gold inside the Tabernacle, is to be interpreted as MARY, and the manna which is in the pot is to be interpreted as the Body of CHRIST which came down from heaven, and the Word of God which is written upon the two tables is to be interpreted as CHRIST, the Son of God. And the spiritual ZION is to be interpreted as the light of the Godhead. The spiritual Pearl which is contained in the Tabernacle is like a brilliant gem of great price, and he who hath acquired it holdeth it tightly in his hand, grasping it and hiding it in his hand, and whilst the gem is in his hand its owner goeth into the Tabernacle, and he is an inmate therein. And he who possesseth the Pearl is interpreted as the Word of God, CHRIST. And the spiritual Pearl which is grasped is to be interpreted as MARY, the Mother of the Light, through whom "'AKRÂTÔS", the "Unmixed", assumed a body. In her He made a Temple for Himself of her pure body, and from her was born the Light of Light, God of God, Who was born of His own free will, and was not made by the hand of another, but He made a Temple for Himself through an incomprehensible wisdom which transcendeth the mind of man.

And on another occasion, when God brought ISRAEL out of EGYPT, they thirsted for water in KÂDÊS, and they murmured and wept before MOSES; and MOSES went to God and made Him to know this. And God said unto him, "Take thy rod and smite this rock"[104]; and MOSES smote the rock lengthwise and breadthwise in the form of the Cross, and water flowed forth, twelve streams. And they drank their fill of the water, their people and their beasts, and when they had drunk that rock followed after them. And the rock is to be interpreted as CHRIST, and the streams of water as the Apostles, and that which they drank as the teaching of the Apostles, and the rod is the wood of the Cross. And the rock is stable, as it saith in the Gospel, "He who buildeth upon a rock shall not be moved by the demons."[105] And again He saith, "I am the gate," and again He saith, "I am the door."[106] And observe ye that when speaking He distinguished between his disciples even as He did between those who [came] after them, the Bishops and the Christian Community. "Thou art the rock," He said unto PETER, "and upon thee I will build the Christian people."[107] And again He said, "I am the Shepherd of the sheep,"[108] and He said unto him thrice, "Feed my sheep."[109] And again He said "I am the stem of the vine," and unto them He said, "Ye are its branches and its clusters of fruit."[110]

And the rod of MOSES by means of which he performed the miracle is to be interpreted as the wood of the Cross, whereby He delivered ADAM and his children from the punishment of devils. And as MOSES smote the water of the river therewith, and turned it into blood, and slew their fish, in like manner CHRIST slew Death with His Cross, and brought them out of SHEÔL. And as MOSES smote in the air with his rod, and the whole land of EGYPT became dark for three days and three nights[111] with a darkness which could be felt so that [the EGYPTIANS] could not rise from their couches, so also CHRIST, being crucified upon the Cross, lightened the darkness of the hearts of men, and rose up from the dead on the third day and third night. And as the rod of MOSES changed itself and transformed itself[112] by the Word of God, being dry yet possessing life, and possessing life yet became a dry thing, even so CHRIST with the wood of His Cross made life for the Christian people who believed on Him, and with the Sign of the Cross made them to drive away devils. For the demons and the Christians became changed; the spiritual beings became reprobates, and through transgressing the commandment of their Lord they became exiled ones by the might of His Cross. And we have become spiritual beings through receiving His Body and Blood in the place of those spiritual beings who were exiled, and we have become beings worthy of praise who have believed in His Cross and in His holy Resurrection. And as MOSES smote the mountains by stretching out his hands with his rod, and brought forth punishments by the command of God, even so CHRIST, by stretching out His hands upon the wood of the Cross, drove out the demons from men by the might of His Cross. When God said unto MOSES, "Smite with thy rod," He meant, "Make the Sign of the Cross of CHRIST," and when God said unto MOSES, "Stretch out thy hand,"[113] He meant that by the spreading out of His hand CHRIST hath redeemed us from the servitude of the enemy, and hath given us life by the stretching out of His hand upon the wood of the Cross.

And when AMALEK fought with ISRAEL, MOSES went up into the mountain, and AARON was with him; they went up to pray because AMALEK was prevailing. And God commanded MOSES and said unto him, "Stretch out thy hand until ISRAEL obtaineth the power [over AMALEK]."[114] And it saith in the TÔRÂH that the hands of MOSES were held out until the sunset; but the hands of MOSES became heavy, and being aweary he dropped his hands that had been stretched out, and then ISRAEL ceased to prevail and their enemies overcame them. And when MOSES kept his hand up and stretched out straight, AMALEK was overcome, and ISRAEL put to flight and vanquished their enemy AMALEK. And when AARON and HÔR (HUR) saw this, they piled up stones on the right and on the left of MOSES, and they made the hands of MOSES to rest on the stones which they had built up, and AARON on his right and HÔR on his left held MOSES up with their shoulders, so that his hands might not drop from their stretched out position.

And now I will explain this to you. The war of AMALEK against ISRAEL is the war of believers against the demons, and before CHRIST was crucified the demons conquered the believers. But when He stretched out His hand on the wood of the Cross because of the sin of ADAM and his children, and when He stretched out His hand and His palm was pierced [with the nails], those who were sealed with the Sign of the Cross of CHRIST conquered them (i.e., the demons). The stretching out of the hand of MOSES indicateth the Cross of CHRIST; and that AARON and HÔR builded up stones indicateth the wood of the Cross and the nails. And AARON indicateth the thief on the right, and HÔR the thief on the left; and AMALEK indicateth the demons, and the king of AMALEK indicateth SATAN. And as concerning that they (the AMALEKITES) were conquered, this indicateth that we have conquered the demons and SATAN by the Resurrection of CHRIST and by His Cross.

And again when ISRAEL went out of EGYPT they came to bitter water, and they lacked drink because the water was bitter; and first of all they murmured because of the bitterness of the water. And God said unto MOSES, "Lift up thy rod, and cast it into the water,[115] and sign it with the Sign of the Cross right and left." Now mark what followeth. Had God said unto him, "Let it become sweet," then would the water not have become sweet? But He made manifest that by the Sign of the Cross everything becometh good, and bitter water becometh sweet, and that by the might of the Cross of JESUS CHRIST every polluted thing becometh good and pleasant.

And here I will declare unto thee yet other matters from the rest of the Prophets concerning His Crucifixion. DAVID saith, "They have pierced for me my hands and My feet"[116]; now this referreth clearly to the nails of His hands and His feet. And again he saith, "They made me drink vinegar for my thirst,"[117] and this showeth clearly that He drank vinegar because of the sin of ADAM. The Breath of Life that had breathed upon ADAM drank vinegar, and the Hand that had founded the earth was pierced with a nail. He Who for the sake of ADAM abased Himself was born, and took the form of a servant.

Footnotes
100. Psalm lxxxvii. 2.
101. Psalm lxxxvii. 3.
102. Exodus xxv. 10, "an ark of shittim wood."

103. Exodus xvi. 33, "take a pot, and put an omer full of manna therein."
104. Exodus xvii. 6.
105. Matthew vii. 24, 25.
106. John x. 7, 9.
107. Matthew xvi. 18.
108. John x. 11, 14.
109. John xxi. 17.
110. John xv. 5, 16.
111. Exodus x. 21, 22.
112. Exodus vii. 10.
113. Exodus vii. 19; viii.
114. Exodus xvii. 11, 12 ff.
115. Compare Exodus xv. 25.
116. Psalm xxii. 16.
117. Psalm lxix. 21.

99. Concerning the Two Servants

Now [it is said] that a certain king had two slaves: the one was arrogant and strong, and the other was humble and weak. And the arrogant slave overcame the humble one, and smote him and all but slew him, and robbed him, and the king upon his throne saw them. And the king descending seized the arrogant slave, and beat him, and crushed him, and bound him in fetters, and cast him into a place of darkness. And he raised up his humble and weak slave, and embraced him, and brushed away the dust from him, and washed him, and poured oil and wine into his wounds, and set him upon his ass, and brought him into his city and set him up on his throne, and seated him on his right hand. Now the king is in truth CHRIST, and the arrogant servant whom I have mentioned is SATAN, and the humble servant is ADAM. And when CHRIST saw how the arrogant servant overcame the humble one, and cast him down in the dust, He came down from His throne and raised up ADAM, His servant, and bound SATAN in fetters in the terror of SHEÔL. And He seated the body of ADAM upon the throne of His Godhead, and magnified him, and exalted him, and honoured him; and he was praised by all the beings whom He had created, the angels and the archangels, thousands of thousands, and tens of thousands of thousands of spiritual beings. For He brought low the arrogant and raised up the humble, and reduced the arrogant to shame and exalted to honour the humble, and rejected the arrogant and loved the humble, and scorned the haughty and had pity on the lowly. He cast down the arrogant from his high place, and lifted the poor up out of the dust. He snatched away the mighty one from his honour, and raised up the poor from corruption, for with Him are honour and disgrace. Whom He wisheth to honour He honoureth, and whom He wisheth to disgrace He disgraceth.

100. Concerning the Angels who rebelled

And there were certain angels with whom God was wroth - now He, the Knower of the heart knew them - and they reviled ADAM, saying, "Since God hath shown love to him He hath set us to minister unto him, and the beasts and creeping things, and the fish of the sea, and the birds of the air, and all fruits, and the trees of the field, and the heavens and the earth also; and He hath appointed the heavens to give him rain, and the earth to give him fruits. And the sun and the moon also hath He given him, the sun to give him light by day and the moon to give him light in the night season. He hath fashioned him with His fingers, and He hath created him in His own image, and He hath kissed him and breathed upon him the spirit of life; and He saith unto him, 'My son, My firstborn, My beloved.' And He hath set him in a garden to eat and enjoy himself without sickness or suffering, and without toil or labour, but He hath commanded him not to eat from one tree. And being given all these things by God, ADAM hath transgressed and eaten of that tree, and he hath become hated and rejected, and God hath driven him out of the Garden, and from that time ADAM hath abandoned his hope, for he hath transgressed the commandment of his Creator."

And God answered the angels who reviled ADAM in this wise, and He said unto them, "Why do ye revile ADAM in this wise? For he is flesh, and blood, and ashes and dust." And the angels answered and said unto Him, "May we declare before Thee the sin of ADAM?" And God said unto them, "Declare ye [his sin], and I will hearken unto you, and I Myself will answer you in respect of ADAM My servant." For God had worked on behalf of ADAM. And God said, "I created him out of the dust, and I will not cast away that which I have fashioned. I brought him forth out of non-existence, and I will not make My handiwork a laughingstock for his enemies." And those angels said, "Praise be unto Thee, O Lord. For Thou, the Knower of hearts, knowest that we have reviled ADAM because he hath transgressed Thy commandment that he was not to eat of one tree after Thou hadst made him lord over everything which Thou hast created, and hadst set him over every work of Thy hands. And if Thou hadst not told him, and if Thou hadst not commanded him not to eat of one tree there would have been no offence [on his part]; and if he had eaten because of a lack of food there would have been no offence [on his part]. But Thy word made him to know, and Thou didst say, 'As surely as thou eatest of this tree thou shalt die.'[118] And he, after hearing this, made bold and ate. Thou didst not let him lack sweet fruits to eat from the Garden, and Thou didst not let him lack one to comfort him and a companion like unto himself. And these things we say and make known unto Thee, and we have revealed unto Thee how he hath transgressed Thy commandment."

And the Merciful One and the Lover of mercy answered them on behalf of ADAM, and said unto them, "You have I created out of fire and air with the one intent [that ye should] praise [Me]. Him have I created of twice as many elements as you - of dust and water, and of wind and fire; and he became [a being] of flesh and blood. And in him are ten thoughts (or, intentions), five good, and five bad.

171

And if his heart inciteth him to good, he walketh with good intent; and if the Devil seduceth him, he walketh with him on an evil path. As for you, ye have no other object in your minds but praise of Me, with the exception of that arrogant one who produced evil, and became an evil being, and was driven forth from your assembly. And now, why do ye magnify yourselves over ADAM? If ye were as he is, and I had created you of water and dust, ye would have been flesh and blood, and ye would have transgressed My commandment more than he hath done, and denied My word." And the angels said unto Him, "Praise be unto Thee, O Lord! Far be it from us! We will not transgress Thy commandment, and we will not oppose Thy word; for we are spiritual beings for life, and he is a creature of dust [doomed] to folly. And now try us well, and put us to the test so that Thou mayest know whether we are able to keep Thy word."

And when they had vaunted themselves in this manner God, the Lover of men, said unto them, "If now ye go astray so far as this in transgressing My word, the wrong will be upon your own heads, [for] JAHANNAM (or, hell), and fire, and sulphur, and fervent heat, and whirlwind shall be your habitation until the Great Day: ye shall be kept in chains which can neither be loosened nor broken for ever. But if ye keep truly My word, and ye do My commandment, ye shall sit upon My right hand and upon My left. For everyone who hath conquered is mighty, and he who is conquered shall be overpowered. Now SATAN hath no power whatsoever, for he hath only what he maketh to germinate in the mind; and he cannot grasp firmly, and he cannot perform anything, and he cannot beat, and he cannot drag, and he cannot seize, and he cannot fight; he can only make thoughts to germinate silently in the mind. And him who is caught by the evil mind he prepareth for destruction; and if [a man] hath conquered the evil mind he findeth grace and hath a reward which is everlasting. And to you, according to what ye wish, there shall be upon you the mind of a man and the body of a man. But take good heed to yourselves that ye transgress not My word and break not My commandment; and defile not ye yourselves with eating, or drinking, or fornication, or with any other thing whatsoever; and transgress ye not My word."

And straightway there were given unto them with His word flesh, and blood, and a heart of the children of men. And they were content to leave the height of heaven, and they came down to earth, to the folly of the dancing of the children of CAIN with all their work of the artisan, which they had made in the folly of their fornication, and to their singings, which they accompanied with the tambourine, and the flutes, and the pipes, and much shouting, and loud cries of joy and noisy songs. And their daughters were there, and they enjoyed the orgies without shame, for they scented themselves for the men who pleased them, and they lost the balance in their minds. And the men did not restrain themselves for a moment, but they took to wife from among the women those whom they had chosen, and committed sin with them. For God hath no resting-place in the hearts of the arrogant and those who revile, but He abideth in the hearts of the humble and those who are sincere. And He spake in the Gospel, saying, "Woe be unto those who make themselves righteous, and despise their neighbours."[119] And again He saith, "God loveth the humble, and He holdeth lightly those who magnify themselves."

And straightway God was wroth with them, and He bound them in the terror of SHEÔL until the day of redemption, as the Apostle saith, "He treated His angels with severity. He spared them not, but made them to dwell in a state of judgement, and they were fettered until the Great Day."[120] The word of God conquered, Who had fashioned ADAM in His likeness (or, form), and those who had reviled and made a laughingstock of ADAM were conquered. And the daughters of CAIN with whom the angels had companied conceived, but they were unable to bring forth their children, and they died. And of the children who were in their wombs some died, and some came forth; having split open the bellies of their mothers they came forth by their navels. And when they were grown up and reached man's estate they became giants, whose height reached unto the clouds; and for their sakes and the sakes of sinners the wrath of God became quiet, and He said, "My spirit shall only rest on them for one hundred and twenty years, and I will destroy them with the waters of the Flood,"[121] them and all sinners who have not believed the word of God. And to those who believed the word of their fathers, and did His Will, no injury came from the waters of the Flood, but He delivered them, saying, "If thou believest My word thou canst save thyself from the Flood." And NOAH said, "O Lord, I believe Thy word, make me to know by what means I can be saved." And God said unto him, "Thou canst be saved from the water by wood." And NOAH said, "How, O Lord?" And God said unto him, "Make thyself a four-sided ark, and build it with the work of the carpenter, and make for it three storeys inside, and go into it with all thy house."[122] And NOAH believed the word of God, and made [the ark], and was saved.

Now hearken ye unto me, and I will explain to you concerning this thing. When God gave the command He could have given unto NOAH a wing like the eagle and transported him to the country of the living, with all his house, until His anger with the sinners who had not believed the word of God and the word of their fathers, had abated, or He could have lifted him up into the air, or He could have commanded the water of the Flood - [which was] like a wall - not to approach the one mountain where He would make NOAH to dwell with his sons and not to submerge the beasts and cattle which he wanted. But know ye this - God was well pleased that by means of wood which had been sanctified the salvation of His creation should take place, that is to say, the ark and the wood of the Cross. God said unto NOAH, "Make that whereby thou shalt be saved," that is to say, the Tabernacle of the Church; and when He said unto him, "Make it foursided," He showed that the Sign of the Cross was fourfold. Now the four corners of the ark are the horns of the altar; and He commanded MOSES to make the ark out of indestructible wood. He said, "I will sanctify thee by that heavenly and spiritual work of My hand. And do thou sanctify thyself from filth, and impurity, and fornication, and vindictiveness, and falsehood, together with thy brother and thy house. And sacrifice unto Me a clean sacrifice with cleanness, and I will accept thee after thou hast sanctified thyself and thy house; command all the people to sanctify themselves, for My holy things [must be offered] by holy ones. And this thou shalt seek, the Tabernacle of My Covenant which I have created for My praise. And if ye come with purity of heart, with love, and with peace, without mockery and reviling, and if ye will make right your hearts in respect of Me and your neighbours, I will hear your prayers, and I will listen to your petitions about everything which ye submit to Me, and I will come and be with you, and I will walk among you, and I will dwell in your hearts, and ye shall be unto Me My people, and I will be your God in truth."

Footnotes
118. Genesis ii. 17.
119. Compare Matthew xxiii. 13, and Luke xviii. 9 ff.
120. 2 Peter ii. 4.
121. Genesis vi. 2-4.
122. Genesis vi. 14 ff.

101. Concerning Him that existeth in Everything and Everywhere
And again God said unto MOSES: "Make for Me an open space before the courtyard of the Tabernacle; no man who is impure sexually and unclean shall come there, and no one who is not pure. For I am there, and not only there, but in every place like thereunto where My Name is invoked in purity. I was with DANIEL in the den [of lions], and I was with JONAH in the belly of the great fish, and I was with JOSEPH in the pit, and I was with JEREMIAH in the well [fed from] the lake. I stand under the deepest deep so that the mountains may not sink down under the waters; and I am under the waters so that they may not sink down upon the fire, and sulphur; I stand under the fire and sulphur so that they may not sink down upon the winds and the rust. I am under the winds and the rusty fog so that they may not sink down under the darkness. And I stand under the deepest darkness and under the abysses, and every created thing supporteth itself on Me, and everything which I have created cometh to Me as a place of refuge.

"I am above the earth, and I am at the ends of the world, and I am Master of everything. I am in the air, My place of abode, and I am above the chariot of the Cherubim, and I am praised everlastingly by all the angels and by holy men. And I am above the heights of heaven, and I fill everything. I am above the Seven Heavens. I see everything, and I test everything, and there is nothing that is hidden from Me. I am in every place, and there is no other god besides Me, neither in the heaven above nor in the earth beneath; there is none like unto Me, saith God; My hand hath laid the foundation of the earth, and My right hand hath made strong the heavens; I and My Son and the Holy Spirit."

102. Concerning the Beginning

As DAVID prophesied by the mouth of the Holy Spirit, saying, "With Thee was the headship on the day of might."[123] Now what do these words, "day of might" mean? Is it not the day whereon CHRIST, the Word of the Father, created heaven and earth? For MOSES saith in the beginning of the Book, "In the beginning God made the heavens and the earth."[124] Understand then "In the beginning" meaneth "in CHRIST"; the interpretation of "beginning" is CHRIST. JOHN the Apostle, the son of ZEBEDEE, saith concerning CHRIST, "This is the first (or, beginning) Whom we have heard and seen, Whom we have known, and Whom our hands have felt."[125] And we will relate unto you how we have a portion with Him, and ye who believe our words shall have a portion with us. And LUKE the disciple saith in the Acts of the Apostles, "In the beginning we make speech concerning everything,"[126] and this that he saith [sheweth] that CHRIST was the redemption of all, and we believe in Him. And MARK the Evangelist in the beginning of his Book wrote, saying, "The beginning of the Gospel is JESUS CHRIST, the Son of God"[127]; and these words mean that CHRIST was the glad tidings for the Prophets and the Apostles, and that we all have participated in His grace. And again JOHN the Evangelist wrote, saying, "In the beginning was the Word, and that Word was with God"; and in another place his word showeth [this] plainly, and he saith, "And likewise in the beginning was God the Word."[128] And now observe that that Word of the Father is CHRIST, whereby He made the heavens and the earth and every created thing. It is He Who created, and without Him nothing that came came into being, nothing whatsoever: "He spake, and they came into being; He commanded, and they were created."[129] And the third glorious thing, hearken [to it]: "Through the breath of His mouth He created all their host."[130] This maketh manifest the Holy Spirit, Who is clearly referred to.

And what shall we say? Let us weep for them. Woe be unto the JEWS and unto the pagans ('ARAMÎ) who have wandered from the truth and have refused to submit to the love of God, with which in His goodness He hath loved man. For after ADAM was rejected through his sin He saved him by the greatness of His mercy, being crucified on the wood of the Cross, His hands being pierced with nails. With His palm stretched out in humility, and His head bowed on one side, for our sakes He, to Whom suffering was unfitting, suffered in the everlasting majesty of His Godhead. He died that He might destroy death; He suffered exhaustion that He might give strength to the wearied being of dust; athirst He drank vinegar, He was crowned with a crown of thorns; He feared not and was not ashamed of the contumely and hatred and spitting of the polluted JEWS. He suffered beating, He was buffeted with fists, He was pierced, He was transfixed with nails, He was reviled and mocked, being God and the King of Death, and the Bestower of glory, and because of this He endured patiently all disgrace. Wearied and miserable, they made Him sad when they rejected Him and hated Him; but strong and glorious, what could sadden Him when they brought false charges against Him? For He Himself knew His Godhead, and He knew His glory, and He knew Himself. And there was none who knew Him, for He was the Creator of everything. And if they had known Him they would not have crucified the Lord of praise (or, glory). And He said in His mercy, "Forgive them, Father, for they know not what they do."[131] They likened their Creator to something that had been created, and they slew a sojourner who did not belong to mortal creatures, and He was not a thing that had been made with the hand. But He Himself was the Maker, and He Himself was the Creator, Light of Light, God of God, Son of the Father, JESUS CHRIST.

He was the Refuge, He was the Feeder, He was the Director; He, Whose domain was above what is on high, and above everything, abased Himself. Even as ISAIAH, the man of keen words among the Prophets, saith, "He was a humble man, and His appearance was rejected, like a root He hid Himself in parched ground, He came in the flesh, a being of the earth, [though He was] the Sustainer of the universe and the Saviour of the universe."[132] And DAVID ascribeth beauty to Him, saying, "On Thy beauty[133] and in Thy goodliness of form." And again he saith, "His form is more goodly than that of the children of men." And again he saith, "Graciousness is poured forth from Thy lips." And again he saith, "Direct aright with prosperity, and reign through righteousness, and justice, and sincerity."[134] And again he saith concerning the JEWS, the enemies of the truth, "Thine arrows are sharp and strong in the hearts of the haters of the King";[135] "it is right that they should transfix their hearts," He saith "unto those who did not wish Me to be King, and they shall be brought before Me and pierced" [with spears]. And again ISAIAH saith concerning the JEWS, "I have sought for them and found them not; I have called unto them and they have not answered Me; I have loved them and they have hated Me."[136] And again DAVID saith, "They returned unto me evil for good, and they hated me in return for my love for them."[137] And again ISAIAH saith, "With their lips they profess love for Me, but in their hearts they keep afar from Me, and their worshipping of Me is an empty thing."[138] And as MOSES saith, "They have moved Me to wrath with their gods, and I will move them to jealousy with that which is not a nation, for they are a people whose counsel is destroyed."[139]

And those who said, "We have no Law," unto them hath the Law been given, for God is the Giver of the Law unto every one. And God rewarded the JEWS according to their wickedness, and He treated the GENTILES according to their simplicity. For He is merciful and compassionate to those who call upon Him and who take refuge in Him, and who purify themselves from all uncleanness in the Church and in the Tabernacle of the Law of God; and He loveth those who weep and repent even as STEPHEN, [one] of the Seventy Disciples saith.[140] Now among the Seventy Disciples there were seven who were chosen for service with the Twelve Apostles, to perform service with SÎLÂS, and BARNABAS, and MARK and LUKE and PAUL. And this STEPHEN spake unto the JEWS whilst he was standing up to martyrdom and the JEWS were killing him, and said unto them as he showed them their folly in not having kept the commandment of God, "Ye have not kept the TÔRÂH according to the ordinance of the angels, as ye received it." And it saith in the Acts [of the Apostles], "When they heard this they went mad with anger and gnashed their teeth."[141] Now hearken ye unto me. In his saying "Ye have not kept the TÔRÂH according to the order of the angels," [we have] a form and a [fore] shadowing of what is in the heavens, that is to say, the heavenly and free JERUSALEM, the habitation of the Most High, whereof the situation and construction are incomprehensible to mortal heart. And in it is the throne of the Most High, which is surrounded with fire, and four beasts bear it in their place, which is the sixth heaven. And a throne goeth up to the seventh heaven, the habitation of the Father, and there dwelleth He Who is with His Father and the Holy Spirit, Who vivifieth everything. And the Tabernacle of the Church is a similitude of the JERUSALEM which is in the heavens, and the Church of the GENTILES is a similitude of the JERUSALEM which is in the heavens.

Footnotes
123. Psalm cx. 3.
124. Genesis i. 1.
125. John i. 1ff.
126. Acts i.
127. Mark i. 1.
128. John i. 1-3; 1 John i. 1.
129. Psalm xxxiii. 9.
130. Psalm xxxiii. 6.
131. Luke xxiii. 34.
132. Isaiah liii. 2 ff.
133. Psalm l. 2.
134. Psalm xlv.
135. Compare Psalms xlv. 5; lviii. 7.
136. Isaiah xlv. 12.
137. Psalm cix. 5.
138. Isaiah xxix. 13.
139. Deuteronomy xxxii. 21, 28.
140. Compare Acts vi. 3; vii. 34.
141. Acts vii. 53, 54.

103. Concerning the Horns of the Altar

Now, the Tabernacle symbolizeth the horns of the altar, where the holy priests offer up sacrifice, whereon they place the tarapîzâ, (i.e., table), the similitude of the grave wherein He (i.e., CHRIST) was buried in GOLGOTHA. And what is on the table, that is, the offering, is a symbol of the firstling, that is to say, the Body of EMMANUEL, [or] "'AKRÂTÔS", the "pure", the "unmixed", which our Saviour took from MARY, of the which He said unto His holy Apostles, "Eat ye My Body[142]; whosoever eateth not of My Body hath no portion with Me, and no everlasting life. But he who hath eaten My Body, even though he be dead, shall live for ever, [for] he is associated with My Body and My Blood, and he hath become My heir, and he shall say to My Father, 'Our Father which art in heaven,'" and the Father shall answer him, saying "Thou art My Son," and the crown (i.e., the covering), which is above the offering, is a similitude of the stone with which the JEWS sealed the grave. And when the priest saith, "Send the Holy Spirit," the Holy Spirit shall be sent, and the Body of our Lord shall be perfect (or, complete). And when we have received we shall be participators in the Body and Blood of our Lord and Redeemer JESUS CHRIST, the Son of the Living God, and the Holy Spirit, henceforth and for ever. Speak ye then to one another so that the JEWS, who are blind in heart, and who are our enemies and the enemies of our Lord God, may not boast themselves over us. And they say, "Your gods are many, and ye worship wood" (i.e., the Cross), and they say, preaching openly the word of ISAIAH the Prophet, "Ye worship the half of it, and with the other half ye cook the body and eat [it]."[143] Now ISAIAH speaketh thus in respect of those who worship graven images and idols. And they say [that we say], "These are our gods, and they have created us"; and that we talk to them and worship them as the Lord our God. And these also are they whom the devils lead into error in their wickedness, and DAVID saith, concerning them, "The gods of the heathen are devils, but God hath created the heavens; truth and goodness are before Him."[144]

Footnotes
142. Matthew xxvi. 26.
143. Isaiah xliv. 16.
144. Psalm xcvi. 5.

104. More concerning the Ark and the Talk of the Wicked

And as concerning the Ark: God saved NOAH in the Ark. And God held converse with ABRAHAM in the wood of MANBAR,[145] that is to say the wood that cannot be destroyed; and He saved ISAAC by means of the ram which was caught in the thicket[146]; and He made JACOB rich by means of three rods of woods which he laid in running water[147]; and through the top of his staff JACOB was blessed.[148] And He said unto MOSES, "Make a tabernacle of wood which cannot be destroyed, in the similitude of ZION, the Tabernacle of the Covenant." And when DAVID took it from the city of SAMARIA, he placed the Tabernacle of the Law in a new Tabernacle, and rejoiced before it.[149] For from the beginning God had made the Tabernacle the means of salvation, and very many signs and wonders were performed through it by its form and similitude. Hearken ye now unto me, and I will show you plainly how God had ordained salvation through the wood of His Cross, in the Tabernacle of His Law, from the beginning to the end.

Salvation came unto ADAM through the wood. For ADAM'S first transgression came through the wood, and from the beginning God ordained salvation for him through the wood. For God Himself is the Creator and Giver of life and death, and everything is performed by His Word, and He created everything, and He maketh righteous him that serveth Him in purity in His pure Tabernacle of the Law. For it is called "mercy-seat", and it is also called "place of refuge", and it is also called "altar", and it is also called "place of forgiveness of sins", and it is called "salvation", and it is called "gate of life", and it is called "glorification", and it is called "city of refuge", and it is called "ship", and it is called "haven of salvation", and it is called "house of prayer", and it is called "place of forgiveness of sins for him that prayeth in purity in it", so that [men] may pray therein in purity and not defile their bodies. God loveth the pure, for He is the habitation for the pure. Those who come into His habitation, and are accepted in the holy Tabernacle, and who pray unto Him with all their hearts, He will hear and will save in the day of their tribulation, and He will fulfil their desire. For He hath made the holy Tabernacle to be a similitude of His throne. But there are some among those whom ye have brought unto us who are like unto us Christians, but who have not abandoned the sin which their father the Devil hath made to spring up in them. And he said, "Thus it is right that we should pray in ZION, the Tabernacle of the Law of God; she was at the first and is even now. The similitude thereof and the fruit thereof are the Mother of the Redeemer, MARY; it is right that we should worship her, for in her name is blessed the Tabernacle of the Law of God. And it is right that we should worship MICHAEL and GABRIEL."

And the Archbishop CYRIL answered and said unto them: And if he hath said this unto them, we also will say unto them: What did our Lord JESUS CHRIST say when He was teaching those who believed in Him? One came from outside and said unto Him, "Behold them, Thy father and Thy mother outside seeking Thee." And CHRIST the Lover of men answered and, stretching out His hand towards those whom He was teaching, said, without making any distinction or difference between man and woman, "Behold them, My father, and My mother, and My brother. Whosoever hath heard My word and hath done the Will of My Father, that same is My father, and My mother, and My sister."[150] O thou blind-hearted JEW, canst thou not see His mercy and His love for men when He spake thus? He neither separated nor made a distinction, but He said unto them, "My brother." For He loveth those who love Him and keep His commandment, especially the martyrs, who for His sake delivered themselves over to death, though they knew the bitterness of death; and the solitary monks who keep the commandment of God, and love Him with all their hearts, and He loveth them. And their graves which are built, that is to say, the martyriums, and the churches which are built in their names, and the tabernacles which the Bishops consecrate in their names; every one is holy in the house of the Sanctuary of God. And the man who prayeth in their names God heareth. And those who pray in purity, without uncleanness and blemish, and in humility and sincerity in a tabernacle which hath been consecrated - whether it be in the name of a martyr, or in the name of an angel, or in the name[s] of the righteous, or in the name of a virgin, or in the name of holy women - if it be consecrated, the Holy Spirit cometh down upon them and changeth the wood so that it becometh a spiritual being. In this wise God transformed the rod of MOSES by His word, and it became a thing of life and made MOSES fear his Lord. And in like manner JOSEPH worshipped the top of the rod of JACOB when he was before him; none forced him, but through the belief of his father he worshipped the top of his rod. And this which MOSES wrote is a prophecy for the last days, so that we may know that tabernacles in the name[s] of martyrs and righteous men are holy, namely, when he saw him he worshipped the top of his rod.

And I will also declare unto you what is written concerning the pride of PHARAOH. MOSES did as God commanded him, and turned his rod into a serpent; and PHARAOH commanded the magicians, the sorcerers, to do the same with their rods. And they made their rods into three serpents which, by means of magic, wriggled before MOSES and AARON, and before PHARAOH and the nobles of EGYPT. And the rod of MOSES swallowed up the rods of the magicians, for these deceivers had worked magic for the sight of the eyes of men. Now that which happeneth through the word of God overcometh every [kind of] magic that can be wrought. And no one can find him to be evil, for it is the Holy Spirit Who guideth and directeth him that believeth with an upright heart without negligence. Even as PAUL saith, "By believing the fathers of olden time were saved."[151] He wished to make known each by his name from ADAM, and NOAH, and ABRAHAM, to RAHAB the harlot who received the spies. And thou, O blind JEW, canst thou not understand from what thou readest in the Law, that is to say, the TÔRÂH wherein thou believest, that inasmuch as thou canst not perform its commandments thou art cursed thereby? For when He saith, "All those who walk therein, if they do not keep what is written therein, accursed shall they be," He saith it to thee. But us, who believe in CHRIST, the Son of God, the grace of God hath chosen, saying, "He who believeth and is baptized shall be saved."[152]

Footnotes
145. Compare Genesis xviii. 1.
146. Genesis xxii. 13.
147. Genesis xxx. 37.
148. Genesis xlvii. 31; Hebrews xi. 21.
149. 2 Samuel vi. 3.
150. Compare Matthew xii. 49; Mark iii. 34 ff.
151. Hebrews xi.
152. Mark xvi. 16.

105. Concerning the belief of ABRAHAM

And thou dost not understand that they were justified by faith - ABRAHAM, and DAVID and all the Prophets, one after the other, who prophesied concerning the coming of the Son of God. And ABRAHAM said, "Wilt Thou in my days, O Lord, cast Thy word upon the ground?" And God said unto him, "By no means.

His time hath not yet come, but I will shew thee a similitude of His coming. Get thee over the JORDAN, and dip thyself in the water as thou goest over, and arrive at the city of SÂLÊM, where thou shalt meet MELCHIZEDEK, and I will command him to show thee the sign and similitude of Him." And ABRAHAM did this and he found MELCHIZEDEK, and he gave him the mystery of the bread and wine,[153] that same which is celebrated in our Passover for our salvation through our Lord JESUS CHRIST. This was the desire and the joy of ABRAHAM as he went round the altar which MELCHIZEDEK had made, carrying branch and palm on the day of the Sabbath. See how he rejoiced in his belief, and see how he was justified by his belief, O blind JEW, who though having eyes seest not, and having ears hearest not, even as the Prophet ISAIAH saith concerning you, "Their eyes are blind, and their hearts are covered with darkness, so that they may not understand and God may not show compassion unto them."[154]

Footnotes
153. Genesis xiv. 18.
154. Compare Isaiah vi. 10; xliv. 18.

106. A Prophecy concerning the Coming of CHRIST

And now hearken how each one of them hath prophesied concerning Him, [for the narrative] is pleasant to hear. ISAIAH the Prophet prophesied concerning His coming and said, "A Son is born unto us. A Child is given unto us. Dominion is written upon His shoulder. He is God, strong in rule, King, great Counsellor is His name."[155] Now the meaning of this is manifest: the Son of God is born, Whose sovereignty was written down before the world was, and He is wiser than anyone else: [this is what] he saith unto thee. And again ISAIAH prophesied and said, "Behold My servant Whom I have chosen, on Whom is the delight of My soul, and the nations shall put their confidence in Him."[156] And these words give us to understand that CHRIST is the Spirit of God, the Word of the Father Who put on our flesh and was born for us: and the peoples of RÔMÊ and ETHIOPIA and all other nations have believed in Him. And he spake unto the people of ISRAEL, and again he prophesied, saying, "Many shall follow after Thee with their loins girded up, and their backs bound with fetters, and they shall pray to Thee and worship Thee, for thou art God, and we have not recognized Thee."[157] Now this he spake concerning the martyrs, and those who became monks in the desert and solitary monks, whose hearts were fettered with His commandment, and who prayed to Him, meaning that reward was meet for both the martyrs and the solitary monks. "And we did not recognize Thee": ISRAEL made itself blind, and crucified Him, and refused to walk in His righteousness. And again ISAIAH prophesied and said, "God shall come, and the heathen shall put their trust in Him and shall know Him";[158] this meaneth that CHRIST shall come, and the JEWS shall reject Him, but the heathen shall believe in Him. And again he prophesied and said, "Be strong ye weak hands and tired knees, and rejoice ye hearts that are cast down, for God hath come, Who shall requite our debt, and save us. And He shall open the eyes of the blind, and He shall make the ears of the deaf to hear, and the feet that are lame shall run, and the tongues of the dumb shall speak."[159] These words are spoken in respect of those who err in worshipping idols, and those who are dead in sin, and those whose hearts are darkened, and of you who do not know that God created you. Rejoice ye this day: He hath come Who will redeem the sin of ADAM, and make ADAM'S debt His own. He was crucified being sinless. He hath killed Death by means of His own death, and the blind see, and the lame walk, and the deaf hear, and the dumb speak unhaltingly, and besides all these things the dead are raised. This is the meaning of this prophecy.

Thus DAVID the Prophet prophesied and said, "God shall come in visible form, and our God will not keep silence."[160]

Thus JEREMIAH prophesied and said, "God shall come down upon the earth, and shall walk about with men like us."[161]

Thus Ezekiel the Prophet prophesied and said, "I your God will come, and I will walk about among them, and they shall know Me that I am their God."[162]

Thus DAVID prophesied and said, "Blessed is He Who cometh in the name of God: we have blessed you in the Name of the Lord."[163]

Thus HABAKKUK prophesied and said, "God shall come from the South, and the Holy One from Mount FÂRÂN and from the cities of JUDAH."[164]

Thus ELIJAH the Prophet prophesied and said, "With a new covenant shall God come unto us."[165]

Thus JOEL the Prophet prophesied and said, "The heavenly EMMANUEL shall come and shall deliver the work which He hath fashioned with His own hand from the hand of the Devil, the deceiver, and his devils which lead astray."[166]

Thus DAVID the Prophet prophesied and said, "The God of gods shall show Himself in ZION.[167] The people say out of ZION, A man is born therein, and He the Most High hath founded it."[168]

Thus SOLOMON his son prophesied and said, "Verily God shall be with men, and He shall walk about upon the earth."[169]

Thus his father DAVID prophesied and said, "He shall come down like the dew upon wool, and like the drop which droppeth upon the earth, and righteousness shall spring into being in his days."[170]

Thus SOLOMON his son prophesied and said, "A Saviour shall be born out of ZION, and He shall remove sin from JACOB."[171]

Thus HOSEA the Prophet prophesied and said, "I will come to thee, O ZION, and I will walk about in thee, JERUSALEM, saith God, the Holy One of ISRAEL."[172]

Thus MICAH the Prophet prophesied and said, "The Word of God shall appear in JERUSALEM, and the Law shall go forth from ZION."[173]

Thus HOSEA the Prophet prophesied and said, "God shall appear upon the earth, and shall dwell with men like us."[174]

Portrait of Our Blessed Lady Mary, the two-fold Virgin, and Child. By her side stand the Archangels Michael and Gabriel

Thus JEREMIAH the Prophet prophesied and said, "A saviour shall be sent from ZION, and He shall remove sin from the people of ISRAEL."[175]

Thus MICAH the Prophet prophesied and said, "God shall come from the heavens and dwell in His temple (or, citadel)."[176]

Thus ZECHARIAH the Prophet prophesied and said, "Rejoice, O daughter of ZION! Behold, I am alive, and I will dwell in thee, saith God, the Holy One of ISRAEL."[177]

Thus MICAH the Prophet prophesied and said, "Behold, God shall come, and shall shine upon those who fear Him; Sun of righteousness is His Name."[178]

Thus HOSEA the Prophet prophesied and said, "God shall come upon thee, JERUSALEM, and shall appear in the midst of thee."[179]

Thus DAVID the Prophet prophesied and said, "And He shall live, and they shall give Him of the gold of ARABIA, and they shall pray for Him continually, and He shall be the stay of all the earth upon the tops of the mountains."[180]

Thus JOB the just prophesied and said, "God shall walk about upon the earth, and He shall travel over the sea as upon the dry land."[181]

Thus DAVID the Prophet prophesied and said, "He bowed the heavens and came down."[182]

Thus ISAIAH the Prophet prophesied and said, "Behold, the virgin shall conceive, and shall bring forth a Son, and she shall call His name EMMANUEL."[183]

Thus DAVID the Prophet prophesied and said, "I brought Thee forth from the womb before the star of the morning."[184] And again he said, "God said unto me: Thou art my Son, and I have this day brought Thee forth."[185]

Thus GIDEON prophesied and said, "Behold, He shall come down like dew upon the earth."[186]

Thus DAVID the Prophet prophesied and said, "God looked down from heaven upon the children of men, and from the temple of His sanctuary."[187]

Thus MOSES the Prophet prophesied and said, "And all the children of God shall say: He is strong, for He avengeth the blood of His sons."[188]

Thus DAVID prophesied and said, "And there will I make a horn to DAVID to rise up, and I will prepare a lamp for Mine Anointed, and I will clothe His enemies with shame, and in Him shall My holiness flourish."[189]

Thus HOSEA the Prophet prophesied and said, "Fear not, for Thou shalt not be put to shame. And be not dismayed because of Thy praise."[190] And again he said, "Hearken unto Me, hearken unto Me, My people, for My judgement (or, justice) is right. I will come and I will dwell with you, and the nations shall put their trust in My light; for the nations shall be the loved ones of CHRIST."

Thus DAVID the Prophet said, "A people whom I do not know shall serve Me; at the mere hearing of the ear they shall answer Me."[191] And to the JEWS he said, "The children of the stranger have been false to me, the children of the stranger have become old and have travelled haltingly on their path. God liveth, and blessed [is] my God."[192] When he saith unto thee, "God liveth," he speaketh of His Godhead, and when he saith unto thee "and blessed [is] my God," he speaketh concerning His putting on the flesh. And again he speaketh concerning His putting on the flesh in ISAIAH the Prophet, saying, "Who is this glorious One who cometh forth from EDOM, ADÔNÂI, Who came down from heaven, and put on the things of BASÔR, glorious in majesty?"[193] When he saith "glorious" he refereth to His sweet odour; and when he saith "ADÔNÂI," he meaneth the Word of the Father Who was before the world, the Son of God; when he saith "He put on the things of BASÔR, the glorious in majesty," he indicateth clearly the body of ADAM.

Thus DAVID the Prophet prophesied saying concerning Christian folk, "Declare ye to the nations that God is King, and that He hath made fast the world so that it shall never be moved."[194] And he also prophesied concerning His coming to the nations, and said, "Before the face of God shall He come, He shall come and shall judge the earth, and He shall judge the world in righteousness, and the nations with justice."[195]

Thus ISAIAH the Prophet prophesied and said, "The Lord of hosts hath planned to destroy the contumely of the nations, and He shall bring to nothing the nobles and the mighty ones of the earth."[196] And continuing his prophecy he said, "He shall come and shall build His house, and He shall deliver His people."[197] And he added other words, saying, "And at that time there shall spring from the root of JESSE One Who shall be set over the nations, and the nations shall put their trust in Him, and the place where He shall abide shall be glorious for ever."[198]

Thus DAVID prophesied, and said, "Sing ye unto God Who dwelleth in ZION, and declare ye to the nation His work."[199]

Thus SOLOMON his son prophesied and spake concerning our Saviour EMMANUEL, the Sun of righteousness, "He brought Me forth before the hills, and before He made the lands and set them in order, and founded Me before the world; before He made the earth, and before He made the abysses, and before the waterfloods came forth, and the beauty of the flowers appeared, and before the winds blew, God created His work before His face, and I existed conjointly with My Father."[200]

Thus his father DAVID prophesied and said, "His name was before the sun, and before the moon, generation to generation."[201]

Thus his son SOLOMON prophesied and said, "When He made strong the firmament above the clouds, and when He set in position the walls of the boundaries of the heavens, and when He set the sea in its appointed place, and before He founded His throne above the winds, and when He made strong the foundations of the earth, I existed conjointly with Him. I was that wherein He rejoiced continually, and day by day, and I exulted with Him at all times before His face."[202]

Thus JOB the Prophet prophesied and said, "The face of my God is in the East, and His light is before [that of] the sun, and the nations put their trust in His Name."[203]

Thus ISAIAH the Prophet prophesied and said, "Remember ye not the things of the past, and think not about the things of olden time; behold, I will make a new thing, which shall now spring up, so that ye may know that I make a road through the desert and water floods in the wilderness; and the beasts of the field shall follow after Me, and the young birds, and the ostriches. For I have given water in the desert, and made streams of water to flow in the wilderness, so that I may give drink to My people and to My chosen ones whom I have gotten, so that they may declare My glory, and perform My commandment."[204]

Thus SOLOMON prophesied and said, "Who hath gone up into heaven and come down? And who hath gathered together the winds in his bosom? And who hath collected the waters in his garment? And who hath measured the waters of the sea in his hand, and the heavens on the palm of his hand? And what is his name and what is the name of his son?"[205]

Thus MICAH the Prophet prophesied and said unto the JEWS, "I have no pleasure in you, saith God Who ruleth all things. And I have no pleasure in your offerings, and I will accept no gift from your hands. For from the rising of the sun to the setting thereof shall My Name be praised among all peoples, and in all countries incense shall be offered up to my great Name among all peoples, saith Almighty God."[206]

And again MICAH the Prophet said, "A new covenant shall appear upon the mountain of God, and it shall be prepared upon the tops of the mountains, and it shall be exalted above the hills, and people shall say, 'Come ye, let us go up into the mountain of God.' And many nations shall go thereto and shall say, 'Come ye, let us go up into the mountain of God,[207] and they shall declare unto us His way, and we will walk therein.'"

Thus DAVID the Prophet prophesied and said, "Hearken unto Me, O My people, and I will speak unto thee, ISRAEL, and will bring testimony to thee; I am God, thy God."[208]

Thus MOSES the Prophet prophesied and said concerning the Trinity, "Hear, O ISRAEL, the Lord thy God is One."[209] And this is to be explained thus: Father, and Son, and Holy Spirit are One God, Whose kingdom is one, Whose dominion is one, and as One men shall worship Them in the heavens and in the earth, in the sea and in the abysses. And to Him be praise for ever and ever! Amen.

Footnotes
155. Isaiah ix. 6.
156. Isaiah xlii. 1.
157. Compare Jeremiah xxx. 6-9.
158. Isaiah lx. 2, 3.
159. Isaiah xxxv. 3 ff.
160. Psalm l. 3.
161. Compare Baruch iii. 37.
162. Compare Jeremiah xxxii. 38; Ezekiel xi. 17, 20; xxxvi. 27, 28; 2 Corinthians vi. 16.
163Psalms cxviii. 26; cxxix. 8.
164. Habakkuk iii. 3.
165. Compare Jeremiah xxxi. 31
166. Compare 1 John iii. 5, 8.
167. Psalms xlviii. 2, 3; l. 2.
168. Psalm lxxxvii. 5, 6.
169. Compare 2 Corinthians vi. 16.

170. Psalm lxxii. 6, 7.
171. Isaiah lix. 20.
172. Compare Zechariah ii. 10.
173. Micah iv. 2.
174. Compare Zechariah viii. 3.
175. Compare Jeremiah xxxi. 11, 12.
176. Malachi iii. 1.
177. Zechariah ix. 9.
178. Malachi iv. 2.
179. Zechariah i. 16.
180. Psalm lxxii. 15.
181. Job ix. 8.
182. Psalm xviii. 9.
183. Isaiah vii. 14.
184. Psalm cx. 3.
185. Psalm ii. 7.
186. Judges vi. 37; Psalm lxxii. 6.
187. Psalm xxxiii. 13.
188. Deuteronomy xxxii. 43.
189. Psalm cxxxii. 17.
190. Isaiah liv. 4.
191. Psalm xviii. 43.
192. Psalm xviii. 45, 46.
193. Isaiah lxiii. 1.
194. Psalm xcvi. 10.
195. Psalms xcvi. 13; xcviii. 9.
196. Isaiah x. 33; Haggai ii. 7.
197. Isaiah xlv. 14; Haggai ii. 9.
198. Isaiah xi. 10.
199. Psalm cv. 1, 2.
200. Proverbs viii. 22 ff.
201. Psalm lxxii. 5, 17.
202. Proverbs viii. 30.
203. Ezekiel xliii. 2.
204. Isaiah xxxv; xliii. 20.
205. Proverbs xxx. 4; Isaiah xl. 12.
206. Malachi i. 10, 11.
207. Compare Isaiah ii. 3; Micah iv. 2.
208. Psalm l. 7.
209. Deuteronomy vi. 4.

107. Concerning His entrance into JERUSALEM in Glory

And the Prophets have prophesied concerning His glorious entry into JERUSALEM, and ISAIAH the Prophet said, "Shine thou, shine thou, JERUSALEM, thy light hath come and the glory of God hath risen upon thee."[210]

Thus the Prophet ZECHARIAH prophesied and said, "Rejoice, rejoice, daughter of ZION, and let JERUSALEM shout for joy."[211]

Thus DAVID prophesied and said, "Out of the mouth of children and babes Thou hast prepared praise because of the enemy, so that Thou mightest overthrow the enemy and the avenger."[212]

Thus SOLOMON prophesied and said, "The children are taught by God, and the peoples rejoice within thee."[213]

Thus DAVID his father prophesied and said, "Blow ye the horn in ZION, on the day of the new moon, on the appointed day of our festival, for it is an ordinance for ISRAEL."[214]

Thus EZRA the Scribe prophesied and said, "Get ye out, make ye a festival in gladness, and say unto the daughter of ZION, Rejoice thou, behold thy King hath come."[215]

Thus ISAIAH the Prophet prophesied and said, "Rejoice thou, JERUSALEM, rejoice thou. Behold, thy King hath come riding upon an ass. His reward is with Him, and His work is before His face."[216]

Thus DAVID the Prophet prophesied and said, "Blessed is He who cometh in the name of the Lord."[217]

Thus JACOB the son of ISAAC prophesied and said, "JUDAH, thy brethren have praised thee. Thine hand is upon the back of thine enemy, and the children of thy mother shall worship thee. And the dominion shall not diminish from JUDAH, and the government shall not depart from his kin, until he shall find Him Who hath been waited for, and Who is the Hope of the nations."[218] And he also prophesied and said, "His teeth are white as with snow, and His eyes are glad as with wine, and He shall wash His apparel in wine and His tunic in the blood of clusters of grapes."[219] And again he prophesied, saying, "JUDAH is a lion's whelp; thou hast lain down, and thou hast slept; no one shall wake him up except him that hunteth until he findeth him; rise up from thy strong place."[220] And again JACOB blessed his son JUDAH, and said unto him, "There is a King who shall go forth from thee and shall wash His apparel in wine, and glorious is the place of rest of the Beloved"; now, by "Beloved" CHRIST is meant, and by "Messiah" CHRIST is meant, and JESUS meaneth "Saviour of the people". Now the Prophets mention CHRIST under a secret name and they call Him "the Beloved".

And ISAIAH spake concerning His Ascension in his prophecy, saying, "On that day the Beloved shall come down from heaven, and shall choose for Himself twelve Apostles."[221] And again he said, "I have seen the ascension of the beloved Son to the seventh heaven, and the Angels and the Archangels receiving Him, He being very much higher than they."

And DAVID said, "The beloved is like the son of the unicorn";[222] and again he said, "And thine only one from the horns of the unicorn."[223] And again he said, "Let my horn be exalted like that of the unicorn."[224] "Horns" meaneth the kingdoms of the world; and "unicorn" meaneth He Who is over His kingdom Whom no one can resist, for He is the governor of kings; He destroyeth whom He will and He setteth up him whom He will. Even as DAVID saith, "I will make thee to rejoice more than those who are mighty through their horns,"[225] which meaneth, "Thou art nobler than the noble kings, and thou dost rejoice."

And HABAKKUK prophesied, saying, "Horns are in his hands,[226] and he hath placed the beloved in the strength of his power," which meaneth, "The palms of the hand, wherein the life of all is held, of the holder of the dominion of kings, are pierced with nails, which CHRIST, the beloved, hath endured in the strength of His might."

Footnotes
210. Isaiah lx. 1.
211. Zechariah ix. 9.
212. Psalm viii. 2.
213. Isaiah liv. 13.
214. Psalm lxxxi. 3.
215. Zechariah ix. 9.
216. Isaiah lxii. 11.
217. Psalm cxviii. 26.
218. Genesis xlix. 8-10.
219. Genesis xlix. 11, 12.
220. Genesis xlix. 9.
221. Compare Ascensio Isaiae, ed. Dillmann, pp.13 and 57.
222. Psalm xxii. 20 (?).
223. Psalm xxii. 20, 21.
224. Psalm xcii. 10.
225. Compare Psalm lxxv. 10.
226. Habakkuk iii. 4.

108. Concerning the wickedness of the iniquitous JEWS

And the Prophets prophesied concerning the wickedness of the JEWS. And DAVID said concerning it, "The man of violence hunteth iniquity to destroy himself."[227] And again he saith, "His sorrow shall return upon his head, and his iniquity upon his forehead" (or, skull).[228]

Thus SOLOMON his son prophesied and said, "The foolish man and the man of iniquity travel by paths that are not straight. He winketh with the eye, and tappeth with the foot, and he giveth a sign by movements of the fingers and motion of the lips, and his perverted heart meditateth evil at all times; a man who is like this will make to come tumult and murder, and the shedding of blood through double-dealing, and he shall not escape the judgement."[229]

And DAVID his father prophesied and said, "They brought forth against me the word of error; he who sleepeth shall he not awake? Shall then the man of my peace (i.e., my friend), whom I trusted, who ate my food, lift up his foot against me?"[230]

Thus ISAIAH the Prophet prophesied and said, "Woe be unto the man of iniquity who bringeth wrath."[231] And again he said, "Let them remove the sinner so that he may not see the glory of God."[232]

Thus DAVID the Prophet prophesied and said, "The sinner speaketh what will condemn him, and there is no fear of God before his eyes."[233]

Thus SOLOMON his son prophesied and said, "The man of iniquity bringeth tumult to the city; and he willingly maketh to come destruction, and beating, and calamity which cannot be healed, for he rejoiceth in everything which God hateth."[234]

Thus prophesied MOSES the Prophet and said, "God wisheth not to forgive him but rather to increase vengeance upon him; and He will make punishments to rest upon him, and the curse which is written in this book shall come upon him; and his name shall be blotted out from under heaven."[235]

Thus DAVID the Prophet prophesied and said, "His heart is ready for slaughter; he preferreth cursing and it shall come to him; he refuseth blessing and it shall be far from him."[236]

Thus JEREMIAH the Prophet prophesied concerning him and said, "The man of iniquity shall be destroyed because of the love of money, and he looketh upon darkness because of his fraud."[237]

Thus JOB prophesied and said concerning him, "His Creator will destroy his fair work, and his root shall dry up under him, and his flower shall be beaten down upon him, and his memorial shall be blotted out from the earth, and his name shall be cast far away, and men shall remove him into the darkness so that he may not see the light, and the house of the man of iniquity shall be blotted out."[238]

Thus HOSEA prophesied and said concerning him, "Hearken unto me, O children of ISRAEL, for there is no righteousness, and no mercy, and no fear of God in his heart, but falsehood, and theft, and murder, and fornication."[239]

And DAVID the Prophet prophesied and said, "SATAN standeth at his right hand"; and again he said, "Let another take his office."[240]

And MOSES cursed in the Law and said, "Cursed be every one who taketh bribes to slay innocent blood; and all the people said, Amen. And Amen."[241]

Thus HABAKKUK the Prophet prophesied and said, "The governor maketh [men] wise concerning this perversion of the Law, and no right judgement cometh forth; for the sinner corrupteth the righteous man, and therefore a perverted judgement cometh forth."[242]

Thus DAVID the Prophet prophesied and said, "The sinner seeth and becometh wrathful, and he gnasheth with his teeth and is dissolved."[243]

Thus SOLOMON his son prophesied and said, "A false balance is a hateful thing to God."[244]

Thus JEREMIAH prophesied and said concerning JUDAH, "My hire is ready (or, weighed) for me - thirty [pieces of] silver."[245]

Footnotes
227. Psalm ix. 15, 16.
228. Psalm vii. 16.
229. Proverbs vi. 13.
230. Psalm xli. 9.
231. Isaiah x. 1, 2.
232. Psalm civ. 35.
233. Psalm xxxvi. 1.
234. Prov. xi. 11
235. Deuteronomy xxix. 20.
236. Psalm cix. 17.
237. Compare Ezekiel xviii. 12, 31.
238. Job xviii. 16 f.
239. Hosea iv. 1, 2.
240. Psalm cix. 6-8.
241. Exodus xxiii. 8; Deuteronomy xxvii. 25.
242. Habakkuk i. 4.
243. Psalm cxii. 10.
244. Proverbs xi. 1.
245. Zechariah xi. 12.

109. Concerning His Crucifixion

And the Prophets also prophesied concerning the Crucifixion of CHRIST.

Thus MOSES, the servant of God, prophesied and said, "Ye shall see your salvation crucified upon the wood, and shall not believe."[246]

Thus DAVID prophesied and said, "Many dogs have seized Me; and they drove nails through My hands and My feet; and they counted all My bones; though they knew Me they despised Me; and they divided My garments among themselves; and they cast lots for My apparel.[247]

Thus ISAIAH prophesied concerning the Incarnation and Crucifixion of CHRIST, and said, "Who believeth our word, and to whom is the arm of the Lord revealed? And we spake like a child before Him: and He is like a root in parched ground, He hath no beauty and no form; and His form is more rejected and abased than [that of] any man. He is a broken man and a man of suffering; for He hath turned away His face, and they treat Him with contempt and esteem Him as nothing."[248]

Thus SOLOMON prophesied and said, "Let us kill the righteous man, for he is a burden unto us; he setteth himself up against our works, he resisteth our intentions continually, and we are an abomination unto him because of our sins."[249] And he continued, saying, "My son, let not wicked men lead thee astray; if they say unto thee, 'Come with us, be a partner with us, let us hide innocent blood and take plunder from him; and let there be one purse common to us all': withdraw thyself from their footsteps, for let it not be through thee that the birds find the net."[250]

Thus DAVID prophesied and said, "They cast gall into My meat, and they gave Me vinegar to drink to [quench] My thirst."[251]

Thus prophesied ISAIAH the Prophet and said, "He hath taken our disease and carried our sickness, and by His wound we are healed; and we saw Him suffering, and wounded in his pain; and He opened not His mouth in His pain, and He came to be slaughtered; like a lamb before his shearer He opened not His mouth in His suffering until they took away His life; and they knew not His birth; through the sin of My people have I come even unto death."[252]

Thus JEREMIAH the Prophet prophesied and said, "And they took the price of the honourable one thirty [pieces of] silver, whom they had honoured among the children of ISRAEL. And God said unto me, Cast it into the melting pot, and test it [and see] if it be pure; and they gave it for the field of the potter; as God hath commanded me I will speak."[253]

Thus ISAIAH the Prophet prophesied and said, "They counted Him with the sinners, and brought Him to death."[254]

Thus DAVID the Prophet prophesied and said, "Those who hate Me wrongfully are many, and they have rewarded Me with evil for good."[255]

Thus ZECHARIAH the Prophet prophesied and said, "And they shall look upon Him Whom they have crucified and pierced."[256]

Now there are still very many passages which have been written and many prophecies which might be mentioned concerning His coming, and His Crucifixion, and His death, and His Resurrection, and His second coming in glory. But we have only mentioned a few of the prophecies of the prophets - we have mentioned one of each kind - so that ye may hear, and believe, and understand, even as it is said in the Acts of the Apostles, "By the Gospel Thou hast guided us, and by the Prophets Thou hast comforted us; for the words of the Prophets make right the faith of those who doubt."[257]

Footnotes
246 Quoted from the LXX (Deuteronomy xxviii. 66). See The Times Lit. Suppl., June 1, 1921.
    247. Psalm xxii. 16.
    248. Isaiah liii. 1-3.
    249. Wisdom ii. 12.
    250. Proverbs i. 10 ff.
    251. Psalm lxix. 21.

How the Jews crucified our Lord. The Virgin Mary stands on His right and St. John on His left. Between the Virgin and the Cross stands Longinus, the soldier who pierced our Lord's side. The Crusaders are said to have found the body of Longinus in the church of St. Peter at Antioch in the XIth century

252. Isaiah liii. 4 ff.
253. Zechariah xi. 13.
254. Isaiah liii. 12.
255. Psalm xxxv. 12.
256. Zechariah xii. 10.
257. Acts iii. 20 ff.

110. *Concerning His Resurrection*

And the prophet DAVID also prophesied, concerning His Resurrection and said, "I will arise, saith the Lord, and I will make salvation and manifest it openly."[258] And again he saith, "Rise up, O Lord, and judge the earth, for Thou shalt inherit among the nations."[259] And he also prophesied and said, "Rise up, O Lord, help us, and deliver us for Thy Name's sake."[260] And again he said, "Let God arise and let His enemies be scattered, and let His enemies flee from before His face."[261] And he also prophesied and said, "God hath risen up like one who hath woke up from sleep, and like a mighty man who hath left [his] wine."[262]

Thus ISAIAH the prophet prophesied and said, "He will remove sickness from his soul, for he hath not committed sin, and falsehood hath not been found in his mouth. And to him that hath served righteousness and good will he show light and he will justify him; and he shall do away the sins of many, for he hath not committed sin, and falsehood is not found in his mouth."[263]

Thus prophesied DAVID the Prophet and said, "For My soul shall not be left in hell."[264]

Thus SOLOMON his son prophesied and said, "The Sun of righteousness shall arise, and shall travel towards the right, and shall return into His place."[265]

Footnotes
258. Psalm xii. 5.
259. Psalm lxxxii. 8.
260. Psalm xliv. 26.
261. Psalm lxviii. 1.
262. Psalm lxxviii. 65.
263. Compare Isaiah liii. 4 ff.
264. Psalm xvi. 10.
265. Compare Malachi iv. 2.

111. Concerning His Ascension and His Second Coming

Thus all the Prophets and many of the early Fathers prophesied concerning His Ascension and His Second Coming to judge the living and the dead.

And DAVID said concerning His Resurrection, "He hath gone up into the heights. Thou hast made captive captivity, and hast given grace to the children of men."[266] And he also said, Having gone forth, I will come back, and I will return from the abyss of the sea."[267] And again he said, "Sing ye unto God Who hath gone up into the heavens, the heavens which are opposite the morning."[268]

Thus AMOS the Prophet prophesied and said, "The Messiah, Who made the time of the morning, hath come and is exalted from the earth into the heights: and His Name is God Who ruleth all things."[269]

Thus prophesied DAVID the Prophet and said, "Thou art exalted, O Lord, by Thy might, and we will praise and hymn Thy strength."[270]

Thus prophesied ZECHARIAH the Prophet and said, "His foot standeth on the Mount of Olives to the east of JERUSALEM. And He rideth upon the Cherubim, and He flieth upon the wing of the winds."[271]

Thus DAVID said, "Open ye the gates of the princes, and let the doors which were from the creation be opened, and the King of glory shall come! Who is this King of glory? God, the mighty and strong One, God, the mighty One in battle." And he also made known and said, "Open ye the gates of princes, and let the doors which were from the creation be opened, and the King of glory shall come! Who is this King of glory? The Lord God of Hosts is this King."[272]

And again concerning His coming - He shall judge the living and the dead -

Christ ascending into heaven and being received by angels. Below are the Virgin Mary and the Apostles

He to Whom belongeth glory for ever and ever. Amen.

Thus ZECHARIAH the Prophet prophesied and said, "That day the Lord my God shall come, and all His saints with Him."[273]

Thus DAVID the Prophet prophesied and said, "God spake once, and this according [to what] I have heard: Compassion belongeth unto God. And Thine, O Lord, is the power, for Thou wilt reward every man according to his work."[274]

Thus spake DANIEL the Prophet and said, "I saw in my vision by night, and behold, there came [one] like unto the Son of man to the Ancient of Days, and there were given unto him dominion, and glory, and sovereignty, and all the nations and peoples and countries shall serve Him, and His dominion shall have no end for ever and ever. Amen."[275]

And all the Prophets prophesied, and nothing that hath happened hath been without the prophecy of the Prophets. And they have declared everything that hath happened, and what shall happen, what hath been done and what shall be done, and that which belongeth to the times of old and that which belongeth to the latter days up to His Second Coming. And this they have done not only by what they have prophesied and declared, but together with their prophecies they have given manifestations of Him in their bodies. And there was a famine in the land of CANAAN, and our father ABRAHAM went down to EGYPT, and came back with much riches and honour without blemish. And in like manner our Redeemer went down and delivered the Church, the Assembly of the Nations, and He went up [again], having gotten honour and praise.

Footnotes
266. Psalm lxviii. 18.
267. Psalm lxviii. 22.
268. Psalm lxviii. 32, 33.
269. Amos iv. 13.
270. Psalm xxi. 13.
271. Zechariah xiv. 4; Psalm xviii. 10.
272. Psalm xxiv. 7, 8.
273. Zechariah xiv. 5.
274. Psalm lxii. 11, 12.
275. Daniel vii. 13 f.

112. How the Prophets foreshadowed Him in their persons

ISAAC commanded his father, saying, "Bind me"; and he was offered up as a sacrifice, though he did not die, being redeemed by the ram which came down from heaven. And in like manner the Son of God was obedient to His Father even unto death. And He was bound with the love of men, and He was nailed [to the Cross] and was pierced, and the Son of God became our ransom, and His Godhead suffered not.

Thus JACOB his son departed to the land of LÂBÂ (LABAN), the country of his mother's brother, with his staff only, and there he made many cattle, and acquired beasts both clean and unclean, and he begot twelve sons, and he revealed baptism, and returned to his own country where he received a blessing from ISAAC his father. And in like manner our Lord CHRIST came down from heaven, the Word of Godhead by Itself; and the staff of JACOB wherewith he pastured his sheep is our Lady MARY our salvation. And moreover, the staff signifieth the wood of the Cross whereby, being crucified upon it, He redeemed His flock and took possession of us from among the JEWS, and the heathen, and the GENTILES. And He chose for Himself Twelve Apostles, and they made the people believe in all the earth and in every country, and He went up to heaven to His Father.

Thus MOSES departed to the country of MIDIAN, and there he held converse with God, Who made him to learn and to know the belief in the resurrection from the dead of his fathers ABRAHAM, ISAAC, and JACOB. And by means of his staff (or, rod) He endowed him with the power to perform miracles; and he begot two sons. And this showeth clearly that we shall be saved by the Trinity. As the mouth of God proclaimed, "I am the God of ABRAHAM" - this of the Father - "and the God of ISAAC" - this of the Son - "and the God of JACOB" - when He saith this it is of the Holy Ghost indicating the Trinity clearly and plainly. "I am not the God of the dead, but the God of the living,"[276] for they all are alive with God; and by this the Resurrection of the dead is to be understood.

JONAH was swallowed up and cast into the belly of the great fish; and our Redeemer went down into the heart of the earth, and rose again the third day. And DANIEL was cast into the pit of the lions, and [the king and the lords] sealed it with their seals; and he rose up therefrom without the lions devouring him. And similarly our Lord was cast into the grave, and the JEWS sealed it with their seals, imagining that they were sealing up the rising of the sun so that it should not shine. O ye foolish, wicked, blasphemous, blind, and weak-minded men, would ye assert that the Spirit of Life should not appear and come forth? And the JEWS were put to shame, and He went forth to illumine us who have believed upon Him.

JOSEPH was sold by the hand of his brethren, and our Lord was sold by the hand of JUDAH. And JOSEPH where he was sold delivered his brethren from the famine, and CHRIST hath delivered us who believed upon Him and hath made us His heirs and His brethren. And as JOSEPH gave an inheritance unto his kinsfolk in the land of GÊSHAM (GOSHEN), so shall [CHRIST] give unto His righteous ones a habitation, an everlasting inheritance.

And moreover, in order that ye may know, and understand, and be certain about the resurrection of the dead, I will give you a sign, which ye shall understand by the guidance of His word. When ABRAHAM had come unto the land of [his] inheritance he bought first of all a tomb wherein to gather together the dead bodies of his kinsfolk, and his children, and his wife, so that he might join them in the resurrection; and there he buried his wife SARAH and he himself was buried. For he was a prophet, and he knew that he would be raised up with his kin. And ISAAC and REBEKAH his wife were also buried there. And it remained their possession from the time when JACOB went down to the land of EGYPT with seventy-seven souls, because of the famine and because JOSEPH his son [was there], until their number became six hundred thousand marching men who were equipped for war, without [reckoning] women and children. And JACOB died in EGYPT at a good old age, and he said unto JOSEPH his son, "I adjure thee by the life of my father and by my God, Who is the renewer of my life, that thou bury me not in this country, but in the tomb of my fathers, so that my death may be with them and my life subsequently with them."[277] Know then by this similitude of the word. And JOSEPH his son carried ISRAEL and buried him by the grave of his fathers, for he reverenced the oath which JACOB had made him to swear.

And again, when JACOB fell sick in EGYPT he called his brethren and his children, and made them to swear that they would not leave his bones in the land of EGYPT, and said, "When God maketh you to return take ye my bones with you and mingle them in the grave of my fathers."[278]

Footnotes
276. Matthew xxii. 32.
277. Genesis xlvii. 29.
278. Genesis l. 25.

113. Concerning the Chariot and the Vanquisher of the Enemy

And the Archbishops (or, Patriarchs) answered and said unto GREGORY, the Worker of Wonders, "Behold now, we know well, and thou hast made us to understand that the Kings of ETHIOPIA have become glorious and great through ZION. And the Kings of RÔMÊ also have become great because of the nails [of the Cross] that HELENA made into a bridle, which hath become the vanquisher of the enemy for the King of RÔMÊ. And the chariot belongeth to the King of ETHIOPIA, and it hath vanquished his enemy. And tell us also how long the vanquisher of the enemy shall remain with the King of RÔMÊ, and the chariot containing ZION with the King of ETHIOPIA. Tell us, for God hath revealed unto thee what hath been, and what shall be, vision and prophecy, like MOSES and ELIJAH."

And GREGORY answered and said unto them, "I will reveal unto you concerning the King of RÔMÊ when he shall transgress and shall provoke God to wrath in the faith. This faith which we have ordered and laid down shall a king transgress who shall come in RÔMÊ, and there shall be associated with him a certain archbishop, and they shall change and pervert the word of the Twelve Apostles, and they shall cast it aside in the desire of their heart[s], and they shall teach what they wish, and they shall turn the Scriptures to suit their own nature, even as the Apostle saith, 'They have behaved themselves like [the people of] SODOM and GOMORRAH.'[279] And our Lord said unto His disciples in the Gospel, 'Guard ye yourselves against those who shall come unto you in the apparel of sheep, and who are inwardly wolves that tear.'[280] And when they have destroyed the faith the vanquisher of the enemy shall be taken away from them, and there shall be none of those who have changed our faith who shall sit upon the throne of PETER, and the bowels of their Archbishops shall be emptied out if they have taken their seat upon it in perverted faith. For the Angel of God hath been commanded to protect the throne of PETER in RÔMÊ. And God shall take away the vanquisher of the enemy from the king who shall not guard the faith, and the PERSIANS shall make war upon him and defeat him, and it seemeth to me that his name is MARCION the Apostate. And the King of PERSIA, whose name is HARÊNÊWÔS (IRENAEUS) shall conquer (?) him, and the king shall carry him away, together with his horse, and by the Will of God the horse on which is the vanquisher of the enemy shall be stirred up, and shall go into the sea and perish therein. But the nails shall shine there in the sea until CHRIST shall come again in great glory upon a cloud of heaven, together with power.

"Now this hath God showed me in the pit. And as concerning the King of ETHIOPIA, and ZION, the Bride of heaven, and her chariot whereby they move, I will declare unto you that which my God hath revealed unto me and hath made me to understand. [ETHIOPIA] shall continue in the orthodox faith until the coming of our Lord, and she shall in no way turn aside from the word of the Apostles, and it shall be so even as we have ordered until the end of the world.

And one answered and said unto the Worker of Wonders (i.e., GREGORY), "Now when SAMÂLYÂL cometh, who is the False Christ (ANTICHRIST), will the faith of the people of ETHIOPIA be destroyed by his attack?" And GREGORY answered and said, "Assuredly not. Hath not DAVID prophesied saying, 'ETHIOPIA shall make her hands come to God?'[281] And this that he saith meaneth that the ETHIOPIANS will neither pervert nor change this our faith and what we have ordered, and the faith of those who were before us, the teachers of the Law of the Apostles."

Footnotes
279. Matthew x. 15.
280. Matthew vii. 15.
281. Psalm lxviii. 31.

114. Concerning the return of ZION

And the Tabernacle of the Law of God, the Holy ZION, shall remain here until that day when our Lord shall dwell on Mount ZION; and ZION shall come and shall appear unto all prepared, with three seals - even as MOSES gave her - as it saith in the Old Law and in the New, "At the testimony of two or three [witnesses] everything shall stand."[282] And then, saith ISAIAH the Prophet, "The dead shall be raised up, and those who are in the graves shall live, for the dew which [cometh] from Thee is their life."[283] And when the dead are raised up, His mercy whereby He watereth the earth shall cease; they shall stand up before Him with the works which they have done. And ENOCH and ELIAS shall come, being alive, so that they may testify, and MOSES and AARON from the dead shall live with everyone. And they shall open the things that fetter her (i.e., ZION), and they shall make to be seen the JEWS, the crucifiers, and they shall punish them and chide them because of all that they have done in perverting the Word of God. And the JEWS shall see what He wrote for them with His hand - the Words of His Commandment, and the manna wherewith He fed them without toil [on their part], and the measure thereof; the GÔMÔR, and the spiritual ZION, which came down for their salvation, and the rod of AARON, which blossomed after the manner of MARY.

Footnotes
282. Deuteronomy xix. 15; Matthew xviii. 16; John viii. 17; 2 Corinthians xiii. 1.
283. Isaiah xxvi. 19.

115. Concerning the Judgement of ISRAEL

And He shall answer and say unto them, "Why did ye deny Me, and entreat Me evilly and crucify Me, [seeing that] I did all this for you, and that by My coming down [from heaven] I delivered you from SATAN and from the slavery of SATAN, and that I came for your sakes? Look ye and see how ye pierced Me with nails and thrust the spear through Me." And the Twelve Apostles shall be raised up, and they shall pass judgement upon them, and shall say unto them, "We would have made you hear, but ye would not hear the prophecy of the Prophets and the preaching of us the Apostles." And the JEWS shall weep and repent when it shall be useless to do so, and they shall pass into everlasting punishment; and with the Devil, their father who had directed them, and his demons who had led them astray, and with the wicked they shall be shut in.

And those who have believed and who have been baptized in the Holy Trinity, and have received His Body and His Blood, shall become His servants with their whole heart, for "there is no one who can hate His Body altogether." The Body of CHRIST crieth out in our Body, and He hath compassion because of His Body and Blood, for they have become His sons and His brethren. And if there be some who have sinned they shall be judged in the fire according to the quantity of their sins; he whose burden of sin is light his punishment shall be light, and he whose burden of sin is heavy, exceedingly great shall his punishment be. One day with God is as a period of ten thousand years; some there shall be who shall be punished for a day; and some for half a day, and some for three hours of a day, and some for one hour of a day; and some there shall be who shall be tested and who shall be absolved from their transgressions.

116. Concerning the Chariot of ETHIOPIA

And the Archbishops answered and said unto GREGORY, the Worker of Wonders, "Behold now, thou hast told us concerning the vanquisher of the enemy of RÔMÊ, and now [tell us] of the chariot of ETHIOPIA and whether it shall remain henceforward, to the Coming of CHRIST, as thou hast told us concerning ZION, and concerning the faith of the people of ETHIOPIA, and likewise if their chariot shall remain." And GREGORY said unto them, "It shall assuredly not disappear. And again, hearken ye unto me and I will declare this unto you: A few JEWS shall lift up their heads against our faith in NÂGRÂN and in ARMENIA in the days after this, and this God will do by His Will so that He may destroy them, for ARMENIA is a territory of RÔMÊ and NÂGRÂN is a territory of ETHIOPIA."

The Last Judgement. God Almighty, holding a standard with flags attached to it, sits in the centre with His angels about Him. On His right are seated the blessed, clothed, and on His left are the damned in the form of naked men and women. At His feet lie " Diabolus, the lover of iniquity " and two other fiends

From Brit. Mus. MS. Orient. No. 510. fol. 93b

117. Concerning the King of RÔMÊ and the King of ETHIOPIA

And the King of RÔMÊ, and the King of ETHIOPIA, and the Archbishop of ALEXANDRIA - now the men of RÔMÊ were orthodox - were informed that they were to destroy them. And they were to rise up to fight, to make war upon the enemies of God, the JEWS, and to destroy them, the King of RÔMÊ 'ÊNYÂ, and the King of ETHIOPIA PINHAS (PHINEHAS); and they were to lay waste their lands, and to build churches there, and they were to cut to pieces JEWS at the end of this Cycle in twelve cycles of the moon. Then the kingdom of the JEWS shall be made an end of and the Kingdom of CHRIST shall be constituted until the advent of the False Messiah. And those two kings, JUSTINUS the King of RÔMÊ and KÂLÊB the King of ETHIOPIA, met together in JERUSALEM. And their Archbishop was to make ready offerings and they were to make offerings, and they were to establish the Faith in love, and they were to give each other gifts and the salutation of peace, and they were to divide between them the earth from the half of JERUSALEM, even as we have already said at the beginning of this book. And for love's sake they were to have jointly the royal title [of King of ETHIOPIA]. They were to be mingled with DAVID and SOLOMON their fathers. The one whom in faith they chose by lot to be named from the Kings of RÔMÊ was to be called "King of ETHIOPIA", and the King of RÔMÊ likewise was to bear the name of "King of ETHIOPIA", and he was to have part in the lot whereby he should be named with DAVID and SOLOMON their fathers, after the manner of the Four Evangelists. And the fourth the one whom they were to choose each in his own country. . .

And thus after they had become united in a common bond, and had established the right faith they were to determine that the JEWS were no longer to live, and each of them was to leave his son there; and the King of ETHIOPIA was to leave there his firstborn son whose name was ISRAEL, and was to return to his own country in joy. And when he came to his royal house, he was to give abundant thanks unto God, and to offer up his body as an offering of praise to his God. And God shall accept him gladly, for he shall not defile his body after he hath returned, but he shall go into a monastery in purity of heart. And he shall make king his youngest son, whose name is GABRA MASKAL, and he himself shall shut himself up [in a monastery]. And when one hath told this to the King of NÂGRÂN, the son of KÂLÊB, he shall come in order to reign over ZION, and GABRA MASKAL shall make his armies to rise up, and he shall journey in a chariot, and they shall meet together at the narrow end of the Sea of LÎBÂ, and shall fight together. And on the same night the two of them shall pray from sunset until the dawn, when the fight waxeth strong upon them. And when they have cried out to Him with tears God will look upon the prayer of both of them, and the penitent prayer of their father, and will say, "This one is the elder and he hath stood up to perform the will of his father, and that one, the younger, hath loved his father, and hath prayed to God [for him]." And God will say to GABRA MASKAL, "Choose thou between the chariot and ZION," and He will cause him to take ZION, and he shall reign openly upon the throne of his father. And God will make ISRAEL to choose the chariot, and he shall reign secretly and he shall not be visible, and He will send him to all those who have transgressed the commandment of God. And no one shall build houses, and they shall live in tents, and none shall suffer fatigue in labouring, and none shall suffer thirst on the journey. And their days shall be double of those of [ordinary] men, and they shall use bows and arrows, and shall shoot at and pierce him that God hateth.

Thus hath God made for the King of ETHIOPIA more glory, and grace, and majesty than for all the other kings of the earth because of the greatness of ZION, the Tabernacle of the Law of God, the heavenly ZION. And may God make us to perform His spiritual good pleasure, and deliver us from His wrath, and make us to share His kingdom. Amen.

And they answered and said unto him, "Verily, thou hast spoken well, for thus was it revealed unto thee by the help of the Holy Spirit. Thou hast told us everything which hath taken place, and thou art in agreement with the book of DAMÔTÎYÔS (DOMITIUS) of RÔMÊ. And thou hast prophesied also what shall happen to the two cities, the brides of CHRIST, the Churches NESTÂSYÂ and 'ARKÂDYÂ, and MÂRÊNÂ, and ETHIOPIA, the great cities of God, wherein pure sacrifices and offerings shall be offered up at all times.

May God show us His grace! The blessing of all the saints and martyrs [be with us] for ever and ever! Amen. CHRIST is our King, and in CHRIST is our life for ever and ever. Amen. And Amen."

Colophon

In the Arabic text it is said: "We have turned [this book] into Arabic from a Coptic manuscript [belonging to] the throne of MARK the Evangelist, the teacher, the Father of us all. We have translated it in the four hundred and ninth year of mercy in the country of ETHIOPIA, in the days of GABRA MASKAL the king, who is called LÂLÎBALÂ, in the days of Abbâ GEORGE, the good bishop. And God neglected to have it translated and interpreted into the speech of ABYSSINIA. And when I had pondered this - Why did not 'ABAL'EZ and ABALFAROG who edited (or, copied) the book translate it? I said this: It went out in the days of ZÂGUÂ, and they did not translate it because this book says: Those who reign not being ISRAELITES are transgressors of the Law. Had they been of the kingdom of ISRAEL they would have edited (or, translated) it. And it was found in NÂZRÊT."

"And pray ye for me, your servant ISAAC the poor man. And chide ye me not because of the incorrectness of the speech of the tongue. For I have toiled much for the glory of the country of ETHIOPIA, and for the going forth of the heavenly ZION, and for the glory of the King of ETHIOPIA. And I consulted the upright and God-loving governor YÂʿEBÎKA 'EGZÎ'Ě, and he approved and said unto me, 'Work.' And I worked, God helping me, and He did not requite me according to my sins. And pray ye for your servant ISAAC, and for those who toiled with me in the going out (i.e., production) of this book, for we were in sore tribulation, I, and YAMHARANA-'AB, and HEZBA-KRESTÔS, and ANDREW, and PHILIP, and MAHÂRÎ-'AB. May God have mercy upon them, and may He write their names in the Book of Life in the kingdom of heaven, with those of all the saints and martyrs for ever and ever! Amen."

A LIST OF THE PASSAGES FROM THE OLD AND NEW TESTAMENTS, QUOTED OR REFERRED TO IN THE KEBRA NAGAST

Genesis i, 1, 170, 191; i, 26, 1; ii, 17, 185; iii, 16, 48; v, 9, 9; vi, 2–4, 188; vi, 14, 188; viii, 21, 7; ix, 4, 6; ix, 25–27, 6; x, 6, 8; xii ff:, 11, 144; xiii, 14–17, 11; xiv, - , 200; xv, 1, 10; xviii, 1, 196; xxii, 13, 113, 196; xxii, 17, 30; xxx, 37, 196; xxxv, 22, 12; xlvii, 29, 221; xlvii, 31, 196; xlix, 4, 12; xlix, 8–12, 210; l, 25, 221.

Exodus iii, 2, 174; vii, 10, 180; vii, 19, 181; viii, - , 181; x, 21, 22, 180; xv, 25, 182; xvi, 35, 178; xvii, 4, 176; xvii, 6, 179; xvii, 11, 12, 181; xix, - , 171; xxv, 10, 13, 178; xxxiii, 18–23, 172; xxxiv, 33, 172.

Leviticus xviii, 18, 32; xxvi, 12, 202.

Numbers xi, 16, 171; xii, 2, 171; xvi, - , 175; xvi, 41, 176; xvii, 8, 176; xxi, 7, 170.

Deuteronomy iv, 1, 156; vi, 4, 208; xviii, 15, 170; xix, 15, 223; xxvii, 15, 158; xxvii, 25, 213; xxix, 20, 212; xxxii, 21, 28, 194; xxxii, 44, 205.

Judges vi, 37, 205.

1 Samuel ii, 29–34, 96; vi, 4, 75, 97; vi, 7, 97; xv, - , 65.

2 Samuel vi, 3, 196; vii, 12, 40, 120.

1 Kings 1, 3, 105; ii, 5, 104.; ii, 35, 43; x, 1, xli; xi, 1, 34.; xvii, - , 65.

2 Kings i, 2, 74.

1 Chronicles ii, 25, 12; v, 1, 12; xxii, 8, 9, 90.

2 Chronicles ix, 1, xli.

Job ix, 8, 204; xviii, 16, 212.

Psalm ii, - , 106; ii, 7, 204; vii, 16, 211; viii, 2, 209; viii, 6, 6; ix, 11, 16; ix, 15, 16, 211; xii, 5, 216; xiii, - , 206; xvi, 10, 216; xviii, 9, 204; xviii, 10, 217; xviii, 43, 205; xviii, 45, 46, 205; xxi, 13, 217; xxii, 16, 182, 214; xxii, 20, 21, 210; xxiii, 8, 213; xxiv, 7, 8, 217; xxviii, 3, 4, 130; xxxiii, 6, 192; xxxiii, 9, 192; xxxiii, 13, 205; xxxv, 12, 215; xxxvi, 1, 212; xl, 7, 169; xli, 9, 211; xliv, 26, 216; xlv, - , 193; xlviii, 2, 3, 203; l, 2, 143, 203; l, 3, 202; l, 7, 208; lviii, 7, 192; lxii, 11, 12, 218; lxviii, 1, 216; lxviii, 18, 216; lxviii, 21, 31; lxviii, 31, 74, 223; lxviii, 32, 35, 217; lxix, 21, 183, 204.; lxxii, 1 ff., 106; lxxii, 5, 17, 207; lxxii, 6, 205; lxxii, 6, 7, 203; lxxii, 9, 10, 74.; lxxii, 11, 95; lxxii, 15, 204; lxxiii, 8, 9, 164; lxxv, 10; lxxviii, 65, 216; lxxxi, 3, 209; lxxxii, 8, 216; lxxxiii, 7, 74; lxxxvii, 2, 3, 178; lxxxvii, 2–4, 75; 5, 6, 203; lxxxix, 3, 4, 95; lxxxix, 35, 120; lxxxix, 37, 120; lxxxix, 27, 29, 95; xc, 3, 191; xcii, 10, 210; xcv, 1, 2, 206; xcv, 10, xlv, 52; xcvi, 5, 52, 196; xcvi, 10, 206; xcviii, 9, 206; civ, 35, 212; cix, 5, 193; cix, 6–8, 213; cix, 17, 212; cx, 3, 204; cx, 4, 106; cxii, 10, 213; cxviii, 26, 202, 209; cxxix, 8, 202; cxxxii, 11, xli, 42, 120; cxxxii, 11–13, 95; cxxxii, 17, 205.

Proverbs i, 10 ff., 214; vi, 13, 211; viii, 22, 207; viii, 30, 207; xi, 1, 213; xi, 11, 212; xxx, 4, 208; xxx, 18, 131.

Song of Solomon iii, 7 ff., 105; iii, 9, 106.

Isaiah ii, 3, 208; vi, 10, 200; vii, 14, 204; ix, 6, 201; x, 1, 2, 212; x, 33, 206; xi, 10, 206; xxvi, 19, 223; xxix, 13, 194; xxxv, 3, 202, 207; xl, 12, 208; xlii, 1, 201; xliii, 20, 207; xliv, 16, 196; xliv, 18, 200; xlv, 12, 193; xlv, 14, 206; li, 16, 75; liii, 1–3, 214; liii, 2 ff., 193; liii; 4 ff., 215, 216; liii, 12, 215; liv, 4, 205; liv, 13, 209; lix, 20, 203; lx, 1, 209; lx, 2, 3, 201; lxii, 11, 209; lxiii, 1, 206; lxv, 1, 74; lxvi, 1, 82.

Jeremiah xxx, 6–9, 201; xxxi, 11, 12, 203; xxxi, 31, 203; xxxii, 38, 202.

Ezekiel xi, 17, 20, 202; xviii, 12, 31, 212; xxxvi, 27, 28, 202; xliii, 1, 174; xliii, 2, 207.

Daniel vii, 13 ff., 218.

Hosea iv, 1, 2, 213.

Amos, iv, 13, 217.

Micah, iv, 2, 203, 208.

Habakkuk iii, 3, 202; iii, 4, 211; iv, 213.

Haggai ii, 7, 9, 206.

Zechariah i, 17, 204; ii, 10, 202, 203; iv, 5, 217; viii, 3, 203; ix, 9, 204, 209; xi, 12, 213; xi, 13, 213; xii, 10, 215; xiv, 4, 217.

Malachi i, 10, 11, 208; iii, 1, 204; iv, 2, 204; iv, 2, 216.

Wisdom ii, 12, 204.

St. Matthew i, 4, 12; i, 20, 121; vii, 15, 222; vii, 24, 2, 5, 179; x, 8, 127; x, 15, 222; xii, 42, 17; xii, 49, 198; xvi, 18, 180; xvii, 4, 82; xviii, 16, 223; xix, 28, 127; xxii, 32, 219; xxiii, 13, 187; xxiv, 35, 7; xxv 22, 159; xxvi, 26, 195.

St. Mark i, 1, 191; iii, 34, 198; xvi, 16, 200.

St. Luke iii, 33, 12; ix, 33, 82; x, 19, 127; xi, 31, xli, 17; xviii, 9, 187; xxiii, 34, 193.

St. John i, 1, 191; 1, 1–3, 191; ii, 19, 105; viii, 17, 223; x, 7, 9, 180; x, 17, 14, 180; xv, 5, 16, 180; xxi, 17, 180; xxi, 25, 167.

Acts of the Apostles i, - , 191; 3, 194; vii, 31, 55, 194; viii, 27, 40; xxx, 20 ff., 215.

1 Corinthians i, 20, 42; vii, - , 31.

2 Corinthians vi, 16, 202, 203; xiii, 1, 223.

Galatians iii, 28, 105; v, 16, 17, 126.

Hebrews xi, 21, 196, 199.

2 Peter ii, 4, 188.

1 John i, 1, 191; iii; 5, 8, 203.

VELLUM 👑 BOOKS

Vellum Books publishes a wide range of titles, from recondite esoteric tomes to classic works on fiction, politics and philosophy and, most recently, our very successful foray into Children's Classics, with vibrant new covers and Black-and-White/Colour illustrations to complement some of the world's very best children's tales. All our imprints are offered to the reader at a competitive price and through as many mediums and outlets as possible.

We are committed to excellent book production and strive, whenever possible, to add value to our titles with original images, maps and author introductions. With the premium on space in most modern dwellings, we also endeavour - within the limits of good book design - to make our products as slender as possible, allowing more books to be fitted into a given bookshelf area.

We are a small, approachable company and would love to hear any of your comments and suggestions on our plans, products, or indeed on absolutely anything. We look forward to meeting you.

mark@ebgb.net

New Titles from *Vellum Books*

Kebra Negast: Book of the Glory of Kings.
The ancient and remarkable tale of Prince Ebna, love-child of the legendary Queen of Sheba and the biblical King Solomon. On reaching adulthood, the Prince seized the two most precious symbols of Israel's unique status before God - the Ten Commandments and the Ark of the Covenant, and carried both to Ethiopia where, it is said, they exist to this day! This is a the classic translation by Wallace Budge, keeper of Egyptian and Assyrian Antiquities at the British Museum.

The Arthashastra
Believed lost for 1000 years, this Indian Classic is a unique guide for Kings on *realpolitik*. Nothing is omitted, from taxes on prostitutes and the use of deception or threat, to methods of 'neutralising' enemies (as well as 'inconvenient' brothers!) by means of ambush, poison, and the use of 'fiery spies'. An eye-opening, amoral discourse on the stratagems to be mastered by any aspiring conqueror!

The Teachings of Zoroaster
Founded in the 6th century B.C. by Iranian prophet Zarathustra (Gk: Zoroaster), this new religion first taught of an individual judgment, Heaven and Hell, a bodily resurrection, the Last Judgment, and life everlasting for the reunited soul and body. This authoritative and accessible introduction explains all aspects of the faith, emphasising Zoroastrianism's place as the precursor of the West's three main religions: Judaism, Christianity and Islam.

Esoteric Buddhism
Alfred Sinnett was an Englishman living in India who studied Theosophy under the tutelage of renowned occultist Madame Blavatsky. First published in 1883, *Esoteric Buddhism* covers topics as diverse as life after death, Karma, the origin of Evil, psychic perception, Nirvana, and Esoteric Cosmogony, highlighting the many ways in which Buddhist esotericism agrees with occult wisdom of other faiths.

Daemonologie
In 1590, three hundred witches were accused of treason against King James VI of Scotland, (soon to be James I of England), leading His Majesty to a deep study of this 'un-Christian' sect. 'Daemonologie' is the result of the King's research, a book that reveals many fascinating aspects of witch-craft, familiar spirits, ghosts and sorcery and concludes with a lurid account of North Berwick's witch trials.

A Dweller on Two Planets
At the age of 18, Frederick Oliver channeled 'Phylos', a being whose remarkable life-story tells of reincarnation, Atlantis, and other planes of existence. If fiction, it is an almost inexplicable achievement for one so young. If truly a message from Beyond, the book provides esoteric information indispensable to all students of the occult.

Common Sense
Disenchanted with Britain, Thomas Paine emigrated in 1774 to the American Colonies, finding there a populace seething against the arrogant impositions of the British Crown,

and ripe for revolution. Paine combined the scattered arguments for Independence into a well thought out plan for change - *Common Sense*. The work struck a deep chord in the Colonists' psyche and sparked the unquenchable, and unstoppable, desire for American independence.

The Age of Reason

The English-born American revolutionary leader Thomas Paine was a Deist, but critical of the priesthood's unthinking acceptance of the 'Authority' of holy books. In *The Age of Reason,* he examines the Christian bible critically and logically. The work was banned in Great Britain; but in America - where the writer was a revolutionary hero - it sold in thousands. Paine's critique remains relevant today, and is a classic in the literature of Free Thinking.

The Spiral Way

The Spiral Way was born of Evelyn Underhill's 10-year struggle to understand the 'spiritual experience'. It describes a contemplative's journey through fifteen Christian mysteries that are to be followed in the soul's ascent to God. She purposely eschews theological terms, describing with great success, and in simple language, 'some of the great truths concerning humanity's spiritual life'. The book has become a well-deserved classic of the genre.

The Complete Brigadier Gerard

One of Conan Doyle's greatest creations, Brigadier Gerard regales his friends - and anyone within earshot - with his adventures in the Napoleonic Wars. He reluctantly admits to being "the finest horseman and best swordsman in the Grande Armée", and shyly concedes that he could indeed win the heart of any female who caught sight of his incomparable figure. Unfortunately, the scrapes and disasters he invariably describes leave one with the unworthy suspicion that our hero's brain was not, perhaps, quite as sharp as his sabre! The inspiration of George MacDonald Fraser's *Flashman* Series.

The Book of the Cave of Treasures

This book is a fascinating 5th century compendium of Jewish and Christian apocryphal lore, a veritable cornucopia of extra-Biblical information. We hear of the 'Wind-Flood' that overthrew Ur, Abraham's original home; of the origin of the Magi, of the mysterious Priest-King Melchizedek, the lives of the Patriarchs, the genealogy of Mary, and many another secret wonder, including Adam's clandestine interment at the very spot where Jesus Christ was later died crucified. Fully annotated with 21 illustrations.

The Meditations of Marcus Aurelius

Despite holding absolute power, Emperor Marcus Aurelius (161–180 A.D.) resisted all temptations to vice or crime - thanks to an unshakable belief in stoic philosophy. In 'The Meditations', we hear the authentic voice of this Stoic Emperor, speaking across a gulf of two thousand years, as he wrestles with the mysteries of life and death and boldly confronts his own inner nature, identifying his flaws and talents, and resolving to live a virtuous life. Meant to be strictly private, it is as well that 'The Meditations' was brought into the light as its timeless wisdom it has continued to influence countless readers across the centuries.

Made in United States
North Haven, CT
14 February 2025

65765982R00114